Parenting *the*
Strong-Willed
Child

Parenting *the* Strong-Willed Child

Fortifying Our Youth and
Healing Our Prodigals

Kevin Hinckley

DESERET
BOOK

SALT LAKE CITY, UTAH

To Cindy,
whose love and constant support
made this book a reality

Library of Congress Cataloging-in-Publication Data

Hinckley, Kevin.
    Parenting the strong-willed child : fortifying our youth and healing our prodigals / Kevin Hinckley.
        p.   cm.
    Includes bibliographical references and index.
    ISBN 978-1-59038-917-1 (paperbound)
    1. Mormon children.   2. Child psychology.   3. Parenting—Religious aspects—Mormon Church.   4. Child rearing—Religious aspects—Mormon Church.   I. Title.
    BX8643.C56H56 2008
    248.8'450882893—dc22   2008005299

Printed in the United States of America
Publishers Printing, Salt Lake City, UT

10   9   8   7   6   5   4   3   2   1

Contents

One

The Premortal Rebellion

Children are natural mimics who act like their parents despite every effort to teach them good manners.—Author Unknown

A few years ago, I was asked to conduct a team-building training exercise for a firm in Dallas, Texas. The employees were having a hard time working together, and their supervisor was anxious to help them become a more cohesive group. I arranged for them to meet me at a local Boy Scout camp where we had a day of team-building exercises and fun.

In order to help them better understand themselves, I began with an activity called the Blind Maze. It consisted of a rope running down through the woods, around trees, over creeks, across logs and so forth, in a maze configuration. The team members were blindfolded and brought to a place at one end of the rope. I instructed each one to hold tightly to the rope, to follow it whereever it led, and to not let go. Finally, I explained they would know they'd reached the end because someone would be there for them.

The purpose of the maze activity, with any group, is to help individuals learn something about how they solve problems. When blindfolded, some become very cautious and tentative; some seek out others they can work with. I've had some participants, in other groups, sit down and cry out of frustration. The simple reality of the Blind Maze is that it is a metaphor for their lives. As I told them that day, "You will do this maze the way you do your life."

After the activity was well under way, I turned to answer a question from one of the other facilitators. When I looked back at the course, I noticed that one adventurous soul was already showing how he dealt with difficult situations. He had let go of the rope and had begun blindly walking across a field. What he did not know was that he was quickly approaching a thirty-foot-high embankment that ran along a creek bed. In horror, I sprinted across the field, tackling him just as he was about to fall over the ledge and down into the creek.

As I helped him up, he never said a word. I took him back to the rope and explained again how vital it was that he not let go again. Then I watched him—much more carefully—until he successfully completed the activity.

Afterwards, we talked about the exercise with the entire group. I explained what had happened. I then asked my wandering friend if this incident was indicative of how he lived his daily life.

"What do you mean?" he asked.

"Well," I explained, "you were given instructions that would lead you safely to the other end of the rope. Instead, you let go, wandered off blindly, and nearly fell down the embankment. You avoided injury only because I happened to see what you were doing. I then had to knock you down to save your life! I'm wondering how often you simply 'let go' during difficult times, leaving everyone around you to guess where you went?"

He thought about it for a moment, then shook his head and shrugged. "I don't think I ever do," he replied.

When I asked the group if this was typical behavior for their colleague, I got a far different response. They all nodded, enthusiastically, in agreement. They explained that he frequently went off on his own during difficult assignments. Eventually, someone would rescue him and bring him back to the rest of the group. They agreed that his behavior on the maze was a mirror image of what they saw him do every day.

When I asked *why* he had let go of the rope, venturing out on his own, and having no idea where he was going, he could only answer, "I don't know!"

Later, as I thought about his behavior, I wasn't sure which aspect was more troubling—the fact that he constantly walked off on his own, or the fact that he didn't know why he did so.

A few years ago, BYU professors Brent L. Top and Bruce A. Chadwick completed a study of LDS seminary students, using a large sample of kids, living in several states. The researchers were able to follow up with fifty young LDS girls, who admitted that they had succumbed to serious morality problems. All these girls had grown up active in the Church. They had heard about the importance of living the law of chastity in untold Sunday School and youth classes. Their LDS parents had endeavored to teach morality in their homes. Yet, in a heated moment, all these teachings and warnings had been discarded, and they had yielded to temptation.

The researchers asked the same question as I had to my friend on the Blind Maze: "Why did you do it?" Amazingly, over 59 percent of them answered the same way he had, "I don't know!" (See *10 Secrets Wise Parents Know* [Salt Lake City: Deseret Book Company, 2004], 88.)

And they didn't. When it came time to say yes or no, they had been persuaded to violate sacred covenants without an explanation as to why.

As parents and youth leaders, we worry constantly about the young people of the Church and their potential for rebellion. We have no illusions about the intensity and persuasiveness of the messages they are exposed to every day. We see their values being challenged on every side. We worry as we watch teens roll their eyes at church assignments or grow restless during spiritual discussions. As they grow older, some seem to become frustrated with Church "rules" and parental restrictions; and they push to see just how far they can extend the parameters. Some go so far as to ask their bishop, "How far can I go without sinning?" Then, when they quit attending church, many will respond with something like, "Hey, it's just not for me!" or "It was boring." Later, they will rationalize their behavior by saying, "Look, I'm not sure I believe all that church stuff anymore."

Having watched such kids over the years, I find myself wishing I could implant a voice in their brain that would shout: "Hey, this is your eternal life you're playing with! Don't you realize what you're doing? What are you thinking?"

As any parent of a wandering child can attest, modern-day prodigals ignore all prior warnings and willfully let go of the safety rope. They think they're immune to consequences, and feeling that no one has the right to tell them what to do, they stumble toward dangers they don't immediately recognize. Blinded by fads, popular opinions, and the invitations of friends, they fail to see the upcoming cliff their parents and leaders have warned them about.

When our children wander, we ask the universal question, "What more could I have done?" We struggle to find answers and the reasons why they did what they did. With our younger children, we modify that question to, "What more can I do?" to fortify them against future rebellious behavior.

In the chapters that follow, we'll strive to get perspective on both questions. Statistics reveal that churches of all kinds are losing kids to Satan's worldly enticements. As Latter-day Saints we do much better than most. But, the tragedy is that we still lose far too many.

Not long ago, while teaching a college-age institute class, I asked the students to reflect back to their deacon and beehive years. I had them recall how many kids were in those classes. I then had them count how many of those classmates were still active in the Church, eight to ten years later. Some students reported that most or all of their classmates were still active. However, there were many who said that large numbers of their friends had completely dropped out or were less active.

In order to better fortify our children against the voices that would entice them away from their eternal safety rope, we need to first understand rebellion and its origins. The better we understand rebellion the more prepared we will be to insulate our kids from its influence.

The Original Rebellion

The Lord revealed to Abraham the circumstances under which the plans for our life on earth were laid. In the premortal or spirit world, Heavenly Father declared, "We will go down, for there is space there, and we will take of these materials, and we will make an earth whereon these may dwell; and we will prove them herewith, to see if they will do all things whatsoever the Lord their God shall command them" (Abraham 3:24–25).

The prospect of our obtaining a physical body was so exciting that we "shouted for joy" (Job 38:7). The 1995 *The Family: A Proclamation to the World*, written by the First Presidency and the Council of the Twelve Apostles, offers this summary of that premortal council: "In the premortal realm, spirit sons and daughters knew and worshiped God as their Eternal Father and accepted His plan by which His children could obtain a physical body and gain earthly experience to progress toward perfection and ultimately realize his or her divine destiny as an heir of eternal life" (paragraph 3).

We have not been told much more than that about our premortal existence, and our limited knowledge raises some puzzling questions—questions that have serious ramifications for our children here on earth. For instance, if we all stood bathed in the glory of our Heavenly Father and were filled with joyful anticipation of the coming earth life, how could anyone—God's sons or daughters—experience the joy of that moment and then willfully rebel against Him? For that matter, how could any son or daughter of God, filled with radiant light and knowledge, do anything that would jeopardize their potential earth life?

The same questions could be asked of youth who stray. How could anyone stand in holy places, feel the Spirit, be taught the eternal plan of happiness, and then trade it all away? How can they not see the danger that lurks just beyond the safety of their lifeline? To better understand, let's look at what actually occurred in that council.

Elder Bruce R. McConkie asks:

> Who created and presented the plan of salvation as it was adopted in the pre-existent councils in heaven? Did Christ offer one plan which would allow men their

agency, and Lucifer sponsor another founded on compulsion?

Although we sometimes hear it said that there were two plans—Christ's plan of freedom and agency, and Lucifer's of slavery and compulsions—such teaching does not conform to the revealed word. *Christ did not present a plan of redemption and salvation nor did Lucifer.* There were not two plans up for consideration; *there was only one; and that was the plan of the Father:* originated, developed, presented, and put in force by him ("Who Is the Author of the Plan of Salvation?" *Improvement Era*, 1953, 1).

It is important our children understand that there is only one plan, in all creation, that brings happiness and joy. That plan was presented before the assembled spiritually begotten sons and daughters of God for their sustaining vote. The one question presented for consideration was not *which* plan to use; it was "whom shall I send" to *implement* the plan? (see Abraham 3:27).

Wait a minute, some say, it does look like Lucifer had a plan in mind! They quote: "And he came before me, saying—Behold, here am I, send me, I will be thy son, and I will redeem all mankind, that one soul shall not be lost, and surely I will do it; wherefore give me thine honor" (Moses 4:1). He says he wanted to save all mankind and wanted Father's glory in return. Isn't that a plan?

Was Lucifer's "Plan" a Possibility?

I recently read an article where the author speculated on what life would have been like under Lucifer's "plan." What the author failed to recognize was that Lucifer's proposal was a lie, an impossibility. It could not have been implemented. Why?

Joseph Smith learned that answer while incarcerated in Liberty Jail.

In 1838, during the final days of Far West, in Missouri, anger grew among the Saints toward several brethren in leadership positions. They felt that these leaders had enriched themselves at the expense of the Saints, leaving many to struggle in poverty. These brethren were the focus of a talk by Sidney Rigdon, given on the 4th of July, 1838. In what has often been called the "Salt Sermon" address, Elder Rigdon declared, "Ye [specifically meaning these leaders] are the salt of the earth, but if the salt have lost his savour, wherewith shall it be salted? it is thenceforth good for nothing, but to be cast out, and to be trodden under foot of men" (Matthew 5:13).

The result of this sermon was that these brethren began to fear for their lives. Under the cover of darkness, they took their families and left Far West for Richmond, Missouri. There they swore out oaths against their former brethren. Those oaths became the final justification for Governor Boggs's infamous extermination order. The stark truth is that Joseph Smith's five months in Liberty Jail and the Saint's expulsion from Missouri were precipitated by brethren who had been leaders within the Church. These tragic events were still on the Prophet's mind as he penned a detailed letter to the Saints, in March 1839. From this letter came Sections 121, 122, and 123 of the Doctrine and Covenants. Near the end of Section 121, Joseph gave inspired direction to priesthood holders everywhere. This revelation, though, could just as easily have been talking about Lucifer. For this purpose we'll interject Lucifer into the verse:

> And why [was Lucifer] not chosen?
> Because [his heart was] set so much upon the things

of this world, and [he aspired] to the honors of men, that [he never did] learn this one lesson—

That the rights of the priesthood [and the creative power of the universe] are inseparably connected with the powers of heaven, and that the powers of heaven cannot be controlled nor handled only upon the principles of righteousness.

That they may be conferred upon [him, as a great son of morning], it is true; but when [he undertook] to cover [his] sins, or to gratify [his] pride [and the pride of his followers], [his] vain ambition, or to exercise control or dominion or compulsion upon the souls of the children of men [in an effort to take their agency], in any degree of unrighteousness, behold, the heavens [withdrew] themselves; the Spirit of the Lord [was] grieved; and when it [was] withdrawn, Amen to the priesthood or the authority of [Lucifer].

Behold, ere he [was] aware, he [was] left unto himself [along with those he deceived], to kick against the pricks, to persecute the saints, and to fight against God (see D&C 121:34–38).

In the premortal world, Lucifer had risen to "authority in the presence of God" (D&C 76:25). For him to have done so, we may assume he had grown in intelligence and understanding, and he is in fact referred to as "Lucifer, son of the morning" (Isaiah 14:12), which sounds like a title of great honor. To achieve that stature and authority would have required knowledge of and obedience to the laws of heaven. As one of the great righteous sons of God, Lucifer would have also presumably been taught obedience to those principles.

Then, in some way, perhaps impossible for our mortal minds to comprehend, a small seed of pride came to be planted into his mind. "For thou hast said in thine heart, I will ascend into heaven, I will exalt my throne above the stars of God: I will sit also upon the mount of the congregation, in the sides of the north: I will ascend above the heights of the clouds; I will be like the most High" (Isaiah 14:13–14). How long that pride grew and took shape we don't know. But pride it was that started him down the road of his eternal role as the adversary. C. S. Lewis observed: "It was through Pride that the devil became the devil: Pride leads to every other vice: it is the complete anti-God state of mind." Furthermore, "Pride is spiritual cancer; it eats up the very possibility of love, or contentment, or even common sense" (*Mere Christianity* [New York: HarperSanFrancisco, 2001], 122, 125).

So pride grew in Lucifer until it began to entirely shape his thinking and drive his every action. No longer would he be content to simply serve God, for pride does not allow competition. He wanted more. President Ezra Taft Benson confirmed this when he declared: "The central feature of pride is enmity—enmity toward God and enmity toward our fellowmen. *Enmity* means 'hatred toward, hostility to, or a state of opposition.' It is the power by which Satan wishes to reign over us" ("Beware of Pride," *Ensign*, May 1989, 4). And, we should add, by which he wished to rule over God and Jehovah as well. From the moment Lucifer began to entertain that germ of pride, he began the process that would place him in opposition to his Creator—and to his glorious brother Jehovah.

At one point Lucifer had great power and righteous influence. He was (and is) a persuasive teacher. But when he began to use that stature to gratify his pride and to hide his sins, he lost whatever priesthood power he had.

As Lucifer began fomenting rebellion, his own intelligence

and knowledge must have told him that the course he was pur-
suing was unrighteous and being followed to gratify his own
pride and vain ambition. In short, he must have known that
what he was proposing would have no priesthood power
whatsoever.

And yet, he preached it anyway. Why? One reason may
have been the natural hatred and enmity pride conjures up.
Hatred is a powerful motivator; it blinds one to inaccuracies
and inconsistencies. When we are filled with pride, we see only
what we want to see and ignore everything else. One current
commentator points to some modern cultures that teach nothing but hate and blame toward everyone around them. These
cultures are:

> so notoriously non-introspective, blaming everyone and
> everything else for its own gargantuan problems . . . [that
> it] renders them literally unable to see themselves and
> their faults. Their hatred acts like a narcotic drug that
> takes away their conscious-pain and recognition of their
> faults that would otherwise naturally impress itself on
> their minds. They are filled with the ecstasy of false righ-
> teousness (David Kupelian, "The Secret Curse of
> Hollywood Stars," *Meridian Magazine*, Feb. 2, 2007, 5).

Satan's focus was simple: he wanted to usurp the power of
God without going through the sacrifice and discipline mortality would require. What he wouldn't acquire by obedience he
sought to obtain by deception and lies. He never volunteered
to be the savior that the plan of salvation required. There was
no mention of submitting his will to the Father. There would
be no Gethsemane for him! He focused only on what he
wanted, and he didn't care whose eternal life was jeopardized

for him to get it. (If you have a child who has already rebelled, this should sound pretty familiar.)

Lucifer could not get what he wanted on his own; he had to rally others to his cause. He was not willing to sacrifice for us, yet his greed required the sacrifice of others—for him. His attempt to acquire power required that other sons and daughters of God had to put in jeopardy their own eternal salvation and turn their backs on their loving Creator. How could he get them to do that?

Lucifer's Logic

To help our youth see through and reject Lucifer's sales pitch, we must never forget just how enticing that pitch is, nor underestimate the powerful effect it had on spirit sons and daughters still filled with premortal glory. Understanding the adversary's approach helps us know what we must do to spiritually insulate our children from succumbing to his wiles.

You can learn a lot about a mentor by studying his students. Listen closely to the words of the student and you'll hear the voice of his master. The scriptural record does not tell us the words Lucifer used to entice others to join his rebellion. However, we do hear his voice in the words of three of his anti-Christ pupils—Sherem, Nehor, and Korihor—recorded in the Book of Mormon. All three were well trained in singing satanic siren songs, the same music that was so seductive and persuasive in those spirit world debates.

Alma describes Nehor as a charismatic, effective communicator and says that Nehor "did teach these things so much that many did believe on his words, even so many that they began to support him and give him money." Reveling in this, Nehor "began to be lifted up in the pride of his heart, and to wear very costly apparel, yea, and even began to establish a church after the manner of his preaching" (Alma 1:5–6).

Brigham Young, no stranger to Satan's buffeting, pointed out:

> The adversary presents his principles and arguments in the most approved style, and in the most winning tone, attended with the most graceful attitudes; and he is very careful to ingratiate himself into the favor of the powerful and influential of mankind, uniting himself with popular parties, floating into offices of trust and emolument by pandering to popular feeling, though it should seriously wrong and oppress the innocent (*Discourses of Brigham Young*, sel. John A. Widtsoe [Salt Lake City: Deseret Book Company, 1954], 69).

Sherem, another influential anti-Christ, "had a perfect knowledge of the language of the people; wherefore, he could use much flattery, and much power of speech, according to the power of the devil" (Jacob 7:4). One stratagem of Satan we see very clearly—he chooses his mouthpieces very carefully. No humble, fourteen-year-old boys for him! He wants great communicators with egos to match the message. Why? *Because the message corrupts the teacher as well as the listener.* Everyone is at risk, especially the teacher, when Lucifer's seductive sales pitch is being made in full glory. His logic is so contagious that it infects anyone who speaks its lies.

What well-oiled sales pitch did these students of Satan use? Here is a portion of their message:

"Ye [meaning Jacob] have led away much of this people that they pervert the right way of God" (Jacob 7:7).

No man can know the future (Jacob 7:7).

There never will be a Christ (Jacob 7:9).

Priests and teachers should be "popular" (Alma 1:3).

Priests and teachers should not have to work but should "be supported by the people" (Alma 1:3).

All mankind will be redeemed at the last day and all will have eternal life (Alma 1:4).

The idea of a remission of sins "is the effect of a frenzied mind" (Alma 30:16).

There shall be no atonement made for the sins of men (Alma 30:17).

"Whatsoever a man did was no crime" (Alma 30:17).

Says one commentator:

> Satan said he would *guarantee* their salvation. He promised salvation without excellence, without effort, without hard work, without individual responsibility, and without obedience to righteous laws. That's the lie that he promulgated in the pre-earth councils. That so-called shortcut to salvation captivated many gullible and lazy spirits. They wanted something for nothing (Robert J. Matthews, *Selected Writings of Robert J. Matthews* [Salt Lake City: Deseret Book Company, 1999], 485).

In order to gratify his own pride and ambition, Lucifer stirred up *their* pride, effectively blinding them to the light. To do so, he spun a tale of ease and "freedom," promising they could do whatever they wanted. And without messy commandments. No restrictive "thou shalt nots." No threats of negative consequences. Only indulgence and gratification. By sowing the seed of pride (which is the opposite of the seed of faith), he could make whatever outrageous promises he needed to make, in order to gain their support and they would believe it. In short, *they believed his lies because they wanted to believe them.*

The appealing promise of easy salvation never goes out of

style for those seeking it. It is still a pleasing doctrine today. Those who don't want to think or study or be held accountable find safe haven in Lucifer's logic. Granted, somewhere deep in their hearts, they suspect the message is too good to be true. But the message is so alluring and the communicator so captivating, they choose to ignore those nagging doubts, let go of the rope, and blindly follow. Over time, their heart hardens, and those nagging doubts finally disappear. They can then follow the easier road, without guilt.

One night I watched a television interview with the successful pastor of a very large church. Each Sunday many thousands pack his auditorium, and his books have become best sellers. The interviewer wanted to know how he had become so successful. With a smile, the pastor explained that he teaches a message of hope. Later in the interview, he was asked about repentance. Quickly, he responded that he does not talk about commandments or repentance. "It just seems to get people down," he commented, "and I try to help them feel good about themselves!" Feeling good about yourself, with no consequences to worry about, will always be a popular message.

The War in Heaven

One common name for Satan or Lucifer is "the devil." When translated from the Greek, the *devil* means "false accuser" or "slanderer." Why false accuser? John, in the Book of Revelation, gives us some insight:

> And there was war in heaven: Michael and his angels fought against the dragon; and the dragon fought and his angels,
> And prevailed not; neither was their place found any more in heaven.

And the great dragon was cast out, that old serpent, called the Devil, and Satan, which deceiveth the whole world: he was cast out into the earth, and his angels were cast out with him.

And I heard a loud voice saying in heaven, Now is come salvation, and strength, and the kingdom of our God, and the power of his Christ: *for the accuser* of our brethren is cast down, which accused them before our God day and night (Revelation 12:7–10; emphasis added).

Pride and enmity lead to contention and attack. The Prophet Joseph Smith observed that apostates from the truth "persecute with double diligence, and seek with double perseverance, to destroy those whom they once professed to love, with whom they once communed, and with whom they once covenanted to strive with every power in righteousness to obtain the rest of God" (*Teachings of the Prophet Joseph Smith*, sel. Joseph Fielding Smith [Salt Lake City: Deseret Book Company, 1976], 68). With his perverted gospel and his lies being exposed, Lucifer and his sons of perdition went on the attack.

During the War in Heaven, many opposed the growing rebellion; namely, Jehovah, Michael, and all the "noble and great ones" who fought for the souls of men. These defenders were met, as they always are, with a hail of lies, slander, and innuendo. While the specific nature of the accusations against them is not recorded, we again hear the echoes of those accusations from one of Lucifer's earthly disciples.

The powerful anti-Christ Korihor was brought before the high priest to explain the things he was preaching. Rather than defend himself, he quickly went on the offensive, spinning lies about church leaders: "Ye lead away this people after the foolish traditions of your fathers, and according to your own desires; and ye keep them down, even as it were in bondage, *that ye may glut yourselves with the labors of their hands"* (Alma 30:27; emphasis added).

In other words, Korihor accused the high priest of wanting to become wealthy off the labors of the people. One can guess this is not the first time he has made this argument. This outrageous lie is consistent with that taught by Nehor, who argued that preachers should be "popular," that is, financially supported by their believers.

Lucifer's strategy has always been thus: accuse the righteous of doing what he, himself, plans to do. He found early that attack and slander are very effective ways to steer attention away from his own destructive intentions. And he moves the focus away from himself by trying to get the righteous to defend principles that need no defending. In the mind of a rebel, the best defense is always a good offense.

As the war in heaven deepened, its eternal effects became more profound. Robert J. Matthews suggests that sin, and its consequent spiritual blindness, were everywhere:

> The war was severe, and it had eternal consequences. Every kind of sin . . . was present in that premortal state, and there were many casualties. Repentance was in order for all who sinned; and forgiveness in that premortal life was available through faith in Jesus Christ and obedience to the plan of salvation. (D&C 93:38)
>
> This was not a war just of words and debate and forensics. It was a war of misdeeds, lies, hatred, pride, jealousy, remorse, envy, cursing, blasphemy, deception, theft, cajoling, slander, anger, and sins of almost every kind that are also known in mortality. The issues were so well defined that coexistence was not possible (Kent P. Jackson, ed. *Studies in Scripture, vol. 7, 1 Nephi to Alma 29,* [Salt Lake City: Deseret Book Company, 1987], 147).

As John suggests, Lucifer was making false accusations concerning Jehovah's motives. As he sought to aggrandize himself at the expense of his brothers and sisters, it can be safely assumed he would accuse Jehovah of doing likewise. He would hope that his slander would sow doubt about other righteous beings, such as Michael and Gabriel. Is it any wonder that the Father could no longer allow Lucifer and his followers to stay in their spiritual home and so marshaled the noble and great ones to cast them out?

The War Continues

The war commenced in heaven has of course not ended; a ceasefire was never declared nor was a treaty written. The struggle continues with the same fervor and intensity as it did there. Only the battlefield has changed. Once Adam and his children began to be born into mortality, Lucifer, now Satan, immediately went to work, sowing more seeds of pride and discontent. He and his sycophants still spin the same lies of deception and accusations. His lies were effective there and they are effective here.

The adversary does not care who is harmed by his lies, caring only that he can persuade as many as possible to help advance his purposes. To follow him is to their eternal detriment, but he does not care. "And thus we see," Mormon concludes about Korihor, "that the devil will not support his children at the last day, but doth speedily drag them down to hell" (Alma 30:60).

The War in Heaven tells us a lot about rebellion. Lucifer succumbed to the power of pride, then used it to rally others to his side. His proposal, an impossibility from the moment it was conceived, was driven by lies, deceit, and accusations. It had, as its sole end, the vain ambition of Lucifer himself. He never offered himself to be a sacrificing savior, only a controlling demigod. Those who supported him did so out of blindness, being fueled by their own ambition and desire for easy salvation.

As we seek to guide the youth of the Church, we should never forget how pride destroyed a powerful son of the morning. In addition, we will need to help growing children understand and recognize that Satan's seductive invitation first comes with soft, comforting flaxen cords that quickly bind. It is the original bait and switch, with the painful chains of hell tucked carefully out of sight.

Modern civilization has provided new tools for Lucifer. Anything developed for the benefit of man, such as the Internet, will be seized by Satan to further his purposes. On the other hand, his message never changes. Children carefully taught how Satan works will spot his handiwork whenever it surfaces, in any modern tool or setting. Youth who fully understand what is at stake, who recognize Satan's tactics, are more likely to resist. Those who are but scantily clad in incomplete spiritual armor are most at risk. At critical moments, only the most prepared will be perceptive enough to ask, as did Moses, "Where is thy glory?" (Moses 1:13) and perceiving him to have none, shun his insidious invitations to abandon the truths they have been taught.

Unfortunately, many of our children and youth remain at risk because they do not understand how the evil one works and why he works. When temptation comes they follow it, often unable to explain why they offered no resistance. Letting go of the rope they may later say, it just seemed like a good idea at the time.

Two

The Swords of Our Rebellion

When you teach your son, you teach your son's son.—The Talmud

The prophet Mormon qualifies as an expert on the topic of rebellion. During his lifetime he witnessed "one continual round of murder and bloodshed" (Mormon 8:8), so much so that the Lord refused to let him preach to the people because they were beyond the reach of any reasoning or spiritual promptings. At some point between wars, Mormon began the arduous task of boiling down a thousand years of history into a book small enough to be read by future generations. To do that, he studied all of what was written by previous authors, such as Nephi and Alma.

What Mormon soon discovered was that other prophets had faced many of the same challenges he did. The pattern he discerned was that the pain and hardships of war resulted in a humility that brought people to God. Their righteousness then yielded peace followed by a season of prosperity. Repeatedly, that prosperity was soon soured by pride and spiritual rebellion, manifesting itself in costly apparel, idol worship, neglect of the poor, and wickedness. At that point, it was only a matter of time before yet another Lamanite army would appear on the borders of the land. This cycle of behavior was repeated over and over, with dreary predictability.

Mormon did discover a shining exception to the cycle—the people of Ammon or the Anti-Nephi-Lehies. One can only imagine the delight Mormon must have experienced as he studied their conversion and subsequent history.

A compelling argument can be made that the conversion story of the Anti-Nephi-Lehies, with the exception of the Savior's visit to the Americas, is *the* story of the Book of Mormon. Their repentance, conversion, and unwavering faithfulness would have been the fondest hope of every prophet/writer who penned any part of the Nephite saga. Located in the heart of the book, at the exact halfway point, it is a success story surrounded on either side by wickedness and war. Their uncompromising, post-conversion zeal proves that the cycle of wickedness can be broken when hearts are completely changed.

What is most astounding is that this remarkable standard of righteousness was achieved by Lamanites, a people cursed for disobedience! Their wickedness and unrelenting warfare was a continual bane to the Nephites, right up to the day of the Nephites' destruction. The descendants of Laman and Lemuel were thought to be incapable of change. Yet, Mormon's abridgment was specifically "Written to the Lamanites, who are a remnant of the house of Israel; . . . that they may know the covenants of the Lord, that they are not cast off forever" (title page of the Book of Mormon).

The story of the Anti-Nephi-Lehies proves that even the most rebellious—present and future—can embrace the gospel if conditions are right. "And thus we see," Alma pointed out, "that, when these Lamanites were brought to believe and to know the truth, they were firm, and would suffer even unto death rather than commit sin" (Alma 24:19).

Armed with this knowledge, Mormon's sacrifice to complete his record must have taken on new significance. *In the midst of destruction and disappointment, his abridgment contained a breathtaking success story.* He could only hope that their descendants would be touched by their deeds, which would whisper to them "from the dust" (2 Nephi 3:20; see also Isaiah 29:4).

The Anti-Nephi-Lehies' remarkable conversion actually began more than forty years before Ammon arrived in the Lamanite land of Ishmael. The Nephites were just emerging from the Nephite "Dark Ages"—hundreds of years filled with little inspiration and gospel knowledge. Mosiah had been warned by the Lord to take his people and "flee out of the land of Nephi" (Omni 1:12), the land of their original inheritance. Traveling through the wilderness, Mosiah eventually settled his followers in the land of Zarahemla. There, he and his son Benjamin labored diligently to restore the people to righteousness. When Benjamin became king he continued to strive "with all the might of his body and the faculty of his whole soul [to] . . . establish peace in the land" (Words of Mormon 1:18). To Benjamin's great joy, his people finally shook off years of spiritual rust and became a righteous people.

Near the end of his life, Benjamin prepared to transfer power to his son Mosiah. He gathered his people before him and delivered one of the great sermons in all sacred writ. Those in attendance at the temple were a righteous people, already striving to keep the commandments. Because of their obedience, Benjamin desired to give them "a name, that thereby they may be distinguished above all the people which the Lord God hath brought out of the land of Jerusalem . . . because they have been a diligent people in keeping the commandments of the Lord" (Mosiah 1:11).

That new name, the name of *Christ*, was given to them as they made covenants. Their righteousness had been a good beginning—a preparation for what was to come. Before bestowing that name, King Benjamin explained the debt of gratitude the people owed to their Creator: "I say, if ye should serve him with all your whole souls yet ye would be unprofitable servants. . . . And now I ask, can ye say aught of yourselves? I answer you, Nay. Ye cannot say that ye are even as much as the dust of the earth; . . . behold, it belongeth to him who created you" (Mosiah 2:21, 25).

He needed them to understand that they were incapable of obtaining their own salvation, regardless of their own personal obedience. Salvation would only come through Jesus Christ, whose name they were about to take. As he explained, this great gift was offered to those who could never do enough to earn such a gift. "Are we not all beggars?" he reasoned (Mosiah 4:19).

The result of his address, as we know, was a dramatic change of heart among his people. Their heartfelt desires and complete submission resulted in a dramatic spiritual transformation. "Yea, we believe all the words which thou hast spoken," they cried together. They declared that the Spirit had "wrought a mighty change in us, or in our hearts, that we have no more disposition to do evil, but to do good continually" (Mosiah 5:2).

What is curious—and tragic—to note is that this spiritual conversion did not carry over into the lives of many of their children. "There were many of the rising generation that could not understand the words of king Benjamin, being little children at the time he spake unto his people; and they did not believe the tradition of their fathers" (Mosiah 26:1).

We have little information as to why the people of Zarahemla struggled to endow their children with a similar level of conversion. It is the same confusion we have today when we see rebellious kids coming from deeply faithful families. We do have some clues, however. We know that the unbelievers grew "more numerous" than their believing parents partly because of "the dissensions among the brethren" (Mosiah 26:5). Mormon does not elaborate on what caused those dissensions or what they were about. We know only that the lack of unity, among the people of God, helped fuel their children's disbelief.

First and foremost among that disbelieving generation, fomenting dissension and discontent, were King Benjamin's own grandsons, the four sons of Mosiah. Ammon, Aaron, Omner, and Himni had teamed with the high priest's son, Alma, in doing everything possible to destroy the Church. This was no mild rebellion by a group of spoiled youth. Mormon describes Alma as "a very wicked and an idolatrous man" who used his words and "flattery to the people" to lead "many of the people to do after the manner of his iniquities" (Mosiah 27:8). The actions of these five young men "became a great hinderment to the prosperity of the church of God; stealing away the hearts of the people; causing much dissension among the people; giving a chance for the enemy of God to exercise his power over them" (Mosiah 27:9).

Their attempt to destroy the Church was halted only by angelic intervention. What parent of a rebellious child wouldn't pray for an angel to stand before him or her and shake the earth? In fact, many parents may wonder why such interventions don't happen more often.

The answer to that question actually has two parts. First, the Lord knew Alma and knew what effect the visit of the angel would have on him. And secondly—as we'll see in chapter 11—it happens more often than we know.

The subsequent conversion of Alma and the sons of Mosiah brought even greater changes than the change of heart their parents experienced. These five young men had destroyed the faith of many Nephites, and their repentance required serious restitution. Following their conversion, they began traveling "throughout all the land of Zarahemla, . . . zealously striving to repair all the injuries which they had done to the church" (Mosiah 27:35).

After they had done so, the sons of Mosiah made a courageous decision. As they worked to heal the damage they had caused to the Church, they were filled with the love of all men that inspires the truly converted. The record declares that "they were desirous that salvation should be declared to every creature, for they could not bear that any human soul should perish; yea, even the very thoughts that any soul should endure endless torment did cause them to quake and tremble. And thus did the Spirit of the Lord work upon them, for they were the very vilest of sinners. And the Lord saw fit in his infinite mercy to spare them" (Mosiah 28:3–4).

Indeed, what they wanted was to preach salvation to the very people who had not yet been given that opportunity—the Lamanites. Filled with the love of God, the sons of Mosiah had a grand, idealistic goal: to establish peace among all the children of Lehi. They believed if they could "cure [the Lamanites] of their hatred towards the Nephites" the result would be "no more contentions in all the land which the Lord their God had given them" (Mosiah 28:2). A pretty ambitious project to say the least!

In relating this missionary endeavor, Mormon desired that the reader understand fully the enormity of their task. His own life had been spent in constant battle against warring Lamanites. Thousands of his friends and companions had been killed by Lamanite ruthlessness. And the sons of Mosiah had "undertaken to preach the word of God to a wild and a hardened and a ferocious people; a people who delighted in murdering the Nephites, and robbing and plundering them; and their hearts were set upon riches, or upon gold and silver, and precious stones; yet they sought to obtain these things by murdering and plundering, that they might not labor for them with their own hands" (Alma 17:14).

In preparation, Ammon and his brethren "fasted much and prayed much that the Lord would grant unto them a portion of his Spirit to go with them, and abide with them, that they might be an instrument in the hands of God." In response, "the Lord did visit them with his Spirit, and said unto them: Be comforted" (Alma 17:9–10). Thus assured, Ammon, being the eldest, then gave each of his brethren a blessing. Then they departed, "every man alone, according to the word and power of God which was given unto him" (Alma 17:17; see also v. 18).

Many of their early attempts went as most had feared. Aaron, for instance, preached the gospel in the synagogues of a city called Jerusalem. Unfortunately, the city was filled with Nephite apostates who had been souring the minds and hearts of the local Lamanites. As a result, Aaron and his brethren were thrown in prison (see Alma, chapter 21).

Ammon, on the other hand, was more successful. Traveling

to the land of Ishmael, he was quickly captured and brought before the king of the land, whose name was Lamoni. As Ammon and Lamoni stood before one other for the first time, little did they know how deep and far-reaching their friendship would ultimately become. When asked his reason for coming into their land, Ammon wisely chose not to begin preaching immediately. Perhaps he sensed how poorly the message would have been received at that point. He chose, instead, to serve the king. That service, of course, ultimately led him to defeat those seeking to scatter the king's flocks at the waters of Sebus, winning for him the king's gratitude and trust. Through Ammon's dedicated service, he won the opportunity to teach and convert Lamoni, as well as his family and servants.

The conversion of King Lamoni and his household is worth closer examination. King Lamoni, as a Lamanite, was guilty of many murders. He had routinely ordered the deaths of his servants who failed to protect his flocks from being scattered. As a king, it was also probable he participated in the ongoing wars with the Nephites.

However, we also know that Lamoni was a direct descendant of Ishmael, the patriarch who had joined Lehi in the desert, and whose daughters had provided Lehi's sons with wives. Like most Latter-day Saints, Ishmael was an Ephraimite (see Joseph Fielding Smith, *Answers to Gospel Questions*, comp. Joseph Fielding Smith Jr., 5 vols. [Salt Lake City: Deseret Book Company, 1957–66], 5:70). Modern revelation explains that the tribe of Ephraim is the recipient of the so-called "believing blood," meaning that those born into this lineage would be more responsive to the message of the gospel. This natural responsiveness was part of the promises made to Father Jacob (see Bruce R. McConkie, *Mormon Doctrine*, 2d ed. [Salt Lake City: Bookcraft, 1966], 81).

When Lamoni allowed Ammon to teach him about "the Great Spirit," the king listened closely and was receptive to what he was hearing. An open heart can quickly trump a lifetime of false traditions. His response to Ammon was "I believe all these things which thou hast spoken" (Alma 18:33). The speed with which he heard and accepted the gospel tells us a great deal about Lamoni's believing spirit. Like Paul or Alma at their moments of crisis, once he finally heard the truth he responded wholeheartedly. The fact that his great spirit had been kept in spiritual darkness so long is a grudging testament to the blindness caused by false traditions.

From childhood, Lamoni had been immersed in a 600-year-old lie. He grew up believing that Nephi had robbed Laman and Lemuel of their rightful birthright, never hearing that their wickedness had caused Lehi to take the birthright from them. That one lie, cleverly repeated, led to the suffering and deaths of countless thousands of Lehi's descendants, including the eventual total destruction of the Nephite nation.

Lamoni, on the other hand, became the source by which thousands were brought into the light of the gospel. This conversion began with his immediate family then soon expanded to his father, the king. Over the next seven years, these conversions continued until the message of the gospel was embraced by the inhabitants of seven Lamanite cities. One can hear the awe with which Mormon observes:

> And thousands were brought to the knowledge of the Lord, yea, thousands were brought to believe in the traditions of the Nephites; and they were taught the records

and prophecies which were handed down even to the present time.

And as sure as the Lord liveth, so sure as many as believed, or as many as were brought to the knowledge of the truth, through the preaching of Ammon and his brethren, according to the spirit of revelation and of prophecy, and the power of God working miracles in them—yea, I say unto you, *as the Lord liveth, as many of the Lamanites as believed in their preaching, and were converted unto the Lord, never did fall away* (Alma 23:5–6; emphasis added).

The unwavering faithfulness of these people has been a continuing source of wonder for students of the Book of Mormon. For our purposes, something in their parenting process seems to have insulated their children from the Nephite cycle of righteousness and rebellion. What made these converts unique?

There are at least three elements that may help explain why their children never fell away. It is first important to understand their "pre-conversion" traditions. Next, following their baptisms, they were willing to transform every aspect of their lives. Finally, they literally buried their weapons of war, along with any residue of rebellion that might inflict pain on someone else. Let's look at each of these three elements in depth.

1—Pre-conversion

At first glance, a mission to the Lamanites appeared to be suicidal. Recall again Mormon's description of them. They were:

A wild and a hardened and a ferocious people; a people who delighted in murdering the Nephites, and robbing and plundering them; and their hearts were set upon riches, or upon gold and silver, and precious stones; yet they sought to obtain these things by murdering and plundering, that they might not labor for them with their own hands (Alma 17:14).

The Lamanites would have appeared to be the least likely candidates on earth to be receptive to the gospel message. Other than the sons of Mosiah, we have no record of any other missionary attempts among them. In fact, most Nephite efforts were focused on trying to avoid them. Also, most of their murderous behavior was driven either by the traditions of their fathers or by the lies of apostate Nephites seeking power. Their hatred toward the Nephites was constantly being stirred up.

It was that hatred that led many in Zarahemla to try to discourage the sons of Mosiah from their intended mission. They reasoned, "Do ye suppose that ye can bring the Lamanites to the knowledge of the truth? Do ye suppose that ye can convince the Lamanites of the incorrectness of the traditions of their fathers, as stiffnecked a people as they are; whose hearts delight in the shedding of blood; whose days have been spent in the grossest iniquity; whose ways have been the ways of a transgressor from the beginning?" (Alma 26:24). On what basis, they reasoned, would there be any expectation that the Lamanites might repent?

The Nephite prophet Jacob, living hundreds of years before Lamoni, called Nephite men to repentance by speaking forcefully against gross immorality. In decrying their behavior, he referred them to the example of the Lamanites, who he said were hated "because of their filthiness." But regardless of their other behaviors, the Lamanites faithfully kept their moral commitments. Jacob explained,

Their husbands love their wives, and their wives love their husbands; and their husbands and their wives love their children; and their unbelief and their hatred towards you is because of the iniquity of their fathers; wherefore, how much better are you than they, in the sight of your great Creator? (Jacob 3:7).

Jacob prophetically concluded that, "because of this observance, in keeping this commandment [of morality], the Lord God will not destroy them." As a result, "one day they shall become a blessed people" (Jacob 3:6).

The truth is that the Lamanites, even at their worst, were a covenant making and covenant keeping people. They did not break oaths they'd made—even with their enemies. This Lamanite characteristic was well known among Nephite generals in times of war. One good example of this fact was the classic battle in 74 B.C. between the Nephites under Captain Moroni, and the Lamanite forces commanded by Zerahemnah. When the Nephites finally gained the upper hand, Moroni commanded the fighting to stop. He warned Zerahemnah that his army would be destroyed "except ye depart with an oath that ye will not return again against us to war" (Alma 44:11).

Judged by modern standards, this is an extraordinary offer. To let an army walk off the field of battle, bound only by an oath, would be unthinkable today. But, Moroni understood the Lamanites. He knew that an oath not to return would be honored. And it was.

Though they were a hardened and bloodthirsty people, held back by a long tradition of lies, the Lamanites also lived by a set of standards they wouldn't break. If they made an oath or a covenant, it would be fulfilled. Those standards helped lay a foundation for their future lives and the transformation that followed. They were covenant making people before and after their conversion.

2—*Complete Transformation*

It has been my joy to serve as a facilitator in the LDS Addiction Recovery Program. Drug and alcohol addictions are difficult to overcome. The difficulty stems from the pervasive way addictions rule every aspect of a person's life. Getting the next drink or the next "high" consumes an addict's every waking thought. It dictates social activities and friendships; structuring holidays and celebrations. The addiction provides comfort during down times and celebrations in good times. The way an addiction takes root is described in the scriptures: The devil "leadeth them by the neck with a flaxen cord, until he bindeth them with his strong cords forever" (2 Nephi 26:22).

To maintain sobriety, an addict must free himself from these entanglements. He will never stay clean if he attempts to maintain the same circle of friends, keep the same social network, or visit the same hangouts. An addict's life has been structured by his drug of choice; and it has to be reconstructed to become free of the addiction. He must learn to live differently, socialize differently, celebrate differently. Nothing can remain the same.

The people of Lamoni faced a similar challenge. The routines of their daily life, their thinking, and their outlook on the world were all dictated or colored by the false traditions they had grown up with. They were raised to believe they had been wronged by the Nephites. They also lived in a culture where robbery and murder were acceptable and where idleness was the preferred way of living. If gold and silver could be stolen from someone else, so much the better.

The message of the gospel required that they alter every facet of their life. Once they rejected the ancient lies, they also needed to change the way they interacted with others. Robbery and murder were no longer acceptable. Neither was a life of idleness.

Symbolic of their complete conversion was their name change. Book of Mormon tradition held that a people took the name of an ancestor or city founder. Lamanites, a thousand years after Laman, still traced their lineage, and their name, back to the son of Lehi. This was the reason, for instance, that King Benjamin gave his people a new name. They had changed the way they lived their lives. They had proved themselves worthy to take on the name of Christ. Their new name signified a new lineage—they were new creatures in Christ.

After their conversion, Lamoni's people no longer saw themselves as Lamanites. But, they would never be Nephites. Though they would soon be "numbered" with them religiously, by heritage they would always be separate. With this in mind, "the king and those who were converted were desirous that they might have a name, that thereby they might be distinguished from their brethren" (Alma 23:16). They chose the name Anti-Nephi-Lehies, a name they would keep as long as they lived among their Lamanite brethren.

This name is a source of curiosity for many readers of the Book of Mormon. On the surface, the common definition of "anti" would suggest they are declaring themselves opposed to the people they now sought to emulate. In actuality, it was just the reverse. Hugh Nibley explained:

> This [anti] means "face to face confrontation" whether it is in the Old Norse, Old English, Semitic, Arabic, Greek, Latin, or in the Book of Mormon. It means

"a face-to-face meeting, a joining together with somebody." We are going to find later on about an Anti-Christ,
who is a person who pretends to be Christ, who matches
Christ, who pretends to take the place of Christ. It's not
somebody who opposes Christ, but someone who pretends to be Christ. . . . They gave themselves this name
Anti-Nephi-Lehies. "And they were called by this name
and were no more called Lamanites." So they were set
apart, but they began to be an industrious people—
getting to work at last (Hugh Nibley, *Teachings of the Book of
Mormon—Semester 1: Transcripts of Lectures Presented to an Honors
Book of Mormon Class at BYU, 1988–1990* [FARMS], 405).

These Lamanites chose a name that described their new
standing. Though they were not Nephites by lineage they had
come to believe in Nephite religious teachings. Consistent with
their new name and lifestyle, they made three covenants:

1. "They never would use weapons again for the shedding
   of man's blood;"
2. "Rather than take away from a brother they would give
   unto him;"
3. And "rather than spend their days in idleness they would
   labor abundantly with their hands" (Alma 24:18).

These solemn oaths would be their guide for generations
to come. The nature of these promises were a clear indication
of just how completely their lives had changed. Lives that had
previously focused on idleness and murder were about to
become an example for every other descendant of Lehi.

The prophet Mormon uses contrasts in order to teach.
In compiling the abridgment of the Nephite records, he
purposefully juxtaposes contrasting stories or characters to

illustrate important truths or doctrines. Thus, the story of wicked King Noah appears immediately after King Benjamin's address. After showing us the contrast, he records King Mosiah's suggestion that given a king's propensity for evil, a government led by judges would be a better form of government than a monarchy. The reader well understands the merit of that suggestion, having just read about both good and evil kings.

The conversion of the Anti-Nephi-Lehies gives us another lesson by contrast. We read earlier about the changes wrought in the hearts of King Benjamin's people but that many of their children refused to believe. Mormon then gives us the story of another rising generation—the children of the Anti-Nephi-Lehies. The contrast between Zarahemla's faithless generation and the Ammonite stripling warriors is stark and instructional.

How do we account for the difference between the two? The answer lies partly in the example set by their parents. It is difficult to know how much life really changed for King Benjamin's people following their conversion. Prior to their conversion, they were already keeping the commandments and already living the law of Moses. They lived in relative prosperity. After their experience at the temple, they obviously felt different, but those changes may have not been that profound. To their children, too young to remember Benjamin's words, nothing was really *that* different. In fact, the only noticeable outside change may have been the additional prosperity resulting from their parents' righteousness.

For the Anti-Nephi-Lehies, conversion was a watershed event for the entire family. It would have been a huge change, one that affected every facet of daily life. In the eyes of their children, it transformed everything their parents did on a daily basis. It also resulted in the deaths of adults they knew; for some, that might have included their own parents. In the end, it necessitated a move through the wilderness to the Nephite land of Jershon. So while the children of King Benjamin probably did not experience any requisite sacrifice at the conversion of their parents, the Ammonite children saw their people sacrifice everything. That example would forever influence how they fulfilled covenants.

If children are to cling to the faith, they must clearly see the differences between a gospel-centered life and how the rest of the world lives. They also need to see and experience the joy that results from living the gospel. Parents whose behavior is barely distinguishable from that of the world around them will find it difficult to keep their children on a higher path. Example is everything.

3—*They Did Lay Down the Weapons of Their Rebellion*

Finally, nothing symbolized the Lamanite's new birth more than the dramatic act of permanently laying down their swords. They actually buried two types of swords: their swords of war and their swords of rebellion.

Burial #1

Their first covenant, to bury their weapons of war, came out of a sense of gratitude for the Lord's mercy. Lamoni's brother, Anti-Nephi-Lehi, put it this way:

> And now behold, my brethren, since it has been all that we could do, (as we were the most lost of all mankind) to repent of all our sins and the many murders which we have committed, and to get God to take them away from our hearts, for it was all we could do to repent

sufficiently before God that he would take away our stain—

Now, my best beloved brethren, since God hath taken away our stains, and our swords have become bright, then let us stain our swords no more with the blood of our brethren (Alma 24:11–12).

This was a deeply symbolic act for these former Lamanites. They had truly repented, and their hearts had been purified and pronounced clean. A clean sword would graphically testify that they were not guilty of any further bloodshed. They appear to have then displayed their bright swords for all to see.

However, that oath would be tested in an unimaginably difficult way. The church of God had grown and prospered for seven years and showed no sign of stopping. Surely that growth must have finally threatened the livelihood of the apostate Nephites living among the Lamanites. They were "Nehors," meaning that they depended on legalistic conflicts for their employment. The peace-loving people of Lamoni would certainly be bad for business. Finally bubbling over, the anger of the unrighteous Nephites "became exceedingly sore against them, even insomuch that they began to rebel against their king, insomuch that they would not that he should be their king; therefore, they took up arms against the people of Anti-Nephi-Lehi" (Alma 24:2).

Ammon met with Lamoni and his brother to determine how they would respond to this upcoming threat. Imagine Ammon's horror when the people refused to take up arms and the king commanded them to "not even make any preparations for war" (Alma 24:6). Even more astonishing is the fact that they also made no attempt to flee the city or to hide. Not only did they refuse to fight, they also refused to run.

To his everlasting credit, their final decision is summed up by King Anti-Nephi-Lehi, Lamoni's brother:

> And now, my brethren, if our brethren seek to destroy us, behold, we will hide away our swords, yea, even we will bury them deep in the earth, that they may be kept bright, as a testimony that we have never used them, at the last day; and if our brethren destroy us, behold, we shall go to our God and shall be saved (Alma 24:16).

John the Revelator could have been talking about them when he explained that Satan's followers would be defeated by those who, "overcame him by the blood of the Lamb, and by the word of their testimony; and they loved not their lives unto the death" (Revelation 12:11).

Some would ask why they refused to defend themselves. If we aren't careful, we can quickly reduce the answer to one of duty or covenant keeping. It is true that the Anti-Nephi-Lehies made covenants to bury their swords deep in the earth. But that decision was driven by a fundamental change in the desires of their hearts.

The desires of our heart can lead us to keep covenants for a wide variety of reasons. For instance, two sisters can faithfully complete their visiting teaching assignment. One sister may be doing it out of a feeling of love and concern for the sisters assigned to her. At the same time, her companion may be angry and resentful and waiting for the visits to end. On the Relief Society roles, both receive credit for having faithfully completed their assignment. But Mormon made this distinction:

> For behold, God hath said a man being evil cannot do that which is good; for if he offereth a gift, or prayeth

unto God, except he shall do it with real intent it prof-
iteth him nothing.

For behold, it is not counted unto him for
righteousness.

For behold, if a man being evil giveth a gift, he doeth
it grudgingly; wherefore it is counted unto him the same
as if he had retained the gift; wherefore he is counted evil
before God (Moroni 7:6–8).

The key to understanding the actions of the Anti-Nephi-
Lehies is to look closely at their heartfelt desires. Ammon was
an observer in that meeting where they decided not to fight
and not to flee. Later, in the psalm of Ammon, he documents
the real reason they kept the oaths they made—even if it meant
their own deaths:

For behold, they had rather sacrifice their lives than
even to take the life of their enemy; and they have buried
their weapons of war deep in the earth, *because of their love
towards their brethren.*

And now behold I say unto you, has there been so
great love in all the land? Behold, I say unto you, Nay,
there has not, even among the Nephites.

For behold, they would take up arms against their
brethren; they would not suffer themselves to be slain. But
behold how many of these have laid down their lives; and
*we know that they have gone to their God, because of their love and
of their hatred to sin* (Alma 26:32–34; emphasis added).

True, they could have fought and prevented themselves
from being killed. But they were filled with the type of love
only the deeply converted know and could not bring themselves to raise a sword at their brethren. Were they inspired to
know that many of their brethren would join the church

because of their sacrifice? We do not know. We do know, however, that they knelt before the oncoming slaughter, buoyed up by Christ-like love, and died in the attitude of prayer.

There is another reason why it was essential that they bury their swords. In accepting the gospel, these Lamanites came to realize just how serious a sin their murders were. Yet, given their false traditions, forgiveness somehow was granted. When any future possibility arose that might involve the shedding of more blood, they recoiled. The king reasoned:

> And now behold, my brethren, since it has been all that we could do, . . . to repent of all our sins and the many murders which we have committed, and to get God to take them away from our hearts, . . . since God hath taken away our stains, and our swords have become bright, then let us stain our swords no more with the blood of our brethren (Alma 24:11–12).

They fully realized the enormity of the forgiveness extended. Even with their ignorance of the law, it had been "all they could do" to become cleansed and to escape the awful hell that awaited them. Now pardoned, they were not about to do anything that might jeopardize the mercy extended to them.

Burial #2

The second type of sword buried by the Anti-Nephi-Lehies—one of particular interest to parents—was the sword of their rebellion. We are told that "they became a righteous people; they did lay down the weapons of their rebellion, that they did not fight against God any more, neither against any of their brethren" (Alma 23:7).

As with most rebels, they had rebelled both against their God and against their brethren. We'll look first at rebellion against God. Then, in chapter 4, we'll see how rebellion expresses itself in our relationships with others.

As we've discussed, the "natural man is an enemy to God" (Mosiah 3:19). The term *enemy* might seem fairly harsh, but it accurately defines the relationship. The prideful "natural man" comes to believe the selfish whimpering of Satan, who vainly cries, "son of man, worship me" (Moses 1:12). It is the same tired message he's attempted to force on God's children from the beginning of time—the song of rebellion.

In the final days of the Nephite nation, Mormon noted "a mourning and a lamentation" (Mormon 2:11) among the people as they realized their fate. Mormon prayed that their sorrowing might lead to repentance. It didn't. It became, instead, "the sorrowing of the damned" (Mormon 2:13), a myopic march devoid of hope. As a result, preaching to them would do no good, for they had hardened to the point they were incapable of hearing the Spirit. Gloomily, he recorded: "My sorrow did return unto me again, and I saw that the day of grace was passed with them, both temporally and spiritually; for I saw thousands of them hewn down *in open rebellion* against their God, and heaped up as dung upon the face of the land" (Mormon 2:15; emphasis added).

Mormon clearly sees their annihilation as the result of their "open rebellion," against God. These "fair ones" were once chosen and blessed. Now they had become enemies to their God. Sadly, as they stood waiting on Cumorah's hill, they believed that their enemy was the Lamanites marching towards them. They would not see it was God against whom they had chosen to fight.

The Lamanite annihilation of the Nephites was driven by a need to correct an ancient wrong. They saw the Nephites as the enemy, children "of a liar." In reality, they too were rebelling against their God. Both peoples had defied the will of God and set aside His counsel. To quote Hugh Nibley, the final battle is "the wicked against the wicked" (*BYU Studies*, 25 [Winter 1985], 27).

When any of us—parents or youth—pick up the sword of rebellion, we do so to defend ourselves against an enemy. The Church is filled with members who refuse to attend because they were offended by someone in the ward. When asked why they no longer attend, they describe wrongs suffered or thoughtless deeds done. In their minds, they must defend themselves against "an enemy," one who would hurt them. In reality, they have moved from "holy places" and placed themselves outside the healing spirit of fellowship. They've cut themselves off from sacred ordinances and blessings of the temple. In doing so, they fail to see that we do not rebel against the bishop or a tactless Church member—we rebel, instead, against God.

The children of Ammon provide parents and youth leaders with a template to follow. They document a deep conversion by parents and show its subsequent effect on their children. That conversion is manifested in a conscious burying of any swords of rebellion we carry, as well as living a life transformed by Christ. It is the example of the transformed life that can inspire a child to surrender his or her own life to Christ.

Three

The Surrendered Life

The tumult and the shouting dies, the captains and the kings depart.
Still stands thine ancient sacrifice, an humble and a contrite heart.
Lord God of Hosts, be with us yet, lest we forget, lest we forget.
—Rudyard Kipling

Elder Henry B. Eyring once told the true story of Jack Steel, a friend of his at Stanford University. During World War II, Jack received the second highest decoration a soldier can receive: the Distinguished Service Cross. He was awarded it because of gallant actions performed while defending his fellow soldiers in battle. Steel's platoon had been assigned to capture an important bridge. As they walked down a long slope, they could see that the bridge was heavily defended. When the enemy on the bridge spotted Jack's platoon they immediately opened fire. A machine gunner trained his gun on the men highest on the hill and began working his way down, with devastating effects. The men of the platoon were rapidly being killed or wounded.

In that moment, Jack Steel saw that the men who began running back up the hill were also being hit. It soon became clear, that if he wanted to live, he would have to charge straight at the bridge. Therefore, grabbing his Browning automatic rifle, he ran toward the bridge, screaming and firing from the hip.

The defenders on the bridge were so surprised by his actions that they immediately deserted the bridge, leaving Jack to capture it single-handedly. His bold attack not only captured the bridge but also saved the rest of his platoon farther up the hill. Elder Eyring concluded the story with this note:

> Now, the reason you need to hear the story is that it turned out to be the wrong bridge. That is what you need to know. The colonel who sent them had given the wrong instruction and it was a useless bridge—it didn't go anywhere. All the people defending it were dealing with the wrong bridge ("We Need a Miracle," an address to CES Area Directors, 6 April, 1981).

Effort and gallantry aside, they had attacked the wrong target! Someone had made a serious mistake in their directives. The bridge they really needed to capture was still out there and still needed to be taken.

I believe that many parents, striving to do the best they can but having less success with their children than they would like, may be following the wrong directives. The result may be that they struggle more than they need to. In the next two chapters we will examine two critical areas that are essential in teaching our youth: first, the connection between building self-esteem and rebellion. Second, we will examine the effect rebellion has on our relationships and marriages, and how those relationships strengthen or dilute our message.

Guilt Warning!

Many of you reading the following chapters have young children and will wish to decrease the chances they will go through significant rebellion in their lives. Our discussion of parenting relationships, discipline, and so forth will help you look more closely at the delicate interplay between parent and child, helping you focus on what it is you're really trying to accomplish.

However, many of you may have children whose pride and rebellion have already led them down destructive paths. Their reckless choices have already brought you grief and second-guessing. As you read these chapters on "prevention" you will be tempted to blame yourself for not following this principle or that. In all likelihood you are already "guilt waiting to happen"!

Please be aware that Lucifer, the great accuser, would have you believe that your child's poor choices are strictly your fault and that you are solely responsible for the resulting chaos. You are also aware that—in saner moments—your heart whispers that though you could have done things differently, you practiced the best parenting you knew how to do. The fact that you are reading these words attests to your desire to do all you can and to be a true blessing when the rebel is ready to return.

That said, let's now turn our attention to the powerful forces that seek to put our youth on faulty foundations.

Generation Me

The last four decades have seen a dramatic shift in societal belief patterns. These changes are best identified by seeing them through the eyes of Baby Boomers, the large demographic group born shortly after World War II.

Immediately before and after World War II, there was a great deal of predictability to life. Soldiers came home, started families, and moved forward with their lives. Their children, the so-called Baby Boomers, were born to parents who had grown up with a clear set of values and expectations. These parents, frequently called the Greatest Generation, had survived the Great Depression and carried on with lives similar to their parents.

The decade of the sixties exploded in a cultural convulsion. The relative prosperity of the fifties had freed up children to question and explore. Growing Baby Boomers were told they were supposed to "do your own thing," "find your bag," and "question authority." Old rules and mores were challenged as never before, giving rise to unprecedented social change and the excesses of the hippie movement.

As the sixties became the seventies, the thrill of unrestrained freedom gave way to disillusionment. The drug culture of the sixties failed to yield the spiritual nirvana it promised. Proud rebels found themselves addicted and miserable. As a result, excess gave way to searching and introspection. That search led to "the journey to find the self," by looking deep inside. And thus was born the self-esteem movement.

Ultimately, boomers came to believe that bliss was found after achieving some type of inner peace. The best indicator of that bliss or peace was their level of "self-esteem." In other words, "Do you like yourself, finally, at the end of your journey?" "Are you," as one psychologist called it, "self-actualized?"

For boomers, the search for self-esteem became all encompassing. They had seen their parents tied closely to societal expectations and didn't always like the results. They weren't sure they wanted to be June Cleaver, wearing a dress and pearls to dinner each night. The journey for self-esteem began to be seen as freedom from the expectations of others in favor of living by your own expectations.

In her book, *Generation Me,* Jean Twenge cites a 1977

teacher's manual that has, as its core philosophy for students, "I am a self and you are a self, and I don't want to be made to feel guilty if I am not like you, nor should you be made to feel guilty if you are unlike me!"

The message was clear—the development of childhood self ego was our most critical task, eclipsing all others. And, like most movements, the self-esteem movement began with the most noble of intentions. Unfortunately, it resulted in unforeseen consequences.

As Baby Boomers became educators (self-actualized educators at that!), they went to work rewriting school curricula. Enlightened boomers made sure that the development of self-esteem became a central theme of education. This was fueled, in part, by the belief that as you increased a child's self-esteem you would increase their academic performance.

Schools moved as never before to help shore up the egos of their students. Twenge writes:

> *Free to Be You and Me*, one of the most popular children's films during the 1970s and 1980s, trumpets individuality in forty-five minutes of catchy songs and stories. Many people I know have it practically memorized; my third-grade class in Irving, Texas, watched it almost every Friday in the early 1980s. One song says, "When I grow up I'm going to be happy and do what I like to do." Another skit gives examples of animals dressed by their owners ("don't dress your horse in a nightgown just cuz he can't stay awake") and concludes, "A person should wear what he wants to, and not just what other folks say" (*Generation Me* [New York: Free Press, 2007], 25).

As part of this effort, children were taught to play the Ungame (where everyone wins) as opposed to Monopoly, a game that fostered competition, hurt people's feelings, and resulted in winners and losers. Honor rolls were taken down from school hallways. If there were any school-yard competitions, such as a 100-yard dash, everyone got a ribbon so they'd know that "everyone is a winner in their own way!"

The logic was (and still remains in many areas), that in any endeavor, some will succeed and others will fail. And though this is gratifying to the winner it is emotionally destructive to the loser. In an effort to shelter kids from that sense of failure, schools and youth programs, such as the Girl Scouts, eliminated any program that might leave a child feeling anything but a winner—regardless of effort or performance.

Unfortunately, as school districts began to evaluate the results of these self-esteem programs, they learned they'd been attacking the wrong bridge. The state of California, for instance, spent $250,000 to raise the self-esteem of California students by promoting self-esteem programs. When a book sponsored by the California Task Force to Promote Self-Esteem and Personal and Social Responsibility was published, it concluded with a surprising, well-documented result: *self-esteem isn't linked to academic achievement,* good behavior, or any other outcome the task force was formed to address! (see ibid., 25).

Why? Shouldn't teaching children to like themselves more improve the way they deal with life? Roy Baumeister has done extensive research in the effect of self-esteem training. His conclusion:

> It is very questionable whether [the few benefits] justify the effort and expense that schools, parents, and therapists have put into raising self-esteem. After all these years, I'm sorry to say, my recommendation is this: forget about self-esteem *and concentrate more on self-control and*

self-discipline ("The Lowdown on High Self-Esteem: Thinking You're Hot Stuff Isn't the Promised Cure-All," *Los Angeles Times*, January 25, 2005; emphasis added).

In the rush to build self-esteem, self-control and self-discipline had been deemphasized. "You are great regardless of what you do" had the effect of telling many kids, "so don't worry about doing too much" (ibid., 25). (Unfortunately for the Church, this attitude may be contributing to the rising rate of missionaries who return home early from their missions. Young men and women who do not see the need for self-discipline, when combined with an increased emphasis on "taking care of me" may be more likely to walk away from stressful situations, such as missions.)

Baby Boomers had sought to find themselves and to feel good about themselves by building their self-esteem. However, they placed the self-esteem cart before the horse. Their children were told they were "great" from the moment they were born, regardless of anything they did or didn't do. Self-esteem had indeed trumped self-control or self-discipline.

BYU professor Catherine Thomas explained at a BYU devotional:

> Whatever the valid uses of the term self-esteem are, however much good is intended, I wonder if self-esteem isn't a red herring . . . *I suggest that the issue of self-esteem is a diversion to distract us from the real issue of our existence.* We might be justified in telling people to fix their self-esteem in order to solve their most basic problems if we knew nothing of man's premortal life, or the spiritual purpose of his earthly probation, or his glorious destiny. But, the fullness of the gospel of Jesus Christ teaches the true nature and true needs of the self (*Selected Writings of M. Catherine Thomas* [Salt

Lake City: Deseret Book Company, 2000], 250; emphasis added).

I agree wholeheartedly with Sister Thomas. For many years, I sought to help those with "low self-esteem" feel better about themselves. Unfortunately, there never seemed to be enough love and support for some people, and that unconditional support seemed to disappear down an emotional black hole. For others, early abuse or trauma seemed to never give up its icy grip on a battered ego. Cheery expressions of "You're great just the way you are!" were greeted with skepticism and pained laughter. Only now, do I better understand the missing pieces to the puzzle and my therapeutic approach is much different.

Like everyone else, I incorporated the same principles that many parents and teachers did concerning self-esteem programs—believing that increasing self-esteem would result in higher discipline and self-control. Unfortunately, in the rush to build esteem independent of anything else, we often fostered the very thing that shook our premortal world—pride.

The full title of Twenge's book is: *Generation Me: Why Today's Young Americans Are More Confident, Assertive, Entitled—and More Miserable Than Ever Before.* Does that sound like any youth you know? As we pump up a disembodied self-esteem—you are great no matter what trouble you get into—we run the risk of developing a generation of narcissists instead.

The generation now in their teens and twenties were raised on a steady diet of self-esteem-ism. Early on, they have been told they are wonderful "just the way you are." And because of that "you can do anything you want to do."

"Wait!" some will ask. "Are you telling me there is something wrong with telling a child 'I love you just the way you are'?" Not at all. Again, what starts out with good intentions can produce the opposite result. Within a home, loving parents build a child up when they honestly express their feelings, independent of anything the child has done.

The difficulty comes when society concludes that any criticism of a child's actions and behavior would irreparably damage the child. This is often paired with the idea that higher self-esteem drives achievement. The false assumption is that we can compliment a child into higher grades, while criticism and critique forever scar their development.

This philosophy is clearly on display on the hit television show *American Idol*. Young people come from all over the country to audition for a chance to become a pop music idol. Without musical accompaniment, they audition for the judges who either reject them or send them on to the national competition. For the first few weeks of the show, we see performer after performer with little or no musical talent. When the judges reject their audition, many stand in stunned silence. Others rush out to be comforted by supportive friends and/or family.

What is astonishing is the amazing gap between these contestants' actual talent and their over-inflated sense of skill. They have little musical talent—but it becomes painfully obvious that no one has ever told them so. Raised with an unrealistic "you can do anything you put your mind to" mind-set, they may spend time focusing on areas other than where their real strengths lie. When rejected, these would-be pop stars stomp off, complaining that the judges just don't understand.

The result of the self-esteem movement has often been just the opposite of what was envisioned. Many young adults, by their own admission, are unprepared to enter a world that will

judge them on the quality of their work and does not give rib-
bons for just showing up. When they are fired, they blame their
boss or the circumstance and sigh, "Hey, it just wasn't for me!"
(If I'm great, then those who don't like me have something
wrong with them!)

This attitude is exemplified in a recent *People* magazine
article about a celebrity who had left his seven months' preg-
nant wife to be with another female celebrity instead. The public's response when the new couple was put on the magazine's
cover? One fan wrote, "I was excited to see [the new girlfriend]
and future stepdaughter, on the cover. It's refreshing to see that
her fiancé chooses to be with her because of love and not with
[the former wife] just because they have children together"
(Kristy Nichols, Letter to the Editor, *People*, Sept. 13, 2004). In
other words, you should just take care of you, regardless of the
effect it might have on anyone else—even your kids.

Our children and youth are swimming in a culture of
me-ism. It surrounds them and forms their thinking and habits.
They are told that no one is more important than they are and
they should always focus first on themselves, putting everyone
else second. Self-esteem, self-worth, self-concept: Satan would
define all of them if he could. After thousands of years, he is
still trying to dictate what we do and what we will be.

Self-esteem-ism, which starts with the greatest of intentions, can easily become Lucifer's plan of deception tied up in a
politically correct wrapper. He teaches that we should like ourselves, just the way we are. When we do something we
shouldn't, it's not our fault. We are not responsible because we
should be able to do anything we want to do. It is the Korihor
plan of self-improvement!

Is there any place for self-esteem? Of course. But first,

children must come to understand how Satan defines esteem when compared with the plan of salvation.

The Divine Paradox

In Latter-day Saint theology we are presented with a series of conflicts. As part of the great plan of salvation, we learn we have the potential to become like our Heavenly Father. In essence, we are gods in embryo. Patriarchal blessings reveal that we are part of a covenant lineage, recipients of all the blessings promised Abraham, Isaac, and Jacob. Our faithfulness results in our becoming the "seed of Abraham" and "the elect of God" (D&C 84:34).

The more we understand, the more we realize the extent to which we've been blessed. As we count our blessings—one by one—we can see that we really are *somebody!* Talk about self-esteem! To see our potential, to know what we know, to be blessed with what we have: truly we are a blessed "royal generation," chosen to come forth in the last dispensation. "Surely," we marvel, "there has never been a generation like us on the face of the earth."

Yet, in the midst of all that spiritual revelry, we turn to the scriptures and might become confused. For example, we read where Moses is brought to stand on a high mountain and is given the glorious and sweeping "vision" of all things (see Moses 1:7–8). This panoramic sweep of God's creation is similar to the one enjoyed by the Brother of Jared, Enoch, Nephi, Abraham, Peter, James, and John, and Joseph Smith. In a wonderful celestial way, the minds of these prophets were expanded to see all God's creations. This vision is the reason the prophet Mormon could say "Jesus Christ hath shown you unto me, and I know your doing" (Mormon 8:35).

After the vision closes for Moses, he is left to himself. Obviously, he is stunned by what he has just seen. Even more, this adopted son of Pharaoh, looks closely at himself and exclaims, "Now, for this cause *I know that man is nothing*, which thing I never had supposed" (Moses 1:10; emphasis added). Nothing? That's pretty harsh. Didn't he mean nothing *when compared with God?* Surely King Benjamin could clarify this idea. Said he: "And now I ask, can ye say aught of yourselves? I answer you, Nay. Ye cannot say that ye are even as much as the dust of the earth; yet ye were created of the dust of the earth; but behold; it belongeth to him who created you" (Mosiah 2:25). Then, so that we wouldn't miss the point, he also said, "For behold, are we not all beggars?" (Mosiah 4:19).

From a self-esteem point of view, these types of statements should scar us for life! However, when we look at prophets like Moses and Mormon, don't these brethren appear to have "high self-esteem"? Weren't they men of great accomplishment? As we look at their lives, we would have to agree that their "nothingness" did not appear to emotionally hinder them in any way.

Curiously, Lucifer's self-esteem would also seem to be in pretty good shape. By all accounts, he likes himself a lot and wants us to be like him, to worship him! The same could also be said of Nehor, Korihor, and Sherem. For that matter, the world's most bloody despots, from Hilter to Stalin, would probably have qualified as men of high self-esteem.

So, if focusing on self-esteem is not the answer, then what?

Divine-Esteem

In chapter 13 we will look closely at the addiction recovery program of the Church. The first step of that program begins with the words, "I admit I am powerless . . ." Recently, a sister stopped to visit after a twelve-step meeting and remarked that she was having a great deal of difficulty with the word "powerless." "I am *not* powerless!" she said earnestly. As we talked she shared some things about her childhood. She described a family filled with dysfunction and pain. Powerless, as defined for her in word and deed, meant being helpless and at risk for abuse. She equated the idea of being powerless with being weak and vulnerable.

I then read her the following quote from Elder Neal A. Maxwell:

> While the egoistic urge of the natural man is to invite others, "Look at me," instead we should increasingly say, "Look to God and live" (Alma 37:47). When our natural instinct is to claim credit, increasingly we should ponder what [God and Christ] have done for us—a rescuing which *we mortals were absolutely powerless to effect for ourselves.* No wonder we are comparatively "unprofitable servants" (Mosiah 2:21).
>
> *Though we are "unprofitable," however, the Lord has not said we are worthless.* In fact, He has said the worth of each soul is great in His sight (D&C 18:13–15). But the vast differences between what He has done for us and what we do for Him truly make us comparatively unprofitable. Nevertheless we are His servants. More important, we are His children! And He is a perfect and nurturing Father (*Men and Women of Christ* [Salt Lake City: Bookcraft, 1991], 31; emphasis added).

Our Heavenly Father does not define powerlessness as worthlessness. This great Being, who loves us more than we can know, pleads that we will become completely and utterly dependent on Him. If we do, He will "mount [us] up with wings as eagles" (Isaiah 40:31). He will not let us fall or fail.

When we admit we can do nothing of ourselves, we are then ready to admit "I can do all things through Christ [who] strengtheneth me" (Philippians 4:13).

On the other hand, what this good sister experienced while growing up was exactly the opposite. To be helpless was to be hurt, to be taken advantage of. To be powerless meant to be unable to stop someone from taking advantage of her. As she grew, she concluded she would never again need anyone— she would not be powerless.

Powerless, in the Lord's lexicon, has an exact definition. The natural man, full of the spirit of pride, believes he is powerful in his own sphere. He takes control, he learns to dominate, he makes sure he gets what he wants. At the same time, this natural powerful man "is an enemy to God." He is not just incompatible—he is an enemy. Why an enemy? Because he does not listen to or follow the whisperings of the Spirit; he listens only to his own set of wants. And he remains at odds with his Maker, "unless he yields to the enticings of the Holy Spirit" (Mosiah 3:19), bringing his will in subjection to the Lord. When we finally place that will on the altar, with a broken heart and contrite spirit, the Lord is then able to make the "mighty change in us, or in our hearts" (Mosiah 5:2).

When the Lord changes a heart, the change is dramatic. The self-powerful "becometh as a child, submissive, meek, humble, patient, full of love." This "new creature in Christ" is "willing to submit to all things which the Lord seeth fit to inflict upon him, even as a child doth submit to his father" (Mosiah 3:19; 2 Cor. 5:17).

I am convinced that if we could help our children increase in divine-esteem (dependency on God), rather than self-esteem (dependency on self), the more confident they would be in solving daily problems and difficulties. They would also be less likely to fall prey to worldly solutions.

As it is, too many children believe in a philosophy best stated by William Ernest Henley's poem "Invictus":

> It matters not how strait the gate,
> How charged with punishments the scroll,
> I am the master of my fate:
> I am the captain of my soul.

Wouldn't we rather want our children to follow Orson F. Whitney's response:

> Art thou in truth?
> Then what of him who bought thee with his blood?
> Who plunged into devouring seas
> And snatched thee from the flood? . . .
> Bend to the dust that "head unbowed,"
> Small part of life's great whole,
> And see in him and him alone,
> The captain of thy soul.
> > (As quoted in Jay A. Parry, Linda Ririe
> > Gundry, Jack M. Lyon, Devan Jensen, eds. *Best
> > Loved Poems of the LDS People* [Salt Lake City:
> > Deseret Book Company, 1996], 42–43)

It was with such knowledge that Moses performed powerful miracles, all the time seeing himself as powerless when compared with his Maker. This is the same spirit that compelled a prophet and a boy—Elisha and his servant—to stand before the approaching army and have Elisha calmly declare, "Fear not: for they that be with us are more than they that be with them" (2 Kings 6:16). They were powerless when compared to man's standards; they were unbeatable when teamed with God.

The notion of complete surrender may seem, to some, at odds with Latter-day Saint belief in self-reliance. We teach that fathers are responsible to provide for their families. We are warned against getting into debt. We have classes in emergency preparedness and food storage. In a temporal sense, we believe we are to be self-reliant. In actuality, even our sense of "self-reliance" is a mirage. We rely, not on ourselves, but on the Lord to provide jobs and financial means to help us accomplish these things. We are instructed to pray for wisdom about how we are to use the means placed into our hands. And, in all things, we give thanks to the Lord for his help. Even in our self-reliance we are divinely dependent.

One Latter-day Saint, struggling to deal with painful addictions, sought to balance the idea of self-reliance against the powerlessness she felt when trying to overcome her weaknesses. As she healed, she came to understand her reliance on the Savior. She also began to see the "vanity" of thinking we were intended to "do it" on our own.

> Of course! This was it! This was the "vanity" and the "unbelief" that brings us into condemnation or bondage. It was the vanity of placing emphasis on self-reliance, self-sufficiency, self-anything above and before emphasis on the reality of seeking salvation in and through the Savior. One of the most damning fallacies Satan had so subtly twisted in my mind during all the years I had listened to church leaders stress self-reliance in temporal concerns, was that I also had to be self-reliant in my own salvation (Colleen C. Harrison, *He Did Deliver Me from Bondage* [Pleasant Grove, Utah: Windhaven Publishing, 2002], 16).

Lucifer would have us believe differently. In a classic piece of anti-Christ wisdom, Korihor taught his followers that "every

man fared in this life according to the management of the creature" and that "every man conquered according to his strength."
These are the justifications for believing that "whatsoever a man
did was no crime" (Alma 30:17). They could do whatever they
wanted to without the inconvenience of consequence. That left
them free to outsmart or outmuscle weaker competitors—it's
just business, after all.

The Surrendered Life

To help insulate our children from Satan's temptations, our
goal, as parents, should be to teach our children how to live a
surrendered life—one directed by the Savior. The more they trust
the Lord, the less they fear. "Look unto me in every thought";
the Savior invites, "doubt not, fear not" (D&C 6:36). Removing
this fear removes one of Satan's greatest tools in the battle for
souls. He will attempt to use fear to entice children to follow
the crowd, to give in to peer pressure.

Not surprisingly, then, surrender and trust are assigned a
negative connotation in today's world. It is not fashionable to
be meek! We are taught that to get ahead in life, you must be in
charge, be self-assured and confident. Dependency and trust
may be harder to learn. Author Richard Eyre explains the
difference between the two:

Living Type A—Taking Charge

Be pro-active, be in charge, be self-confident,
Take control of your life.
Depend on yourself and go get the things you want.
Act, don't react.
Plan your work, then work your plan.
Only you can know what you want,
    and only you can decide what your life will be.

Set your goals, make your plans, and let no one
    change them or stand in your way.
Cultivate strength and knowledge, for these are the
    differences between man and Maker.
View your life as a series of competitions that you
    can win, and as an ongoing effort to prove your-
    self, and rise above your rivals.
Understand that achievements are life's measure,
    and wrap your identity in positions and
    possessions.
Acquire, Achieve, Accumulate, Accomplish, Attain!
    (Richard Eyre, "A Poetic Clue to the Three
    Alternatives," *Meridian Magazine*, March 23, 2007).

This is the formula for every success workshop imaginable! Anything less is an invitation for failure. The only thing missing is the "dress for success" and "power tie" combination from the 1980s!

On the other hand, what is it the Savior invites us to do?

Living Type B— A Surrendered Life

Brother Eyre continues:

Be spiritually active,
Seek guidance, be humble, turn your life over to
    God, and depend on Him.
Strive to understand His plan and seek His will,
    for only He knows what is best for your eternal
    soul.
Be aware of His nudges and impressions.
Notice the needs of those around you,
    and try never to win at someone else's expense.

Cultivate awareness and perspective,
>for these are the differences between man and
>Maker.

View your life as a series of opportunities to serve
>and an adventure in discovering who God wants
>you to be and what He wants you to do.

Understand that relationships are life's measure,
>and wrap your identity in your family (ibid.).

There is nothing in a surrendered life that suggests that this is to be a life of mediocrity and misery. On the contrary, this path leads to service and joy. Children are bombarded daily with Type A images. Those images, from sport stars to celebrities, look appealing and sound like the path to happiness. The media rarely features Type B Saints. For this reason, the best examples of a surrendered life will always come from within the walls of children's homes and in the lives of their Church leaders and in our testimonies.

One disclaimer: If we or our children say to the Lord, "I'll go where you want me to go," then we need to be prepared to go to places other than where we'd planned. For those of us who prefer tightly structured lives, this willingness to be "led by the Spirit," not "knowing beforehand" (1 Nephi 4:6) may be uncomfortable at first. For many Latter-day Saints, this may be the most difficult part of living a surrendered life.

Is There Any Place for Self-Esteem in the Surrendered Life?

If we look at Church leaders who have lived surrendered lives, self-esteem and self-confidence appear not to be an issue. There is great power in a Joseph Smith, standing chained and shackled at Richmond Jail and rebuking his guards for their vile comments (see *History of the Church,* 3:208), or in a youthful Joseph F. Smith, with a gun to his face, when asked if he were a Mormon, who boldly responded, "Yes, siree; dyed in the wool; true blue, through and through!" (*The Life of Joseph F. Smith* [Salt Lake City: The Deseret News Press, 1948], 189).

Latter-day Saints should be filled with self-confidence; the question is whether it comes from trusting ourselves, "the arm of flesh," or whether we have surrendered that confidence to the Lord, knowing that "in his strength I can do all things" (2 Nephi 4:34; Alma 26:12). With that surrender we have the quiet confidence that we are living the life the Lord intends of us. Doubt dissipates and faith remains.

As a church, how are we doing in this regard? Earlier, I referred to the excellent study by Brent Top and Bruce Chadwick in which the authors explored the effect of religion in the lives of LDS youth with regard to self-esteem. While they concede that a number of factors—friends, clothes, physical appearance—all play a role for teenagers, the influence of religion had been ignored by most researchers who study teenage self-esteem.

To this end, they gathered information from nearly six thousand LDS high school students in the United States, Great Britain, and Mexico. Their findings provide solid evidence of the increased sense of self-worth by youth who understand the idea of the surrendered life. The researchers concluded:

> First, we found that religiosity is directly linked to academic achievement. The more religious and spiritual an LDS teenager is, the better he/she will do in school and the greater will be the desire for additional education.
>
> The second finding was even more stunning. We found a very powerful relationship between LDS teen's

religiosity and their self-esteem. *The more religious they are, the higher their self-esteem—the better they feel about themselves and the more self-confidence they possess* ("Spirituality and Self-Esteem: The Role of Religion in the Lives of LDS Teens," *Meridian Magazine*, March 10, 2003; emphasis added).

The study points out that the strength of this religiosity is more a function of *internal* factors (spiritual experiences, personal prayer, scripture study) than it is of *external* behaviors (professed religious beliefs, family religious practices, attendance at church). They found that *the greater number of private spiritual experiences a child has and the more the child understands what they are experiencing, the better they feel about themselves,* and the more they achieve. They also found striking correlations to self-esteem and the role of parents, which we will discuss in a later chapter.

These findings cannot be overemphasized. Their implications should drive much of what we do as parents. When children learn to rely on the Lord, on their own, they report higher self-esteem, increased self-confidence, and greater happiness.

These findings run counter to conventional psychological wisdom that tries to paint religion as a demeaning and restricting force in people's lives. To the contrary, it points to the power of a surrendered life and the positive effect it has in all other aspects of a child's daily living.

The Wrong Bridge?

At the beginning of this chapter we alluded to Elder Eyring's friend Jack Steel and his gallantry in attacking the wrong bridge in World War II. In trying to strengthen our youth, parents and youth leaders might mistakenly attack the wrong bridge—resorting to constant praise in an effort to build up their child. Parents and leaders may foolishly avoid giving any criticism so as to not damage tender egos. Conversely, rebelling youth often face an avalanche of criticism in an attempt to stop their destructive course. Between the two extremes is support and accountability.

Elder Richard G. Scott once shared a sacred experience. Strong impressions came to him during a period of time when he was struggling to do a work the Lord had given him. In prayer, he told the Lord he feared the assignment was beyond his personal capacity to fulfill. In response, the Lord told him, "Testify to instruct, edify, and lead others to full obedience, not to demonstrate anything of self. All who are puffed up shall be cut off." And then the Lord said to him, "You are nothing in and of yourself, Richard." That was followed by counsel on how to be a better servant ("Acquiring Spiritual Knowledge," in *Speeches of the Year, 1993* [Provo: Brigham Young University Press, 1994], 8).

Helping our children find inner strength through surrender is a delicate dance. When they are very young, teaching them to obey is easy; simple compliance is assured if you are punitive enough. However, simple compliance is not our goal. Teaching our kids to recognize and rely on the Spirit is much more difficult because it is more art than science. Learning to trust the Lord and surrendering to His guidance may be something even we as parents struggle with. As a result, we may be hesitant to stress it with our family. May I humbly suggest our children may understand this concept better than we do?

King Benjamin became king just as the Nephites were emerging from the great Nephite dark ages. At least three hundred years separated King Benjamin from Enos, during which there was little known spiritual guidance among Lehi's descendants. After so much time, it took the preachings of many "holy men" to overcome "the stiffneckedness of the people." Finally, through persistence, Benjamin succeeded in achieving "peace in the land" (Words of Mormon 1:17–18). They became a righteous people, worthy to take upon themselves the name of Christ.

Earlier we wrote about how the natural man is an enemy to God. The Lord's goal is for us to become "as a child" (Mosiah 3:19). In other words, King Benjamin recognized that the opposite of the prideful man is the naturally submissive child, already meek and humble. It is only as children grow older that they become otherwise.

While serving as president of Ricks College, Henry B. Eyring observed that as parents "we make the mistake, too often, of putting our efforts and concerns as parents into keeping [children] submissive *to us and to our leadership.* The real question is, 'How do we transfer that natural submissiveness of our children to the Lord Jesus Christ? How do we help our children follow the Savior in submissiveness?'" ("Family Followership," *Ensign,* April 1973, 30; emphasis added).

This may be the greatest challenge in all parenthood. When children are small we can control them in a variety of ways. Again, if our goal is their strict obedience, we can find many approaches—even detrimental ones—to keep them obedient. But, as President Eyring suggests, the ultimate goal is not to have them submissive *to us.* We want them to become independent, functional adults. We want them to transfer that submissiveness to the Lord. Elder Eyring goes on to suggest that, early in their lives, we need to "see the problem as helping them to fall in line behind us, in a line led by the Savior" (ibid.).

Let's now talk about how we do that, starting with ourselves.

Four

Marriage and Relationships

Parents are not interested in justice; they are interested in quiet.—*Bill Cosby*

Lisa and Mike have been married for eight years. They have two boys, five and three. Mike grew up with a father who was a high school football coach. His father believed that, above all, children should be obedient. Mike has carried that philosophy into his marriage. He tends to be very strict with the kids, raising his voice when they do wrong and spanking them when he feels it is warranted.

Lisa, on the other hand, came from a home that was much more relaxed. Her parents were both teachers. She worries frequently that Mike is too hard on the kids. She often approaches the children after Mike has disciplined them and changes some of the consequences. For instance, when Mike grounds one of the boys for five days, Lisa will later tell him it will only be for two days. The boys have learned to ask Mom when they want something or quietly go to her after Dad says no, looking for a "second opinion."

It is no surprise, then, that discipline is a constant source of irritation between Mike and Lisa. Mike believes Lisa is too soft, so he tends to be more strict. Lisa under-disciplines, anticipating that Mike will go too far. Both accuse each other of not understanding what the kids need. When they try to discuss it, Mike becomes angry; Lisa withdraws and is sullen for a couple of days afterwards. As a result, both are reluctant to bring the topic up, and the discipline problem never gets resolved.

The quality of our parenting is limited by the quality of our marriage relationships. It is difficult to deal lovingly with our children when there is anger or resentment between Mom and Dad. Negative (and positive) emotions spill over into parenting decisions, clouding and magnifying any problems we may have.

For children to embrace a surrendered life they need to begin by observing a surrendered marriage. That life is best demonstrated in the way parents relate to each other. Much of a surrendered life centers on how we treat one another; it is a reflection of how the Lord deals with us. Like the Lord, we begin to see others in the best possible light, especially members of our own families.

"Be Ye Not Unequally Yoked"

The Lord intended the marriage relationship to rest on equal footings. Those footings come from a wide variety of sources. The first week Cindy and I were married, we had just finished eating dinner when she looked over at the full trash can.

"The trash is full," she said.

"I know," I said.

"Aren't you going to take it out?" she asked.

"No." I stated. "My job is to put the garbage out before they collect it."

"No," she returned, "it's your job to take the trash out. It's my job to take the garbage out to the curb."

In that moment, we realized we were basing our chores on what we'd seen our own parents do. As we started a new family, we had to decide which rules to keep and which rules to change. As it turns out, in our home, husbands take the trash *and* the garbage out!

Many of the conflicts in a marriage stem simply from what we saw while growing up. How our parents related to one another was on constant display. If we grew up in a situation with just one parent, then we guess how things ought to be, basing our beliefs on everyone else we saw around us.

Conflicts also result from differences in personalities. Quite simply, if we tend to dominate others in our daily relationships, we will probably try to dominate our marriage relationship. Marriage does tend to moderate extreme aspects of our personality, but it does not eliminate them. We grow, but remain basically who we are.

Most would agree that marriage partners must work together to solve problems. To do that, the marriage yoke must be equally applied. A psychologist named Eric Berne suggests that the different aspects of our personalities interact, in predictable ways, with the personality traits of our spouse. Though oversimplified, he believes that three major personality states dominate our interactions with others. They are: a parental or authoritarian part (P); an adult part, dealing with others as equals (A); and a child part, that side of us that defers to another adult (C). (See figure 1.) Further, he suggests that when we relate to other people, each aspect of ourselves causes a reaction in the Parent, Adult, or Child in someone else. For instance, the adult part of us relates to the adult part in someone else. A wife's adult behavior is most comfortable (and compatible) with the adult behavior of her husband.

We cycle through all three aspects on a daily basis. For instance, a working mother may get her kids out the door for school (P), then get to work and talk to a coworker (A), report to a boss (C), teach a skill to someone (P), order lunch from a cafeteria worker (P), learn a skill from someone else (C), come home and help her children with their homework (P), then spend time with her husband (A).

During those times when we are more in control or in authority, our parental aspect predominates (P), forcing those around us into more of a child's (C) role. At other times we defer to someone else, such as a boss or teacher, placing ourselves in the child role, while he or she assumes the parental role. When we do that, we are no longer in an equal Adult-to-Adult relationship, but one that is unequal.

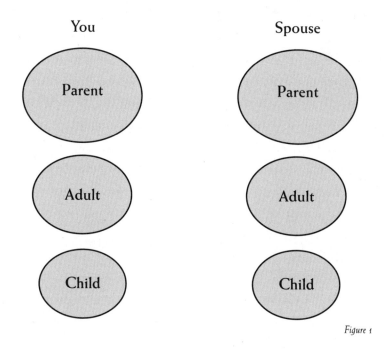

Figure 1

In a relationship, we cycle between all three personality states. In the morning, a husband may show his wife something on the car, placing him in the Parent (P) role and her in the Child (C) role; he is teaching; she is learning. Later, she might share with him something she learned, placing her in the P role and him in the C role.

Difficulties arise when in a relationship we begin to relate, most of the time, from a position other than Adult to Adult. For instance, as demonstrated in Figure 2, when one spouse often expresses outward anger, it has the effect of frequently putting his or her spouse in a child role. Anger, by its nature, dominates and controls a relationship.

When continually put into a Child role, an individual may react to anger in a variety of ways. One response is to withdraw whenever anger is present. When that happens, a spouse will either physically walk away or emotionally withdraw. Another response, as in the case of many wives who are abused, is to accept or to "own" their spouse's anger. They assume that whatever "caused" the anger must be their fault. They respond with guilt and constant attempts to fix the problem, whether they caused it or not. "Owning" the anger is a way to calm it, to make it go away. If they can find the cause of the anger and remove it, their spouse won't have to be angry.

What C spouses fail to recognize is that the problem is not a dirty house or a noisy child or the extra weight or any other presumed "causes" for their spouse's anger. Constantly angry spouses, perpetually remaining in the P position, use anger because it gets them what they want; in short, they use anger because it works.

Another common C response to anger is to retaliate. One client of mine had a controlling husband who became angry when he didn't get what he wanted. When angry, he would become more demanding and was difficult to live with. Then, when he went off to work, she would "get even" with him by spending "his" money, buying things she didn't need, in order to punish him. In her mind, it was the only way to fight back.

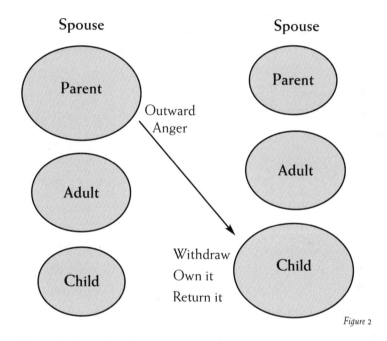

Figure 2

Another example is when one spouse is overly perfectionistic. He (or she) assumes the parental role because he requires perfection from everyone around him, including his spouse. When confronted by an overly perfectionistic parent, children (adults or actual children) can either comply or rebel. There is very little middle ground.

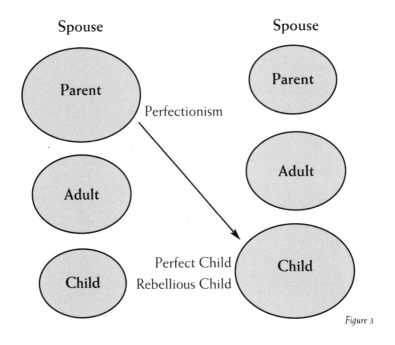

Figure 3

Many relationship dynamics exist, but this gives us a sample of the problem. A couple in the examples above are anything but "equally yoked." P-spouses may control their husband or wife, but they are not happy. C-spouses constantly feel manipulated and frustrated. When it comes time to parent their actual children, both parties are anything but calm, loving, and structured.

When we find ourselves in a consistently lopsided relationship, one in which we spend the majority of our time in a dynamic other than Adult to Adult, what do we do? As we see in Figure 4, a shift requires changes from both spouses. In order for a Parenting spouse to become more Adult-like, he or she has to be willing to give up control. Conversely, a spouse constantly being placed into a Child role, enjoys the benefit of not being responsible should something go wrong. Spouses will sometimes choose a Child role in order to avoid blame, especially when they come into a marriage with a poor self-concept.

Movement by one spouse necessitates movement by the other. There is no such thing as an effective or satisfying Parent-Adult or Child-Adult relationship between two adults. If one spouse begins demonstrating Adult relationship skills, the other spouse typically will slowly mirror those same traits. But someone must instigate the move!

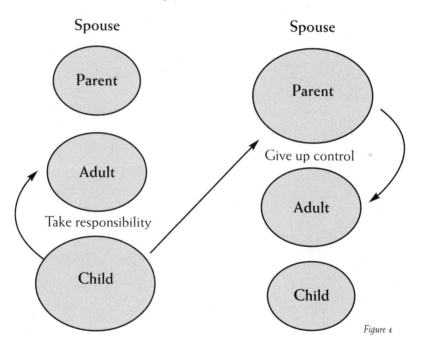

Figure 4

Below are the desired aspects of an Adult-Adult relationship. There should be no real surprises here. Whenever I have asked a group to identify the traits they would expect to find in an Adult-Adult relationship, there is never any hesitation. We know, instinctively, when our relationship with someone, especially a spouse, is equally yoked. We know what it feels like to be an equal contributor in any friendship.

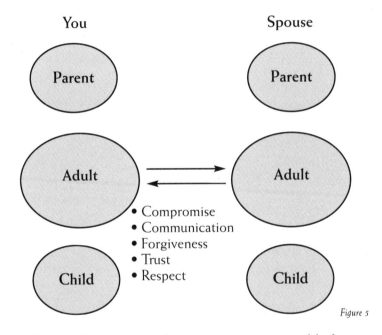

Figure 5

The paradigm shown above gives us one possible framework to help identify what it is we are doing. Again, marriage relationships are far more complicated, with many more dynamics than I have just shown. However, these examples underline how a marriage can become unequal and ineffective when trying to parent.

Our Example

The most visible sign of a surrendered life is seen in the way we interact with others. Our relationships set an example for our children to follow. We want them to learn how to serve, and they will learn that by watching us. As we submit our will to the Lord, our children will see that we forgive easily, treat others equally, and, finally, *we refuse to compromise our standards, without offending* those who have different standards.

1. We Forgive Readily

Twice in the Sermon on the Mount, Jesus teaches the same concept. "Blessed are the merciful," he explains, "for they shall obtain mercy" (Matthew 5:7). Later on, as he is providing a pattern for prayer, he instructs, "and forgive us our debts, as we forgive our debtors" (Matthew 6:12).

The implications of those statements are staggering when we consider their full ramifications. The Lord explains that *our* salvation, *our* access to his mercy, and *our* own forgiveness, is dependent on being merciful and forgiving toward others—regardless of how they may have harmed us.

As a psychotherapist, I am especially in awe of this principle. Some of my clients have had histories of abuse and dysfunction. Some will carry deep emotional scars the rest of their lives. At times, I have personally struggled with this requirement as I've witnessed the emotional damage caused by the abuse. It seems a lot to ask of people who have been brutally victimized.

I will be forever grateful to Elder Bruce C. Hafen, who helped me understand why this forgiveness of others is so vital to spiritual growth. Said he:

What are we doing when we are willing to absorb a terrible trauma of the spirit, caused not by our own doing but by one who claimed to love us—and we absorb the trauma even to help the sinner? That picture somehow has a familiar look—we've seen all this before. Of course, because this picture depicts the sacrifice of Jesus Christ: he took upon himself undeserved and unbearable burdens, heaped upon him by people who often said, and often believed, that they loved him. And he assumed that load not for any need of his, but only to help them.

So to forgive—not just for abuse victims, but for each of us—is to be a Christ figure, a transitional point in the war between good and evil, stopping the current of evil by absorbing it in every pore, thereby protecting the innocent next generation and helping to enable the repentance and healing of those whose failures sent the jolts into our own systems (Bruce C. and Marie K. Hafen, *The Belonging Heart: The Atonement and Relationships with God and Family* [Salt Lake City: Deseret Book Company, 1994], 123).

That is a remarkable concept. In asking us to forgive others, the Savior not only asks us not to harm others, he asks us to fully forgive those who have harmed us. In essence, he asks that we follow him and do what he did. None of us have earned, or will ever earn, the forgiveness of our sins. Despite our best efforts, we will always be "unprofitable servants" (Mosiah 2:21). And yet, he extends forgiveness anyway.

When someone has harmed us in some way, memories and effects tend to linger, sometimes for a lifetime. As the Savior did, we are to extend our forgiveness, whether our tormenter asks for or deserves it. "Vengeance is mine," the Lord instructed Mormon, "and I will repay" (Mormon 3:15). And he could have added, "And your job is to forgive them seventy times seven" (see Matthew 18:21–22). In return for extending forgiveness, we receive the peace of mind that replaces the anger or hurt we have been carrying.

I know a successful lady who seems to have the proverbial Midas touch—whatever she puts her hand to grows and prospers. Years ago, her mother died prematurely. The daughter became angry at some family members over the disposition of some property her mother had owned. Due to some unpaid back taxes, the land was sold to meet the outstanding debt. She was furious that the land she had hoped to inherit was now gone. In her wrath, she drew away from the rest of her family and swore she would not speak to any of them again. Year by year her grudge ate at her, eventually souring her relationship with her own children as well. In frustration, they eventually also drew away from her. At this point, she has kept her promise, not speaking with the family for almost thirty years. How has such anger and resentment served her well?

If we carry a grudge or nurse an offense towards those who have offended us, we draw on the power of the evil one, who is still angry about what happened in the Council in Heaven. He will be eternally miserable because he could not "let it go" there, and will not "let it go" here. His goal is for us to be as miserable as he is. He knows that true forgiveness takes a Savior, and we who are striving to become Savior-like draw on His atonement to forgive those who have harmed us.

It should be noted that forgiving someone does not mean continuing to put ourselves in positions where we can be hurt again. If someone has offended us and continues to offend because they do not see a problem, forgiveness does not require that we look for every opportunity to spend time with them. We can love them and pray for them, but the Lord doesn't require that we put ourselves in a position to be constantly reinjured.

2. We Treat People Equally

School yards can be brutal places. Children can be merciless to one another. As children grow, they sometimes find that the fastest way to build up their ego is to tear down someone else's. Call it the Lucifer Principle. It is for this reason that children must see something different modeled for them at home and at church by adults. If they witness, through our gossip or casual comments, that we treat people differentially, they will adopt that standard into their teens and adulthood.

In the early days of the Restoration, there was a tendency to exclude some individuals from Church meetings. By way of instruction, the Lord chastised them, telling them "never to cast any one out from your public meetings," especially those "earnestly seeking the kingdom." It was important for the Saints to understand that though "all have not every gift given unto them . . . every man is given a gift by the Spirit of God" (D&C 46:3, 5, 11). And each of these gifts, though different, are equally valuable to the building up of the kingdom of God.

This is the same concept the Apostle Paul taught to the Corinthians:

> If the whole body were an eye, where were the hearing? If the whole were hearing, where were the smelling? But now hath God set the members every one of them in the body, as it hath pleased him.
>
> Nay, much more those members of the body, which seem to be more feeble, are necessary: and those members of the body, which we think to be less honourable, upon

these we bestow more abundant honour; and our uncomely parts have more abundant comeliness (1 Corinthians 12:17–18, 22–23).

Eugene England has observed:

> This is strange doctrine, of the kind Paul knew would be "foolishness to the Greeks"—that is, to the rational, worldly mind: What? we should honor *more* the feeble, the uncomely among us? Scandalous! But Paul has a good reason for us to do precisely that—if we can see the matter from God's perspective, which is not concerned with emphasizing comparative, individual excellence but with helping *all* his children become like him and also helping those children learn how to help each other reach that goal. . . .
>
> The "comely gifts"—such as knowledge and wealth— will normally get much honor in human society, . . . On the other hand, we must seek to appreciate *all* each other's gifts, however feeble or uncomely they seem in the world's eyes. We must learn to suffer together and share honor together, so that we can all be blessed by all our diverse gifts. That mutual blessing, in fact, has much to do with why God gave the gifts in the first place (*Why the Church Is As True As the Gospel* [Salt Lake City: Bookcraft, 1986], 73–74; emphasis in original).

Children know our real opinions about the bishop or the new family in the ward. They see our reactions and listen to our conversations. They mentally record the biting remarks or angry reactions, as well as the loving admirations. They understand when our teachings of "love one another" do not match our daily attitudes. Teens are especially sensitive to any behavior that seems hypocritical as they decide who to trust.

Early in my counseling career, I worked as an aide on

a hospital unit that treated mental health emergencies. Individuals would be brought to our unit for a short period of time, stabilized, and then released to other programs for follow-up. When someone came to us in crisis, they were generally absorbed in solving their immediate needs: in seeing the doctor, in getting the appropriate medication, in contacting family. However, as their emotional crisis eased, I would watch a remarkable change. They would begin to worry more and more about others on the unit and less about themselves. I always knew they were ready for discharge when they moved from a complete self-absorption to a concern for their fellow patients.

If you love me, the Lord admonishes, "feed my sheep" (John 21:16). Who we feed, and how we feed them, tells our youth the state of our hearts.

There is a segment of society, fueled by Lucifer himself, which roots against anyone who has achieved anything. Languishing in their own misery, such individuals are perversely cheered when any achievers fall or self-destruct. It is as if there is some sense of justice or satisfaction when the successful "finally get their due." While it may provide the detractors some moments of amusement, it does not take into account the misery being experienced by the one who is wallowing in despair.

In the chapters to come, we will discuss ways to cultivate a meek and teachable attitude in our children. We will look for ways to instill in them a desire to love and serve those around them. In their lives, those they will serve might include the rich (who have a larger house than they), the proud (including those who routinely attack the Church), the famous (who flaunt their disobedience to every commandment), as well as the poor and socially unskilled. Regardless of their personality or station in life, everyone needs our love—not just those who are much easier to love.

The things we say and our attitudes toward those less easy to love, all reveal the true state of our hearts. Our behavior demonstrates the extent to which we have turned our will over to "my Jesus" (2 Nephi 33:6). To do that, we must subdue the natural-man urge to attack or demean others, whether they are a famous celebrity or a socially insensitive member of our ward.

3. We Refuse to Compromise Our Standards, but Seek Also Not to Offend Those with Different Values

I believe the Lord expects us to respond to one another in love, meekness, and humility. We are to focus on changing or improving our own emotions and personality traits that interfere in our relationships with others.

However, "burying weapons of rebellion" does not mean compromising values and standards we know to be right. The Lord does not expect an abused wife to allow that abuse to continue without doing something about it. In fact, should she fail to do something about it, she is guilty of surrendering to evil. Being submissive does not mean standing idly by while being fleeced by an unscrupulous con man. It is not an act of love when parents, under the guise of being humble, provide little or no structure and discipline for their children.

Too many young women have surrendered their virtue because they did not know how to say "no" firmly and clearly. Each of us needs to know that we do not appease or compromise with evil intentions. Young people may not know how to stand against peer pressure, knowing that "friends" will be unhappy or condescending when they choose the right course. And they need to see that same firmness in their parents and youth leaders. It is for this reason that parents cannot allow themselves to be abused in any way by their spouses or by their children. Any abuse: verbal, physical, or sexual, sends a clear message that values and beliefs can be surrendered if confronted by force or anger or peer pressure.

The many ways to be firm and assertive, in the face of coercion or abuse, is a topic for another discussion. But so serious is its implications to our children, that if there is a problem in this area, we may need to utilize professional help to assist us. We can be firm without being angry but still leave no misunderstanding about where we stand.

As with so much of what we do, we will be judged as much by the desires of our hearts as by our actions. When our interactions with each other are prompted by pride or anger, we draw from our emotional armory behaviors that are far from the love of Christ. When we use coercive means, there are never any winners.

In the early 1960s, the world lived in great fear of the Soviet dictator Nikita Khrushchev. Having observed the international conflict, Elder Mark E. Petersen arose in general conference and declared:

> Is it a sign of strength to be quarrelsome and unpleasant? Does might make right in a nation or in a shop or in a family? Are any of us so blind that we think that one member of the family can always be right and nobody else? Can we be so deceived by our egotism that we suppose that like the king we can do no wrong, that we can be domineering and tyrannical in our own little circle with impunity?
>
> If you quarrel with your wife, have you thought that you might be motivated by the same spirit which moves Khrushchev when he quarrels with the President of the United States?
>
> If you are contentious in your family, or quarrelsome

with your neighbors, or even with your brethren and sisters in the Church, have you thought that you might be motivated by the same spirit which also moves Khrushchev? How different from him are we if the same evil spirit motivates us both?

. . . People can be kind if they want to be kind. They can be considerate if they want to be. They can be peaceful if they would but try. They can be thoughtful and considerate of others if they but have the desire. Why even Khrushchev can smile and polish apples when he wants to (in Conference Report, Oct. 1961, 49).

Finally, it was the Savior himself who explained:

He that hath the spirit of contention is not of me, but is of the devil, who is the father of contention, and he stirreth up the hearts of men to contend with anger, one with another.

Behold, this is not my doctrine, to stir up the hearts of men with anger, one against another; but this is my doctrine, that such things should be done away (3 Nephi 11:29–30).

Given the eternal nature of relationships, we must do all we can to improve our daily interactions with one another. This is especially true in dealing with those with whom we do not get along. It is a difficult task to permanently bury the emotional crutches we use to contend with one another. To return anger with a smile, contentiousness with love, requires a heart at peace. Such are the peacemakers the world sorely needs. And such peacekeeping measures are what permit parents to deal effectively with their rebellious children, as we shall see.

Five

Covenants: What We Teach

He has all the virtues I dislike and none of the vices I admire.
—Winston Churchill

W hen our first child was born, my mother-in-law flew in from Texas to help us. A week later, I took her to the airport to fly home. When I returned, Cindy and I nervously looked at each other, then at our new daughter, and gulped. At that moment we still felt as though we were just kids, with a tiny baby who depended on us. It was a terrifying moment. We felt overwhelmed and unsure. She had come with no instruction manual, no directions printed on her tiny back. All we had to go on was a smile from both of our mothers, suggesting we would soon figure things out.

The great challenge of parenthood is that there is no exact formula, no guarantees. Just when you think you're beginning to understand a child, they change. Then, when you've learned what to do with the first one, the second one shows up, and you have to throw all the rules out and start over. The longer we parent, the less we feel we know.

If we just had a pattern to follow, wouldn't that help?

As it turns out, we do. Recently, I was invited to speak to a university audience about the Church. A professor raised his hand and asked me to describe the Mormon concept of the gender of God. I began by telling him that we believe in a God we address as "Heavenly Father." I described how He is the Father of our spirits and that we lived with Him before this life. Finally, I explained that our earthly homes are intended to be a reflection of our heavenly home. It was a concept the class had not considered.

The great God of the universe has requested we address Him as Father. It appears to be the title He desires most. We hear it in the way Jesus addressed Him—"Abba." Elder Russell M. Nelson explains, "The word *Abba* is significant. *Ab* means 'father'; *Abba* is an endearing and tender form of that term. The nearest English equivalent might be *Daddy*" (*Perfection Pending and Other Favorite Discourses* [Salt Lake City: Deseret Book Company, 1998], f.n. 171).

The good news for all of us is that the scriptures and the modern revelations give us valuable information into the divine parenting pattern, one that provides a template to learn from. And while it may seem simplistic to some, in order to be successful, we need to learn to parent as Father in Heaven parents. His approach provides a grand key of how to raise a surrendered generation. It is "my work and my glory," He explains, "to bring to pass the immortality and eternal life" of all His children (Moses 1:39).

Let's begin by asking some basic questions:

- How does Heavenly Father parent?
- How does He deal with His children?
- What does He want His children to know, to learn?
- How does He instruct and teach?
- When we rebel, what is His reaction?
- How does His discipline work?

The goal of Heavenly Father's parenting is to teach us the things we'll need to know and do to "live with him someday" (*Children's Songbook*, p. 3). His teaching pattern, the way He handles His children, is all focused on helping us reach that goal—a goal put in jeopardy by rebellion.

"I give unto you these sayings," says the Lord, "that you may understand and know *how* to worship, and know what you worship, that you may come unto the Father in my name, and in due time receive of his fulness" (D&C 93:19; emphasis added). Clearly, if we desire our children to develop divine-esteem as opposed to self-esteem, we need to follow that divine template. Our children must understand—accurately—who and how we worship.

Who We Worship

During the months leading up to the dedication of the Kirtland Temple, Joseph Smith worked feverishly to prepare the Saints for the blessings of the temple. For instance, he met long into the night to help the brethren understand gospel concepts related to the temple. The School of the Prophets was one such place where these great trainings took place. Part of this training is recorded in the *Lectures on Faith*. Speaking of faith, the prophet taught,

> Let us here observe, that three things are necessary in order that any rational and intelligent being may exercise faith in God unto life and salvation.
>
> First, the idea that he actually exists.
>
> Secondly, a *correct* idea of his character, perfections, and attributes.
>
> Thirdly, an actual knowledge that the course of life which he is pursuing is according to his will. For without

an acquaintance with these three important facts, the faith
of every rational being must be imperfect and unproduc-
tive (Lectures on Faith [Salt Lake City: Deseret Book
Company, 1985], 38).

When I first read the *Lectures on Faith* as a new missionary, I
believed that the second principle, the need to have a correct
idea of His character, meant we needed to understand that
Heavenly Father had a physical body, separate from the Son. It
seemed to be saying that one can't have a fullness of faith without having a complete knowledge of His *physical* attributes.

Though we do need to understand those physical characteristics, I should have remembered that these lectures were
being given to a group of men who already had a correct
knowledge of God's physical attributes. However, by their
behavior, those early Saints misunderstood some of God's most
basic characteristics—the same ones many of us struggle with
today.

In a class a few years ago, we discussed reasons why we
often stubbornly keep "leaning to our own understanding" (see
Proverbs 3:5), rather than submitting and surrendering all our
weaknesses to God. Someone pointed out the oft-repeated
quote from Stephen E. Robinson that we *believe in* Jesus Christ,
we just don't always *believe* Him (see *Believing Christ* [Salt Lake
City: Deseret Book Company, 1992], 9). In other words, while
we believe He exists, we just don't believe He knows and intervenes with us personally.

The question I posed was along these lines, "If God is really
all-knowing and all-powerful, if He really loves us more than
we love ourselves, if He really has our best interests at heart, if
He really is smarter than us and more powerful than us, and
if He really wants to exalt us in the celestial kingdom, then why

is it so hard to completely trust Him? Why is it such a difficult problem for all of us?"

Out of that discussion came a startling reality: even though we say we believe in Him, our daily behavior suggests that most of us still don't have a correct belief in Heavenly Father's characteristics. We think we trust Him, but then we keep trying to live life *our* way, contrary to what He asks of us. It was a sobering idea for all of us. The following questions came as a result of our discussion.

Often—though we would initially deny it—we may find we harbor some of the following beliefs:

- God appears to love some people more than others.
- The spiritual gifts of others appear to be "more excellent" than mine.
- God teases or tests me by withholding needed answers just to see how I'll react.
- He doesn't understand me or He would have answered my prayers differently.
- God is looking for "loopholes" or reasons not to bless me.
- He can't love me as much as He does others, because of some past sin of mine.
- I believe that wickedness never was happiness, but some "harmless" wickedness is more fun than being seen as too "straight" or rigid.
- If I follow Him exactly, I'll have to do things differently; and I'll be less happy.
- Completely obeying God means being a puppet and giving up my agency.
- The Atonement covered the collective sins of the universe; He doesn't understand my *individual* pain or depression.

One class member put it this way: "I feel like there is a secret formula for getting answers to prayers, and I just haven't figured it out yet. There must be something I'm saying, or not saying, that gets in the way. It's as if the answers to my prayers are locked behind some ATM in the sky, and I don't have the PIN number." In that moment, he realized that he believed Heavenly Father had answers for him, but they were being withheld because he hadn't yet figured out the right combination of "fast, pray, ponder, trust, stupor, pray, burning," and so forth.

When I asked how he knew he didn't have the right combination, he smiled, realizing what he was saying. "Because I haven't gotten the answer I've been looking for!" It was true. We may harbor the idea that the Lord should confirm the course of action we want to pursue; in other words, we want the Lord to tell us to do what we already want to do. We aren't praying for answers; we're looking for a heavenly endorsement. For that reason, any answer contrary to our wants is not an answer at all!

The result is that we may be withholding our complete trust and obedience, based on false notions that He loves us less or is deliberately withholding blessings or answers from us. Our evidence? Again, we have prayers that are not answered, or crushing adversity that comes despite our faithfulness. We have no answers for why these things occur, so we begin to suspect our Heavenly Father has some ulterior motive we have yet to figure out. These thoughts, spurred on by the great accuser, Lucifer, cause us to hesitate to trust in the boundless love God has for us.

Recognizing this kind of erroneous thinking will help us evaluate where we put our trust—and where we will teach our children to place their trust. If we struggle with doubts or mis-understandings about Heavenly Father, we will hesitate teaching our children to place their trust in Him. We may unconsciously be steering them toward trusting themselves, rather than relying completely on the Lord.

To illustrate, if I asked a group of Saints to rigidly live 100 percent of the commandments for a week, promising that the Lord would bless them, I would probably get mixed results. Some would try; most would struggle. If I then took the same group of Saints, placed one million dollars on their kitchen tables, and promised them the money if they were 100 percent obedient all week, the rate of success would likely be much higher. At the end of the week, if I didn't get 100 percent obedience, I'd be shocked.

Why the difference? As natural men and women, we believe in the power of money in this life. We see effects of money all around us. The outward differences between those who have it, and those who don't, are considerable. It is easy to see the tangible benefits of wealth all around us.

I think it fair to say: *Our behavior is driven by who or what we believe in; and that behavior has a major impact on what our children believe in.*

We are spiritually begotten sons and daughters of God. The eternal joy and blessings that await us far exceed any earthly amount of money we could assemble in this life. The great God of the Universe has declared His work to bring to pass the exaltation and eternal life of His children. He looks for, pleads for, any opportunity to bless us and to be our God. He takes the least obedience on our part as a chance to shower blessings upon our heads. We are all equal in His sight and are limited only by our lack of faith. Anytime we find ourselves believing one of the falsehoods we've just discussed, we demonstrate our lack of understanding of *who* He is and *what* He will do for us—if we'll just let Him.

How Does Heavenly Father Parent?

The Lord's pattern of parenting is best understood when we attend the "house of learning," the temple (D&C 88:119). The endowment of spiritual power we receive there comes only after we are properly taught, and then make and keep sacred covenants.

1. We Are Taught

What are we to teach our children? The Lord was very clear in speaking to one father, the Prophet Joseph Smith. "Children," He revealed, are to be brought up in "light and truth" (D&C 93:40). To Adam, He clarified what that light and truth was. "Teach . . . unto your children, that all men, everywhere, must repent, or they can in nowise inherit the kingdom of God" (Moses 6:57).

It is interesting to note that the Lord didn't say, "Teach them knowledge," or "Make sure they know that there's no such thing as a free lunch." He was very clear that our parental stewardship requires us to bathe our children in the light of repentance.

Always conscious of his future readership, Nephi wanted us to understand that his people followed the Lord Jesus Christ. "And we talk of Christ, we rejoice in Christ, we preach of Christ, we prophesy of Christ, and we write according to our prophecies. . . ." Why the intense focus on Jesus Christ? So that " . . . *our children may know to what source they may look for a remission of their sins*" (2 Nephi 25:26; emphasis added).

We might think that looking toward the Savior for repentance would be fundamental. Where else could we look? That answer might not be as simple as you might think.

> A bishop recently related a truly disturbing incident. He said that while making his way through the hallway toward the chapel to begin sacrament meeting, a young woman from his ward stopped him and said, "Bishop, I really need to talk to you. It will just take a minute." Thinking it would be some minor item he stopped and listened. "Last night," she blurted out, "I was involved in a violation of the law of chastity." She said just enough more that he knew it was a major violation of the law. Before he could stop her and set up an appointment for a proper interview, she continued, "But it's okay because I stayed up all night going through the steps of repentance. Confessing to you is the only one I had left on the list. So now I think I am ready to partake of the sacrament" (Lawrence R. Flake, "Beyond 'Recipe Repentance' and 'Formula Forgiveness,'" *Religious Educator* [Provo: Brigham Young University Press, Vol. 7, No. 1, 2006], 13).

This young woman could repeat the "Seven Rs of Repentance"; she had learned them in Primary and Sunday School. However, despite annual lessons on the subject, she demonstrated that she did not understand the True Source of the remission of her sins. She had come to believe, as she recited the seven Rs, that repentance was something she did on her own by working her way down the list. Repentance was just a series of quick "action items" to be checked off. Without a true understanding of the Lord's role, repentance had been reduced to a do-it-yourself affair, and she was the one setting the terms.

Our rising generation needs the same thing we do; that is, to fully understand the True Source of forgiveness and comfort in their lives. Elder Jeffrey R. Holland eloquently expressed his concern about what we miss. He warned:

> When crises come in our lives—and they will—the philosophies of men interlaced with a few scriptures and poems just won't do. *Are we really nurturing [our children] in a way that will sustain them when the stresses of life appear?* Or are we giving them a kind of theological Twinkie—spiritually empty calories? President John Taylor once called such teaching "fried froth," the kind of thing you could eat all day and yet finish feeling totally unsatisfied ("That Our Children May Know," in *Speeches of the Year, 1980* [Provo: Brigham Young University Press, 1981], 82; emphasis added).

It is possible to fill our children with a steady diet of worldly platitudes and church poems, only to have them wither from spiritual malnutrition. We might hesitate to speak of the Atonement because they consider it a boring topic. Well-intentioned youth leaders may try to raise future priesthood leaders on a steady diet of basketball and broom hockey, rather than service, because the youth see the activities as fun and are more likely to show up. We cannot expect that one week of Especially for Youth or a handcart trek, no matter how powerful the experience, will make up for a year's steady diet of "fried froth." They will need real nourishment if they are to withstand the urgings to rebel.

Elder Holland goes on to describe the travails of some close friends. Their teenage daughter was diagnosed with cancer. Despite a long and valiant effort, that cancer finally claimed her life. Throughout her ordeal, this young girl maintained her testimony of Jesus Christ and lived her life to the fullest—right up to the last day. In fact, she passed away as the family was making its way to Disney World for one last family trip. Elder Holland concludes their story by commenting:

> These are my childhood friends, Stan and Barbara. I grew up with them, and my daughter has not had cancer. But, theirs has and she's gone. And how do you tell a child that life isn't entirely a Disneyworld? *Will there be times in your life or theirs that they will need the substance of the gospel in a way that only you can teach it?* (ibid.; emphasis added).

Joseph Smith was very clear on how children gain this substance that Elder Holland refers to:

> We have now clearly set forth how it is, and how it was, that God became an object of faith for rational beings; and also, upon what foundation the testimony was based which excited the inquiry and diligent search of the ancient saints to seek after and obtain a knowledge of the glory of God; and we have seen that *it was human testimony, and human testimony only, that excited this inquiry,* in the first instance, in their minds. *It was the credence they gave to the testimony of their fathers, this testimony having aroused their minds to inquire after the knowledge of God;* the inquiry frequently terminated, indeed always terminated when rightly pursued, in the most glorious discoveries and eternal certainty (*Lectures on Faith* 2:56; emphasis added).

There is no substitute for vital testimony bearing. When Alma the Younger was enduring the torment of his sins, he says, "I remembered also to have heard my father prophesy unto the people [and, we can assume, his own family]

concerning the coming of one Jesus Christ, a Son of God, to
atone for the sins of the world" (Alma 36:17). Children need to
be taught about their Savior. And they need to hear it most
from the lips of their believing parents. When they do, the
memory of that teaching will be brought to their hearts at the
moment they need it most.

There are many parents, in the Church, who could step
forward and exclaim, "But we did that! We did teach them
those things. We bore our testimony! And they rebelled anyway!" True, these parents did teach correct principles, only to
see their children rebel as did Alma the Younger. But, as we will
discuss in chapter 6, *what* we teach is heavily filtered by *how* we
teach. The essence of the gospel message is often discounted
(or enhanced), based on how it is presented. We will also see
that our "parental style" plays a major role in how we teach and
how our message is received.

2. We Make Covenants

President Marion G. Romney explained the importance of
covenants:

> Traditionally, God's people have been known as a
> covenant people. The gospel itself is the new and ever-
> lasting covenant. The posterity of Abraham through Isaac
> and Jacob is the covenant race. We come into the Church
> by covenant, which we enter into when we go into the
> waters of baptism. The new and everlasting covenant of
> celestial marriage is the gate to exaltation in the celestial
> kingdom. Men receive the Melchizedek Priesthood by an
> oath and covenant (in Conference Report, Apr. 1962, 17).

In the temple, as soon as we have been given knowledge,
we next make covenants. These covenants detail things we

promise to do and describe the attendant blessings the Lord is willing to impart, based on our obedience. The temple endowment consists of a series of spiritual contracts we enter into.

One promise Adam made was to multiply and replenish the earth. He also promised to make sacrifices to the Lord, though he did not completely understand why. As parents and youth leaders, we would do well to ask: "Just what is it I've promised to do? Exactly, what is my covenant responsibility to these children?"

I once heard a loving parent explain a simple reality to his teenage daughter. She was asking—no, pleading!—for a pair of expensive designer jeans. Responding to her pleas, this wise father told her, "When you were born, one of the things I agreed to do was to clothe you, so you wouldn't run around naked. But, I didn't agree to *decorate* you. My commitment to clothe you means I've done my job when I've covered you in a $25 pair of jeans. Designer jeans are decoration. After the $25, you are welcome to decorate yourself through earning the money yourself!"

Like this daughter, children need to understand what our responsibilities are, as parents; and what their responsibilities are, as children. Before we can have any discussions about family rules, we must define what our responsibilities are to one another and covenant to do them. Family rules then revolve around helping each of us fulfill covenant responsibilities.

Parents' Responsibilities

What, exactly, does the Lord expect of us as parents? I posed that question in an institute class and asked them to come up with a consensus. The students brainstormed for a while and then compiled a number of ideas. In the end, they agreed that parents' main responsibility was to help their children gain the skills necessary to become responsible adults. They concluded that responsible adults had a variety of skills, including: how to get answers to prayers, how to solve problems, how to work, how to socialize, and so forth. Once the group defined these things as goals, they agreed that they would give them a starting place for how to raise their kids in the future.

If we agree that we have covenanted to bring up our children to become responsible adults with strong testimonies, it should become easier to see beyond any distractions. We will also have a better idea of what a surrendered life might look like. President Spencer W. Kimball taught that "If we live in such a way that the considerations of eternity press upon us, we will make better decisions" ("The Things of Eternity— Stand We in Jeopardy?" *Ensign,* Jan. 1977, 3). It is those considerations, and the considerations of what our children are to become, that help us make better parenting decisions.

Years ago, I attended a "manners dinner" sponsored by our ward's Young Women presidency. As leaders, we acted as waiters and waitresses while our youth learned about appropriate behavior at a formal dinner. The tables were decorated with fine china and crystal goblets. The food was gourmet in nature and tasted wonderful. The cultural hall was set up to resemble an elegant restaurant, and the music was live and tasteful. It was a wonderful evening. The youth laughed and had fun learning how to act appropriately. Afterwards, they felt they'd had a great time. They all learned valuable lessons they could take on their missions and elsewhere.

And yet, I came away from the evening greatly saddened that it could have been far greater than it was. Why? I was struck by the fact that the youth had not been involved in any aspect of the planning or the carrying out of the activity. They were not consulted about putting on the evening, nor did they aid in the event—not even the cleanup. What the youth leaders had done was put together a "beautiful event," unspoiled by potential mistakes youth often make in setting up complex activities like that one. They had agreed that the night would go more smoothly if they did not delegate any of the planning to a group of unpredictable teenagers, especially where the sisters' fine china was involved. It had been decided it would be easier and much more efficient to do it themselves.

Youth leaders of the Church, like parents, also covenant to help youth develop into responsible adults with strong testimonies. In order to learn responsibility, the young people must be allowed to make mistakes they can learn from. The youth programs of the Church were never intended to provide flawless activities, professionally written road shows, or perfectly staged fashion shows, organized by youth leaders who are more concerned with the appearance of the activity than the growth of the youth. If these youth are to grow and learn, they must be put into monitored situations where they can develop the tools they will need in the future. An activity or family home evening that "flops" may be the best activity of the month—if we take the time, afterwards, to walk them through "what happened?" and "what would you do differently next time?"

As Young Men's president, I had the following conversation with one of my priests:

Me: So let's talk about the youth joint activity last Wednesday. How do you think it went?

Priest: It was awful. All we had was water for refreshments!

Me: I saw that. What happened?

Priest: The deacons were supposed to bring some cookies and they didn't! Dumb deacons!

Me: Did they get the assignment?

Priest: Yeah, I called the deacons quorum president last Sunday and told him.

Me: Did you ask him what happened?

Priest: He says he called some guys to bring the cookies, and they all forgot.

Me: So, what did you learn?

Priest: Don't call the deacons?

Me: Well, that's one approach. . . . What else would you do differently?

Priest: Next time I'd call and remind them the night before.

Me: That's a pretty good idea. People do forget, and that's why you have to follow up with them. Unless you want water for refreshments next time. . . .

The ultimate goal of youth activities is to help train our youth. We do that by helping them organize everything from spiritual experiences, to service projects, to responsible fun. Programming provides a wonderful chance for them to gain valuable experience learning how to plan and organize these events. Again, we covenant to *prepare*, not *entertain*.

For example, a young woman I know came from humble circumstances. Through hard work and study, she was able to earn a college scholarship. Her roommates also earned similar academic awards. Their scholarships were contingent on maintaining a certain grade point average. At the end of the first semester, she was the only one of her roommates who kept her scholarship. Her roommates had all lost their scholarships due to poor grades. What happened to these formerly good students? They sheepishly acknowledged that their mothers had gotten them up every morning and made sure they finished their homework. Once they went away to school and their mothers were no longer around, they discovered they lacked the self-discipline to do those things on their own.

Recently a colleague and I cornered a gifted teacher who is also a former mission president. We asked him about his experience and the kind of things he looked for in his missionaries. He smiled thinly and shook his head. "You know," he said, "I just wanted missionaries who knew how to work. I didn't even care if their testimonies weren't that strong, because that was something I could teach them. What I couldn't teach them was how to work!" He concluded that lack of work ethic was his number-one challenge during his time as mission president. He had been dismayed at how many an elder or sister approached him about quitting, the moment they faced a challenge or difficulty. His belief was that many parents had been too quick to insulate their kids from difficulty and challenge. As a result, these good, active kids arrived in the mission field prepared to have a great time, but totally unprepared to handle difficulty.

If we stay focused on the long-term goals of parenting, we will make better decisions about how to prepare our children for the challenges of adulthood. If children understand that these are our goals, they will have a clearer sense of why we make the parenting decisions we do. In addition, they will have a clearer sense that a surrendered life involves accountability to the Lord and to those around them.

When we covenant to bring our children up in light and truth, we agree to bring them up in a home free from ambiguity. We promise to raise them with a clear sense of right and wrong; good and evil. Children should never have to guess where we stand or where the Lord stands. Nor should they see a difference between what we profess and how we behave. For instance, the father who teaches his children to tell the truth, but calls in sick at work so he can play golf, does serious damage to his credibility. He is teaching his children that you tell the truth, unless it is inconvenient.

When parents take *our* covenant promises seriously, and hold our children to *their* agreements, we demonstrate that there are clear "rights" and "wrongs," where compromise is unacceptable.

Let's look at one last example of parental covenant-keeping. In chapter 2, we spent time coming to understand the Anti-Nephi-Lehies and the example they set by burying the swords of their rebellion. There is one aspect of their example we may not have considered. Some two thousand of their children, the stripling warriors, were instrumental in helping defeat the Lamanite army. Helaman explains that they believed that "our God is with us, and he will not suffer that we should fall" (Alma 56:46). Where did this great faith come from?

> They did think more upon the liberty of their fathers than they did upon their lives; yea, they had been taught by their mothers, that if they did not doubt, God would deliver them.
>
> And they rehearsed unto me the words of their mothers, saying: We do not doubt our mothers knew it (Alma 56:47–48).

The sobering footnote to the belief is this: before the Anti-Nephi-Lehies could leave the land of Nephi and join with the Nephites, they were attacked and martyred; not once, but twice. Thousands of men and women allowed themselves to be killed rather than break the covenant they had made with their Redeemer.

Due to the sheer numbers of those who were martyred, it would be difficult, if not impossible, to raise an army of two thousand young men without including some of those boys who had lost parents to that horrific slaughter. In all likelihood, then, many of those young men who remembered the words their mothers had taught them, would also have remembered that their mothers and fathers gave the "last full measure" to that faith. For the rest of their lives, these young men would know and understand the extent to which they must go, rather than break sacred promises.

As we're talking about covenant making and keeping, we should also note that our marriage covenant will be the most noticeable, binding agreement in the house. What of those homes, then, where divorce has occurred? In the midst of learning about covenants, children have watched a relationship struggle, fail, and finally end. Though much could be said here, children in these settings need to be reminded of the power of eternal covenants the Lord makes with us. Where we sometimes fail, He does not. The tragedy of divorce does occur, with all its sad implications; but the love of the Lord remains constant and unchanging.

High rates of divorce is another reason that children need to grow in their divine-esteem. Parents are fallible, struggling with their own foibles and issues; God is not. The sooner our children learn to comfortably lean on the Lord as their source for answers, the more immune they are from any difficulties our weaknesses may cause.

Children's Responsibilities

Parents have been given their stewardship; children have as well. What do children covenant to do? In order to become responsible adults, they need to learn early the importance of obedience and accountability. In other words, they must learn how to accept assignments, carry them out, and then return and report. Learning these steps is a long-term process, one in which they become more accountable as they grow older. The process looks something like this:

Age Range	Children Learn	Accountable To
Age 3–5	Obedience	Parents
Age 6–9	Stewardship	Heavenly Father
Age 9–12	Discipline	Self
Age 12–15	Service	Others
Age 15–18	Love/Charity	Another Individual

(See Linda and Richard Eyre, *Teaching Children Responsibility: A Guide for Latter-day Parents* [Salt Lake City: Deseret Book Company, 1982], 10).

This chart highlights a very important principle, one that underlies one of the most difficult tasks a parent may face. If you will notice, very young children are first responsible to be obedient to their parents. In the child's very early years, parents set all the rules and children obey them—or face uncomfortable consequences. When they are young, children are completely dependent on parents to set the rules they must follow.

However, as they mature, a critical shift begins: children must begin to transition from complete "obedience to parents" toward a "stewardship to Heavenly Father." This step is cumulative, in that there is still a need to be obedient to parents. However, as they age, they need to shift more and more of their accountability to Heavenly Father. Learning to be accountable to God will carry them, long after they've left home. How do we do that? Elder Henry B. Eyring explains that "the opportunity lies in their sensing what they knew [before this life], that the power to choose is a gift from God to bring them happiness in life and in the life to come with Him. We can help in the way we react to their determination to choose for themselves" ("A Life Founded in Light and Truth," in *Speeches of the Year,* 2000 [Provo: Brigham Young University Press, 2001], 4).

To be accountable to God is much harder to teach than simple obedience to Mom and Dad. The process is more art than science. Children need to learn both what to ask and how to trust the answers they receive. The ease with which a child makes this transition is also highly dependent on our level of parental control, as we will discuss later.

This is the transition that enables children to develop the "divine-esteem" we've talked about. In this process they begin to recognize they "can do all things through Christ which strengtheneth me" (Philippians 4:13). The more thoroughly children understand this principle, the more they develop the problem-solving skills that will aid them in adulthood.

This early transition also prepares them for those teenage moments when parents are trying to enforce the unenforceable. It lays the foundation for adulthood. Elder Eyring continues:

> The teenager who begins to say "it's my life to live, my choices to make" is speaking the truth, a wonderful truth. The choice to do good is the only way to build a life on this foundation of truth and light.
>
> *Yet those words can strike fear* into a parent or a bishop or a Young Women leader who loves the teenager. That

outburst of independence usually comes when a rule is announced or something is forbidden. It may come with the mere appearance of authority, with anyone telling them what they must do or even with just a look at a hemline (ibid.; emphasis added).

This critical transition depends heavily on parents seeing their roles as teachers. We reinforce and remind our children that family rules, just as the commandments themselves, guide them as they are learning their stewardship duties to Heavenly Father. Again, the rules are based on commitments the child has already made to God and to the rest of the family.

Elder Eyring captures the essence of this responsibility when he explains that "a morning prayer and an early search in the scriptures to know *what we should do for the Lord* can set the course of a day. We can know which task, of all those we might choose, matters most to God and therefore to us. I have learned such a prayer is always answered if we ask and ponder with childlike submission, ready to act without delay to perform even the most humble service" ("This Day," *Ensign*, May 2007, 89; emphasis added).

How then do we teach this most essential transition? They will learn it by watching the example of those around them and as they find answers in the scriptures.

Growing up, I learned a great deal about trusting the Lord from the example of my parents. My father had a consistent way to purchase new cars. When he found one he liked, he would arrange to bring the car home overnight. He would then have a trusted mechanic do a complete evaluation of the car and give him a recommendation in the morning. Secondly, in our family prayers, I would hear my father humbly ask the Lord if this car was right for us. If he felt right about it, the next morning, my father would take the car back and complete the transaction.

Our example demonstrates to our children whether we lean more to our own understanding or whether we rely on the Lord's guidance. To do this effectively, our decision-making process needs to be "transparent" to our children. True, we could receive answers to our problems as a couple or in individual prayer. But we cannot underestimate the effect of pleading with the Lord while our children listen. Allow them to hear our concerns, our gratitude—our surrender to His will. The more transparent we are in the way we seek guidance, the more clearly our children will see the link between our behavior and divine accountability.

At a key moment in my career, we received a kind offer to join a friend in his business out of state. Cindy and I flew out and interviewed for the job. After the interview, we went to the temple and spent time in the celestial room, praying about the offer. As we prayed, we both felt peace and calm, confirming our decision to take the new job. When we returned home, we gathered our children and announced we would be moving out of state. It meant uprooting them from their friends and schools. It meant starting over in many different ways. But as we described the answer we'd received in the temple, they understood and were able to accept the Lord's decision in our behalf.

As parents in the gospel, we have a potential for a rich family legacy of the Lord's dealings with us. The testimony of receiving answers to prayers can help establish in our children's hearts both an understanding and an expectation that the Lord does answer prayers. That example will teach them that answers are possible and that Heavenly Father can be active in their lives.

One LDS researcher found that there is strong evidence that narratives, the stories we tell or hear, are the most natural way we learn from one another. This research confirms that people transfer their most fundamental beliefs through stories, stories in which the listeners and the storyteller participate together in the recognizable, "Oh-I-know-what-you-mean" elements of the story (see *Writing His Law in Their Hearts: The Development of Religious Faith in Children*, BYU Forum, 31 January 1995, 3).

Someone once said that everyone in the scriptures is either an example or a warning to us. In the scriptures are story after story of people who trusted Heavenly Father for answers and were then able to do things far beyond their ability. Nephi, Gideon, Enoch, Abraham, Paul, Mormon, Joseph Smith, and President Hinckley all faced hard tasks and drew on the Lord to help them. More important, He was able to bless them as they stayed true to covenants they had made.

Nephi tells us he "did liken all scriptures unto [his people]" (1 Nephi 19:23). I take that to mean he taught them to apply lessons learned by their scriptural ancestors to their own daily situations. The scriptures are rich with stories of ordinary people who have made and kept sacred covenants. They also tell us of those who broke their promises. The key is making the scriptural examples relevant in the lives of youth who face their own set of challenges.

Are there answers for:

• Your ten-year-old son, who is dealing with a bully at school?

- Your thirteen-year-old daughter, who wants to wear more revealing clothing?
- Your nine-year-old son, who saw some disturbing sexual images on the Internet?
- Your fifteen-year-old son, who has been asked by a non-member to a girl's-choice school dance?

Are there answers in the scriptures for these problems? Can your children find them? Have the covenants they've made—to you, to the Lord, to themselves—helped your children determine how to handle these situations? And, can those in our sacred history, those who kept their covenants, serve as a guide?

The scriptures can and will help, if we know where to find the examples and create the forums to share them with our kids. If we are skillful, we can help scriptural accounts or stories from Church history come alive. We can help them see that boys such as Nephi or Ammon or Joseph Smith struggled to find answers and courage in difficult situations. How would our daughters benefit from knowing the story of the two courageous young women, clutching printed pages of the unpublished Book of Commandments, and being pursued across the cane breaks by a drunken mob in Missouri? Then, and more important, can we ask them, after they have read or heard these stories, how they *feel* about them? When they read Joseph's First Vision, did they feel "something," such as a calm or a peace, even for a few moments? Do they understand what it was that they felt?

The Church has worked hard to surround us with reminders of the covenant-making in our rich history. They've made sure that Church history sites are well-preserved, beautiful, and worth visiting. These sites stand as monuments to those who understood the eternal significance of the promises they had made. And, as we will discuss in chapter 12, there is real power in those places, hallowed by blood and sacrifice, that has the potential to "turn the hearts of the children" in a way nothing else can (see Malachi 4:6).

One last example of covenant-making is found in the family legacy of our patriarchal blessings. In them, we have received personal revelations from the Lord to us. He makes promises and covenants and describes the great possibilities available to us if we are obedient. Do our children know what the Lord has promised their parents? Have we explained, in loving terms, how our child fits into the Lord's promises to us? Have we worked to generate excitement for the day when they will find out the specific blessings the Lord has in mind for them, under the hand of an inspired patriarch?

When our children were young, we had some enjoyable family home evenings where Cindy and I shared our patriarchal blessings with our children. In our blessings, the Lord had revealed specific promises about our four kids, and Cindy and I enjoyed pointing out those promises to them. We were able to testify that our patriarchal blessings are evidence that the Lord knows Cindy and me and that He knows our children. By sharing our blessings with our children, the kids were able to see the sacred promises that had been made and learn how those promises were being fulfilled. For parents in Zion, these personalized revelations constitute a unique tool that can be used to build faith and help our children learn to trust and love Heavenly Father.

In conclusion, God has been in the parenting business for countless millennia. There is no parental problem He has not seen or dealt with. In fact, the Savior, by "suffering pains and afflictions and temptations of every kind . . . his bowels [are] filled with mercy . . . that he may know according to the flesh how to succor his people" (Alma 7:11–12). He knows what we need as parents, and He knows the needs of our children. His divine example teaches us an eternal pattern of parenting, based on making and keeping covenants. The sooner children develop divine-esteem, through covenants, the more quickly they will learn how to live a surrendered life. And the less likely they are to rebel.

Covenants, responsibility, and repentance are what we teach. The extent to which children internalize these concepts depends a lot on how effectively we teach these truths. We know the WHAT, let's now look more closely at the HOW.

Six

Parenting 101: How We Teach

Before I got married I had six theories about bringing up children; now I have six children, and no theories.—John Wilmot

It is 8:30 on Sunday morning. Church begins in thirty minutes. Jan finally has herself ready and the baby dressed. She is just sitting down to a quick breakfast when ten-year-old Shawn wanders into the kitchen still dressed in his pajamas.

"Shawn," Jan says, looking up, "hurry and get dressed. We need to leave in just a few minutes."

"Not going," mumbles Shawn.

Scenario #1:

"Shawn!" Jan yells, "You march right back to your bedroom and get into your Sunday clothes. I don't have time for this right now."

"But I don't want to," whines Shawn, his voice rising.

"Go!" says Jan firmly, pointing toward his room. "Unless you want to be grounded all week . . ."

Shawn stares, then slowly turns around and heads back to

his room. A few minutes later, he comes back dressed without saying a word.

Scenario #2:

"Okay," says Jan, "you can choose if you go or not. But just remember that when you don't go, you make Heavenly Father sad. When we don't go to church we tell Him that we just don't love Him anymore. I'd be really disappointed in you too because you know better. So think hard before you let everyone down like that."

With that, Jan turns back to her breakfast. Out of the corner of her eye she sees Shawn hesitate, then turn and shuffle back to his room to get dressed.

Scenario #3:

Jan puts down her fork and puts her arm around Shawn.

"Shawn, you've always liked going to church. What's the matter?"

Shawn stares down at the floor and doesn't say anything.

"Is something going on with your teacher or the other kids in your class?" prompts Jan.

After a moment of silence, Shawn finally admits that a couple of the deacons have been teasing him about his new glasses.

In each of these scenarios, Mom is trying to help her son get to church. In each case, she makes it clear that attendance at church is important. In each case, though her goal is the same, there are different approaches to accomplish the same thing. In the first scenario, Jan enforces obedience by threatening consequences; in the second, she uses guilt. In the third, however, she recognizes a change in Shawn's behavior and wants to understand what's happened.

To this point in the book, we've pursued our goal of preventing future rebelliousness by helping children develop divine-esteem or reliance on the Spirit. We've concluded that they are able to develop that reliance only when they have a correct understanding of their Heavenly Father. We've also examined the importance of having a clear understanding of covenanted responsibilities.

Most children who rebel have been taught correct principles in the home and at church. They know they are supposed to keep the commandments. Many rebellions are not a rejection of the message as much as they are a rejection to our approach and our authority.

We can reduce the possibility of that rejection by creating a proper environment, one in which spiritual experiences can and do occur. Elder Joe J. Christensen has pointed out:

> One of the most important strengths our children can develop is to have their own personal spiritual experiences. We should stress the value of our children's having a direct personal involvement in such activities as reading the scriptures and praying on their own, thus developing their own testimonies. When they become personally involved in spiritual experiences, they are much more likely to avoid harmful behaviors such as cheating, lying, shoplifting, taking drugs, and breaking the law of chastity. *We really have come to the day when neither we nor our children can live on "borrowed light"* (One Step at a Time: Building a Better Marriage, Family, and You [Salt Lake City: Deseret Book Company, 1996], 88; emphasis added).

Brent L. Top and Bruce Chadwick have written:

> As parents, we should recognize that it is important not only to hold family home evenings, family prayers, and family scripture study, but also to find ways to help our children have their own personal spiritual experiences. *When we hold family religious activities only to be holding them, our youth do not seem to gain the benefit needed to deter delinquency.* It appears that if we are only "going through the motions," our children recognize that fact and in turn only "go through the motions" of religiosity themselves. As parents, we can demonstrate to our children that the gospel is an essential part of our lives by providing opportunities not only to learn what the gospel is, but also to experience for themselves what the gospel does ("Special Report—Teens Out of Trouble," *This People*, Fall 1995, 24).

As we look at the inventive ways Satan is using to snare our youth, it's easy to appreciate the prophetic vision of Heber C. Kimball who warned that "the difficulties of this work will be of such a character that a man or woman who does not possess this personal knowledge will fall" (as quoted by Elder Harold B. Lee, in Conference Report, October 1955, 56).

Our children can gain knowledge they need, but we must teach it in a way that encourages their receptiveness. A few years ago, I wrote a small training manual I titled, "Lectures Are Lethal Things." I tried to stress that children retain very little from lectures, shutting out most of what they hear. Ninety-five percent of what we say to anyone is promptly forgotten an hour later! The longer we lecture, the more we begin to sound like the adults in the *Peanut* cartoons on TV. Instead of hearing what we have to say, our children hear only "wha, wha, whawhawha!" I have frequently joked that we can tell children something one hundred times, but they need to hear us at least once.

Lectures, especially angry parental ones, *are* lethal things. How we parent, our style and approach, is key to establishing home environments that are conducive to spiritual experiences. Our approach sets the tone and temperature of the home. Let's now look at some of the factors that influence how we teach and the effect these styles have on the gospel message we hope is being written on our children's hearts.

Parental Styles

The "how" of parenting is really a function of three core factors. These three factors, in some combination, form distinct patterns in the way we parent (see A. Lynn Scoresby, *Bringing Up Moral Children* [Salt Lake City: Deseret Book Company, 1989], 179–208).

Anxiety

The first of these factors is the level of *anxiety* or emotion shown during parent/child interactions. A parent with consistently low levels of anxiety comes across as calm and even-tempered. They rarely yell or exhibit extreme emotions when dealing with their children. As the level of anxiety increases, so does volume. And stress. In addition, parents with higher levels of anxiety tend to make decisions that are more reactionary in nature, ones they often regret or have to change. ("Young man! That's it! You are grounded for the rest of your life!")

Contrast this with the voice of our Heavenly Parent. It is described as "not a harsh voice, neither [is] it a loud voice; nevertheless, and notwithstanding it being a small voice [that does] pierce [us] that . . . hear to the center" (3 Nephi 11:3).

While His voice clearly and firmly explains what He expects, His voice also whispers peace. The result of hearing that voice is peace. Instinctively, we all respond more favorably to a calm tone.

It should be noted the "anxiety" component of parenting is also directly related to the stress of the adult trying to parent. As our level of personal stress increases, so does the anxiety with which we parent. Highly anxious parents are also highly stressed parents.

Control

The second parental factor is the amount of direct *control* we seek to impose in our children's lives. Control is seen as the extent that rules and structure define our daily family living. In high control homes, for example, rules are very clear-cut and daily life is highly organized. These rules are "top-down," set by parents, followed by kids. Breaking a rule brings immediate consequences. Rules are rarely suspended or negotiated. Conversely, low control parents have few rules, little structure, and are more likely to involve their children in decision-making.

Nurturing

The third factor of parenting is warmth and affection or *nurturing*. This describes the level of affection and positive interaction demonstrated by parents toward their kids. The greater the affection the more likely a parent is to use physical touch and hugs. Affectionate parents tend to spend more time with their children in nondiscipline situations and have closer relationships. Low nurturing homes are colder, more formal, with less interaction between parent and child.

The level of these three factors tends to remain pretty constant without a focused effort to change them. Rarely do parents choose or decide their parenting style. Our parenting relationships are an extension of our interpersonal style, combined with our own personality, and often are an extension of how we were treated by our parents. We tend to interact with our children the same way we respond to those subordinate to us. As a result, we may or may not recognize the long-term effect our style is having on them as they mature. As a parent, it is important we examine our parental style, making sure it best facilitates our stewardship goals.

Let's now look at how these three factors combine in ways that result in distinct, recognizable patterns of parenting—and the predictable reactions they have on children.

1. Overprotective Parents (High Anxiety, High Control, High Nurturing)

This is a highly controlled, highly charged form of parenting. When structured parents also exhibit high degrees of anxiety and nurturing, children tend to become overly bonded to their parents. While this may create a close-knit family—very close—it also may negatively affect a child's sense of autonomy. As they mature, children from these homes may have difficulty making independent decisions. Missionaries and college students from these homes, for instance, may pass through difficult bouts of homesickness as they adjust to life away from their families.

One former client of mine described himself as a Navy brat: his dad was in the Navy most of the time my client was growing up. Dad's assignments rarely took him away, so he was home most of the time, running it with tight military precision. Dinner was always at 6:00 P.M., homework was to be completed by 9:00 P.M. if at all possible. Both Mom and Dad were very involved in his life—PTA, coaching—and were active in the Church. But Dad also had a temper and could quickly hand out harsh punishments on the spur of the moment. Their unwritten but well-understood family rule was: "Don't make Dad mad." His parents, especially Dad, dominated decision making within the home. Today, as an adult, my client still feels he must call his father before he makes any large decision.

How Overprotective Parents Teach the Gospel

One phrase that applies here is a favorite of mine: "beware of what works." Just because an approach produces results in the short-term doesn't mean we'll like the long-term effect. Over-protectiveness and excessive control work well if the goal is simple obedience. In the long run, however, children from controlling households tend to grow into either compliant adults who struggle with self-esteem, or they ultimately rebel, rejecting the control and the gospel message. In either case, they are probably uncomfortable at church. This occurs because the "high anxiety" component of this parenting style lends itself to using guilt as a form of control. Children comply because they don't want to make their parents mad but also because they don't want to hurt their feelings or see their mother cry. Liberal use of guilt to force compliance can confuse a child's understanding of love and the Atonement, especially as they grow older and sense some manipulation in their parents' emotional reaction.

2. Controlling Parents (High Control, Low Affection, Low Anxiety)

Parenting with a high level of control tends to be goal/result focused. Decisions are based on what is logical. Punishment is swift and consistent. The drive toward perfectionism may put an overemphasis on outward appearance. As with overprotectiveness, children growing up in this environment become either very obedient or they take the first opportunity to rebel as soon as they are old enough. They may be shy and fearful of making mistakes. Our motto, "beware of what works," is also applicable in this case because this style is a very efficient way to produce compliant children but, like the overprotective style, may be a disaster in helping prepare autonomous adults. For example, this approach could put some young women, who are seeking nurture, at risk for predatory males who feign love and approval in return for intimacy.

How Controlling Parents Teach the Gospel

LDS parents who stress rules without much affection create a gospel focused on the "letter of the law"—much like the Pharisees of the New Testament. Children begin to believe in a God who metes out punishment but very little love. They may have a difficult time learning to love the vengeful God they've been conditioned to fear. Controlling parents tend to classify feelings and emotions as illogical weaknesses. Because of that, children who attempt to learn to trust the nuances of the Spirit will become confused at best and may dismiss spiritual promptings as "just emotions."

3. Democratic Parents (Low Control, High Affection, Low Anxiety)

Parents who demonstrate high amounts of affection, along with low regulation and anxiety, create a home that is warm, fun, and supportive. Family rules are limited and children have great input into helping form them. Because there are fewer rules inside the home, consequences tend to come more from outside organizations such as schools. For instance, a democratic parent may allow a child to fail classes and have them deal with the school's consequences. Children growing up in these homes can be more nonconformist than their peers but are also more likely to be self-directed. This kind of home environment is ideal for creative or artistic children.

It should be noted that not all children are happy in a democratic environment with little or no structure. As we will discuss later, some children, by their innate nature, are born needing or craving a structured environment. If so, they will find this parental style frustrating and too chaotic for their nature.

How Democratic Parents Teach the Gospel

LDS homes presided over by democratic parents create an atmosphere where children can learn the gospel well. High warmth, combined with their self-regulation, can enable children to shine in gospel settings. If regulation is too low or consequences too rarely applied, it is also possible for children to remain active in the Church structure, but "slip through the cracks" as far as gospel knowledge is concerned. If this happens, they may grow too casual in their relationship with Heavenly Father or view the Church merely as a social organization.

4. Organized Parents (High Control, High Affection, Low Anxiety)

If there is a formula for creating high achieving children, this is it. This style of parenting produces an environment for children who grow to be goal oriented and feel well supported in all their many activities. They are respectful of leadership and those in authority. The lack of anxiety gives them room to make mistakes and learn from them.

In an organized style, children benefit greatly by being able to participate more in the establishment of rules as they grow older. They then become part of the process and internalize the reasons for the rules. At the same time, they can learn the importance of divine-esteem and surrendering their will to Heavenly Father.

How Organized Parents Teach the Gospel

This parenting style most closely approximates how the Lord explains the priesthood is to be administered. In teaching the Prophet Joseph Smith, the Lord describes how priesthood and authority are meant to work. The Prophet was told:

> No power or influence can or ought to be maintained by virtue of the priesthood, only by persuasion, by long-suffering, by gentleness and meekness, and by love unfeigned; [**High Affection**]
>
> By kindness, and pure knowledge . . . [**Low Anxiety**]
>
> Reproving betimes with sharpness, [**High Control**] when moved upon by the Holy Ghost; and then showing forth afterwards an increase of love toward him whom thou hast reproved, lest he esteem thee to be his enemy (D&C 121:41–43).

Covenant-making inspires us to voluntarily subject our self to a Grand Being who loves us and wants the best for us. In return, He simply requires our obedience. Children learn to covenant with God because they first learn to covenant with parents who love them and require their obedience. This is ideally done in a low anxiety setting that invites the whisperings of the Spirit.

5. Anxious Parents (Low Control, Low Affection, High Anxiety)

In a word, this is chaos. Homes with high levels of anxiety and stress, combined with low control and low affection, say more about the parents' needs than the children's. Parents in these settings may be dealing with serious issues that occupy their time and focus. In addition, they may be overwhelmed by the needs of their children and are at a loss as to what to do about it. Children in these homes can develop serious problems, including trying to parent their parents. This style can lead to unhealthy coping skills that can spill over into a child's schooling and relationships.

One common situation where this style may occur is in a contentious or painful divorce. The custodial parent, usually the mother, may become so absorbed in daily survival and stress that the child's emotional needs are overlooked. Regardless of what parenting style was in play before the divorce, the children are now placed into a less structured situation with changing rules and dynamics.

High anxiety parenting styles can cause a chain reaction that impacts the parent/child relationship (see below). The

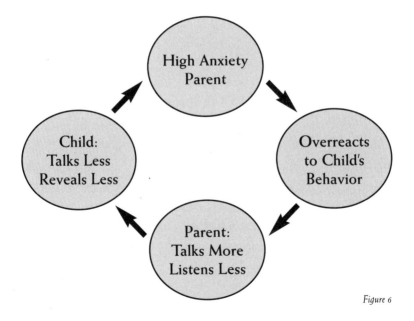

Figure 6

more anxious we are, the more reactive we are. Also, the more reactive we are, the more we lecture and less we listen. Our children respond by sharing even less. As they share less, a high anxiety parent reacts more because the child is providing less information. It is a vicious cycle with no winners! This ongoing pattern results in a parent knowing less about what a child is doing.

How Anxious Parents Teach the Gospel

Depending on the severity, these may be special needs situations. In a setting where anxiety and fear rules, it is difficult for young people to experience the joy and happiness inherent in the gospel of Jesus Christ. Callings and Church programs can be perceived as just one more stressful situation to be avoided. This style may also be a byproduct of a parent who does not understand the gospel well or finds their basic assumptions about God being challenged by adversity. For these reasons, a supportive ward organization is vital in providing supplemental gospel training and loving support to children from such families.

6—Overindulgent Parents (Low Control, High Affection, High Anxiety)

An overindulgent parent is one who doesn't want to say "no." They may be more invested in trying to be their child's friend as opposed to being their parent. They are afraid that if they impose rules, it will somehow negatively impact their child's growth and/or their relationship with their child. All rules are negotiable and consequences rarely applied. Discipline tends to be an overreaction to crisis situations that have escalated because they weren't dealt with earlier. Unfortunately, the threatened discipline may also be reversed later given the child's reaction.

Children in such homes learn to become manipulative, trying to charm their way around the rules. In more extreme cases, they begin to believe that rules just don't apply to them.

How Overindulgent Parents Teach the Gospel

The great plan of happiness requires our obedience in a "strait and narrow" way of living. Children who are not taught consequences will have a difficult time learning to covenant. They may acknowledge the love of their parents and youth leaders but chafe at any rules, such as dating standards that limit what they want to do.

One mother I know used Joseph Smith's quote, "I teach them correct principles and let them govern themselves" (*Millennial Star* 13:339) as justification for not holding her young children to attendance at church, etc. She felt she'd taught them and they were now responsible to govern themselves from that day forward. When her older children quit going to church and later developed Word of Wisdom problems, she would shake her head and remind anyone that would listen that her children had been taught. "What else can you do?" she would add with a shrug. This overindulgent mother refused to see that her children had been *told* what to do but had never been properly *taught* what to do.

All of these concepts and scenarios we have thus far mentioned, hinge on a single factor: the relationship between parent and child. We can recover from a lot of parental mistakes if we are able to keep the lines of communication open. Parents whose style is warm, consistent, and low anxiety find time to talk to their kids—and then listen carefully to what they are saying. They are also more aware of a child's daily activities and friendships.

Child's Personality Styles

As any parent can quickly attest, each child is different, doing things for their own reasons. At a very early age, they begin to develop the unique personalities they will carry with them into adulthood. They have their own temperaments and are motivated by their own goals, likes, and dislikes. These unique differences help form their individual personality styles. As we will discuss later, these individual personality styles interact with our parenting styles to help define the delicate interplay between parent and child. Let's look first at these personality differences.

Our personalities may be grouped into four major categories. I've tried to define them into four quickly identifiable types. These four personality styles act as a window through which our children respond to the world around them.

Personality Styles

Talkers

Socializer
Friend oriented
Bedroom: disorganized, pictures
Future Job: sales, people-oriented
Spiritual Strength: sensitive
 to the Spirit
Spiritual Weakness: comparisons

Doers

Achiever
Goal oriented
Bedroom: awards
Future Job: boss, owner
Spiritual Strength: action,
 worker
Spiritual Weakness: patience

Thinkers

Analyzer
Object oriented
Bedroom: cluttered with projects
Future Job: computers, mechanics

Spiritual Strength: understanding
Spiritual Weakness: mistrust of
 feelings

Planners

Organizer
Process oriented
Bedroom: organized
Future Job: office manager,
 engineer
Spiritual Strength: service
Spiritual Weakness:
 spontaneity

When our own children were young, we learned just how different they were as soon as we tried to discipline them. For instance, Cindy and I often used "time-outs" when we wanted to curtail some behavior. One of our sons is a *talker*. For him, timeout was uncomfortable, and he disliked it a lot. It cut him off from the rest of the family and from his friends. In his mind, time-out was the worst punishment we could do to him.

Another of our sons is clearly a *thinker*. He enjoys time alone, thinking and analyzing problems. Time-out in his room turned out to be more reward than punishment. When he was being "punished," he would hole up in his room and think or read. Time-out was not a deterrent for him. However, if we had a long talk with him and helped him understand *why* he shouldn't be doing something, the behavior stopped.

Understanding a child's personality style helps us know the kind of consequences that would help them learn responsibility. Understanding their personality also helps us know how they learn. This is valuable as we teach gospel principles. A talker, for instance, is traditionally seen as more "right-brained"; meaning that they are creative and visual. They learn by observing others and illustrations more than they do by long explanations. Doers and thinkers learn better by completing projects and hands-on activities.

How Do We Individualize Our Parenting?

Parenting describes the interaction between parent and child. Parenting occurs in thousands of words, looks, reactions, nonverbal body language, punishments, encouragement, and so on. The parent/child relationship happens within the parental styles we've just described, but it happens with children who have their own personality and personality styles.

Depending on his or her personality, each child reacts or meshes with a parental style. What makes the difference? Each parental style, at its core, is a reflection of our own personality style. It should come as no surprise that a parent who is a planner would parent with a higher level of control than a parent who is a talker. Again, as we parent, we develop our own style based on our own personality.

A child's personality style, then, will be reflected in their reaction to the way we parent. Planners are naturally more comfortable with a parenting style that emphasizes organization, predictability, and consistency. A talker, growing up under the same parenting, may chafe under the rules and long for more spontaneity.

At this point, you might be asking: what if my spouse is one personality and I am another? What then? The short answer to this most critical question is that husbands and wives generally tend toward some level of compromise so that their parental style is a combination of the two. When that compromise is not achieved, children grow up in a home where they have to change their behavior, depending on which parent they are interacting with. And, given how important unity is, we'll leave this topic for another chapter where we can explore it more in depth.

What we need to realize, then, is that our parenting will be reflective of who we are, but it also must take into consideration the individual personality styles of our children. Parents operating in a democratic style (high nurture, low control, low anxiety) may find they need to provide more structure for children who are naturally planners or thinkers. And democratic parents shouldn't be surprised when their doer child steps out and makes bold decisions without consulting them.

The following grid shows how a child's personality style may or may not complement our parental style. And though we may work to modify our parental style somewhat, it will always be a reflection of our own personalities.

The grand key is recognizing whether our parenting style complements or clashes with the enduring, ingrained personality style of each child. If the two, our style and their style, are similar, they will understand more completely what we're trying to do. They will be more likely to agree with our approach and be less likely to rebel.

On the other hand, if their personality and our style are opposites, then the responsibility falls to us, as parents, to modify our approach in a way that takes into consideration our child's own style.

Complementary?

Parenting Style	Talker	Doer	Thinker	Planner
Overprotective	No	Yes	No	Yes
Controlling	No	Yes	Yes	Yes
Democratic	Yes	Yes	No	No
Organized	Yes	Yes	Yes	Yes
Anxious	No	No	No	No
Overindulgent	Yes	Yes	No	No

Individualizing our approach to our children requires that we keep the following points in mind:

1. Recognize their personality style (talker, doer, thinker, or planner)

Remember that the child's style is the lens through which they view the world—especially relationships. For instance, you're not surprised when your talker is much more verbal, telling you everything that's going on. Your thinker, on the other hand, may be saying very little and causing concern. Hint: If you want to discuss a serious topic with a thinker, try leaving him/her a note expressing your concerns. Let them digest your thoughts for a couple of days, then approach them. Conversely, keep your conversations with a doer short— they generally tune out after ten minutes. Also, just tell them what you need; don't drive them nuts by beating around the bush.

2. Try to identify their needs as they see them

We are all motivated by those things most relevant to us. The world of a child can be surprisingly small. With the benefit of adulthood, we know that bullies grow up and most high school popularity contests end with graduation. But our children do not yet understand that. Their immediate concerns command their fears and their focus. Even thirteen-year-olds will open up if we are discussing things most on their mind. Do we know what they are worried about?

One way to know what a child is concerned about is to keep in mind *childhood universals*. A universal is a concern that most or all children have at certain stages.

Age	Stage	Universals
0–5	Object relations	Security, safety
6–9	Law and order	Rights and wrongs
9–12	Hero worship	Learning to follow hero's actions
12–15	Peer	Friends, fitting in
15–18	World view	Their place in larger society

These broad stages vary depending on the developmental growth of a child. But they are still broad universals that come with each stage of their development.

3. Talk less and listen more

As parents, we all talk too much! It is an illness we all share. Somehow, we've learned to confuse teaching and lecturing. If we're telling them, we're parenting them! We are concerned about a child's behavior, so we launch into a lecture and think we're having a discussion. We end up telling them what to do rather than collaborating with them. Telling and lecturing are easier and they take less of our time. However, a parent's universal is this: when we visited with our child, and we talked more than they did, we probably still don't know what is really going on.

4. Learn to ask the right questions

"How is school going?" is an invitation for a one-word answer: "Fine!" And, you still don't know how school is going. "Tell me about your math class" is better. "Are you OK?" will again get you a one word, "Yes." "You look really down, can you tell me what's going on with you?" is much better.

Learning to ask the right questions, "Tell me how math is going," helps you gather information about their life. Remember, though, that there is always something else going on, things they may not bring up spontaneously. Try this: "And what else is going on?" or "And what other classes are you having a hard time with?" or "And what other friends are getting into trouble?" And what else? And what else? And what else?

On average, teens require about three prompts to get to the full story. The first two answers are the parent answers; things they just tell adults. You have to dig—and then quit talking—to get the real story.

5. Allow them their feelings

As parents, we sometimes want to step in too quickly and tell a child how they should be feeling. Or we react to an emotion we disagree with or that scares us. When a child says, "I hate everybody," we may respond with, "Honey, that's not a good feeling to have. We're not supposed to hate!" If we jump in too quickly, they'll be less likely to tell us what caused the feeling in the first place. When they tell us how they're feeling, it is a great opportunity to find out what is causing those emotions.

6. Remember, all behavior is purposive

People do things for their reasons and that reason is often different than what they say it is. It may even be different from what *they* think it is. As parents, we need to understand why our children behave the way they do. For instance, when your mild-mannered fourteen-year-old son punches a hole in the wall, do you immediately (A) point out how inappropriate his behavior is and talk about repairing the wall or (B) sit down with him and explore why he's so frustrated?

Finally, we need to remember that as teacher/parents, we are not alone in this sacred endeavor. It was never intended for parents in Zion to teach responsibility, let alone gospel principles, without the aid of the Spirit. The Lord has promised:

> Seek not to declare [lecture] my word [unto your children], but first seek to obtain my word, and then shall your tongue be loosed; then, if you desire, you shall have my Spirit and my word, yea, the power of God unto the convincing of [your children] (D&C 11:21).

What a comforting promise. Specifically, if we call upon Him, the Lord will teach us *how* to teach. All that we have studied and learned will then be brought to our mind. As Elder Neal A. Maxwell reminded us:

> When we speak about teaching by the Spirit it is not about a mystical process which removes responsibility from the missionary or teacher [or the parent] for prayerful and pondering preparation. Teaching by the Spirit is not the lazy equivalent of going on "automatic pilot." We still need a carefully worked out "flight plan" (*That Ye May Believe* [Salt Lake City: Bookcraft, 1992], 40).

Seven

Problem Solvers and the IGeneration

Too often we give children answers to remember rather than problems to solve. —*Roger Lewin*

Lisa is a cute fifteen-year-old Mia Maid. The youngest of four children, she has her own cell phone, TV, and computer. Referred to by her parents as "the princess," she spent last summer's handcart trek riding on top of one of the handcarts, pulled by two adoring young men. At girls camp, she refused to drink the water since it tasted "funny" and soon became dehydrated and had to go home early. Like many of her friends, she dresses in tight, revealing clothes. She will turn sixteen, six months after prom, but already she and her mother have been out looking at expensive prom dresses.

Greg is eleven and a loner. Though his school is two blocks away, his father drives him there every morning. Greg hates doing homework, so his mother sits by him each night until he finishes. He also has his own computer, video games, and a cell phone, but complains constantly that they are "junk" and that he needs the latest versions. He's quick to follow fashion trends at school, though he refuses to admit that his current haircut looks pretty strange. He's not looking forward to being a deacon because he says he hates to camp out or go anywhere he can't play his video games. He has a season pass to the local amusement park but refuses to go because "it is so boring!"

Lisa and Greg are part of the IGeneration or the "Indulged" generation. Their parents have given them pretty much everything they've asked for, only to discover that the child always wants more. Much of their pampered status comes as their parents seek to match all the things their friends have. Even though they have all the latest electronic toys, it never seems to be enough. And when they don't get what they want, they complain and pout until they do.

Lisa and Greg's malady has been around for a long time. Their problem is how they see themselves and their place in the world. As seen in the diagram below, when children begin to feel entitled, they begin to see only two groups of people around them: those who will give them what they want and those who won't. ("Those who are cool and those who are mean!") Meeting their needs is defined as "giving me what I want and not making me do things I don't want to do."

How They See Their World

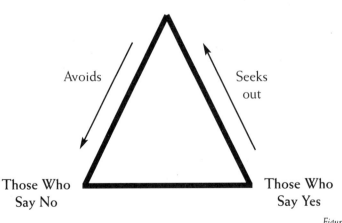

Figure 7

This pattern of thinking can be reinforced by parents wanting to befriend their children rather than parent them. Though it is a faulty way of thinking, it can remain unchallenged by parents who simply try to avoid arguments, as well as those who excessively focus on a child's social status among their peers. The result can be the same in each case: we try to buy approval, for them or for us, with material things.

In reality, their world is much different than they would believe. IGeners, those who have been indulged in the majority of their wants, end up with a fragile self-image. They feel good about themselves as long as their "needs" are being met. What they quickly realize, however, is that they don't have the means to finance their endless indulgences. Others, specifically parents or grandparents, are seen as having the financial ability they lack to purchase each new toy they "need." As a result, they are dependent on others to "understand"—and purchase—their needs.

In addition, since their sense of self-worth is tied to worldly goods, they live in a house built on shifting sand. Fads change constantly, technology is always upgrading, and fashions re-invent themselves overnight. For the overindulged, it is as if they are chasing smoke—happiness based on moonbeams. In the end, there is no happiness, only emptiness with the hope that the next gadget will make them happy.

If we are to avoid raising such a child, as parents, we need to constantly make an honest self-inventory of our actions and our motivations. We might ask the following:

- Do the things I purchase for my children leave them *internally* stronger or weaker?
- As a result of my parenting, are my children more

able or less able to solve their own problems through reliance on the Lord?

- Am I afraid my children won't like me if I fail to give them what they are asking for?
- Do I want my kids to be popular with their friends, even those who might have much different values than ours?
- Do I find it easier to give them what they want rather than listen to them whine and complain?
- Do I find myself "letting them off the hook" or waiving the consequences of family rules they've broken?

In Reality

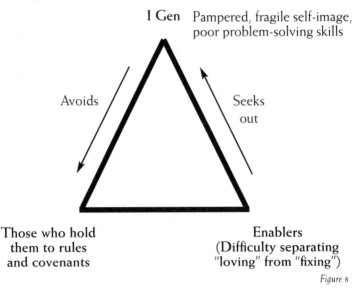

I Gen   Pampered, fragile self-image, poor problem-solving skills

Avoids

Seeks out

Those who hold them to rules and covenants

Enablers (Difficulty separating "loving" from "fixing")

Figure 8

The long-term result for the overly pampered can be seen in the way they approach adulthood responsibility. *Time* magazine recently ran a feature article on a growing pattern of behavior among young adults which experts are calling "twixters."

Social scientists are starting to realize that a permanent shift has taken place in the way we live our lives. In the past, people moved from childhood to adolescence and from adolescence to adulthood, but today there is a new, intermediate phase along the way. The years from 18 until 25 and even beyond have become a distinct and separate life stage, a strange, transitional never-never land between adolescence and adulthood in which people stall for a few extra years, putting off the iron cage of adult responsibility that constantly threatens to crash down on them. They're betwixt and between. You could call them twixters.

Where did the twixters come from? And what's taking them so long to get where they're going? Some of the sociologists, psychologists, and demographers who study this new life stage see it as a good thing. The twixters aren't lazy, the argument goes, they're simply reaping the fruit of decades of American affluence and social liberation. This new period is a chance for young people to savor the pleasures of irresponsibility, search their souls, and choose their life paths.

More historically and economically minded scholars see twixters differently. These scholars explain that adulthood is being delayed because they lack the skills. Whatever cultural machinery used to turn kids into grownups has broken down, so that society no longer provides young people with the moral backbone and the financial wherewithal to take their rightful places in the adult world ("Grow Up? Not So Fast!" January 24, 2005, 42).

The twixter phenomenon is partially a function of the IGeneration, a generation having difficulty learning to focus beyond their own self-indulgent wants. As they carry that myopic view of life into their adult years, they struggle to solve the basic problems of their lives and have little tolerance for jobs or activities that require sacrifice or self-discipline. Instead, they continue to live at home, drift from college to jobs, or from major to major, and stall their entrance into society. Marriage and raising a family is then put off well into the future.

The IGeneration has raised sufficient concern within the Church to bring this strong counsel from Elder Dallin H. Oaks concerning dating and marriage:

> This tendency to postpone adult responsibilities, including marriage and family, is surely visible among our LDS young adults. The average age at marriage has increased in the last few decades, and the number of children born to LDS married couples has decreased.
>
> Men, if you have returned from your mission and you are still following the boy-girl patterns you were counseled to follow when you were 15, it is time for you to grow up. Gather your courage and look for someone to pair off with. Start with a variety of dates with a variety of young women, and when that phase yields a good prospect, proceed to courtship. It's marriage time. That is what the Lord intends for His young adult sons and daughters. Men have the initiative, and you men should get on with it ("The Dedication of a Lifetime," CES Fireside, May 1, 2005).

Pampered youth postpone taking on responsibility. They shun it in favor of focusing only on their own wants. Adulthood, and its attendant complexities, are avoided because these youth are used to being consumers, not problem solvers.

This is a sensitive subject due to the number of twenty-somethings still living at home within the Church. Certainly each situation is different. However, as we each do an honest reappraisal, we may find that we need to change the way we parent older "children" as well as our younger ones!

Raising Problem Solvers

With these concerns in mind, it should become obvious just how important proper structure, genuine warmth, and calm consistency are to effective parenting. They help establish a setting where the Spirit can be present as we teach responsibility. Parents are—above every other description—teachers. As educators, we must strive to teach without lecturing, love without indulging, and lead without force.

Children need to learn how to be problem solvers. Responsible adults solve problems in a productive way. We all cope in one way or another, healthy or unhealthy, consistent with or destructive of our goals. Our children, with us or without us, will learn coping skills that may be functional or not. The child who learns to cope with a schoolyard bully by hiding under the slide every recess is "coping." She has found a way to not be attacked. The son who does not study but becomes "ill" every time there is a big test has also learned to cope. They will learn how to get their short-term needs met, but they will not reach their potential without developing effective problem solving skills.

I once worked as the program manager for an adolescent unit at a psychiatric hospital. In this program we had kids with a wide range of emotional and behavioral problems. Many were dealing with the consequences of the poor choices they had made and having to learn more functional ways of coping.

One of our treatment goals was to help them establish a connection between their behavior and consequences. For whatever reason, they had not learned to evaluate their actions based on what they wanted in the future. They focused only on what they immediately wanted. As a result, they rarely got what they wanted and were frustrated and depressed. The idea of behavior and consequence was a hard concept for most of them to learn. They had very little insight into the personal devastation caused by their small, daily decisions.

To help them see better the impact of their decisions, we had them do experiential, "hands-on" therapy activities on a regular basis. My goal for these team building activities was to "take the covert (behaviors, beliefs, attitudes) and make them overt (seen clearly)." Taking the covert and making it overt became our unit mantra.

Struggle is in fact a great teacher. For this reason, the Lord does not shield us from adversity. We learn by resolving the myriad of trials and challenges life throws at us. We flex our spiritual muscles as we struggle in our search for answers to problems. As adults, our success in life is largely dependent on learning these valuable lessons and being able to apply them to new challenges. Though it is painful at the time, without that "effectual struggle" we limit what we can do in the future.

Like us, our children must learn how to solve life problems as well as spiritual ones. We are not doing them a favor when we rob them of their struggles. Their ability to deal with life will be largely dependent on understanding the connection between their actions and the consequences of their behaviors. Thus, in our roles as parent/teacher, we want to help them learn how to (1) gather information, (2) make decisions, (3) see the results, (4) then accurately evaluate their choices. This process is vital to their growth. Remove the struggle and we remove the growth.

Four Easy Steps

Joseph McConkie tells of his experience as a new chaplain in Vietnam. He was overwhelmed by the many personal and spiritual problems a chaplain is called upon to solve. He was grateful to receive a visit from Victor L. Brown, the Presiding Bishop of the Church. As they visited various installations, Brother McConkie and the branch president would pepper Bishop Brown with questions about how to solve the problems placed before them.

In response, Bishop Brown told them a true story. He explained that a few years earlier, a young man had been confronting a serious issue. Unable to solve it, he went to his bishop. The problem was thorny enough that the bishop told the young man, "I do not know what to suggest, but I will be seeing the stake president tonight and I'll ask him." That night he presented the problem to the stake president, who also deferred, but promised to run it by a member of the Quorum of the Twelve, with whom he would be meeting later in the week. As he did so, the apostle listened attentively, then promised to take it to President David O. McKay.

Later that week, the apostle presented the problem to President McKay. He listened to the problem, then replied, in essence, "That is quite a problem. I wonder how the young man will solve it!" As he concluded the story, Bishop Brown explained that the Lord expects each of us to work together with the Lord to solve our own problems. Brother McConkie finished by saying they then quit asking Bishop Brown to solve the problems of their own stewardship (see "Finding Answers," *BYU Magazine*, Spring 2007, 1).

Teaching children to problem solve is not complicated. However, it is infinitely more time-consuming than doing the task ourselves. Each time a child has a problem in life, we need to see it as a teaching opportunity. We then have the opportunity to lead them through four questions that will help them evaluate their actions. They are:

What happened?
What have you tried?
Have you prayed about it?
What do you feel you should do now?

These questions lead to the outline successful adults use to problem solve. We learn to first gather information about the situation and ourselves. We seek divine guidance and plan what needs to happen next. Finally, formally or informally, we evaluate whether our approach was effective or not. We can teach children how to walk through the same process.

Example #1:

Your nine-year-old daughter comes home from school in tears. After a little encouragement, she explains that a small group of her friends have begun excluding her at school. She's being left outside their little clique. Every time she has attempted to be included, they have walked away from her. As she sits and cries, she wants to know what she should do.

Warning! Regardless of our parenting style it is always hard to watch our children be hurt. It's even harder when we know someone is deliberately doing something that is causing them pain. However, this is the exact moment, especially for those of us with controlling tendencies, to take a deep breath and focus on our long-term goals for our children:

Mom: Wow, honey, I had no idea. *What happened?*
Daughter: I don't know, Mom! I just know that they

weren't doing it until that new girl, Mandy, moved in. She made friends with my friends. Pretty soon they started ignoring me. I didn't even do anything!

(Note: At this point, Mom knows what is probably going on. NOT diving in and solving it will be her biggest challenge.)

Mom: That would be really hard. *So what have you tried, so far?*

Daughter: I tried being nice and they just ignored me. I even wrote Mandy a note and she didn't write back!

Mom: I'm sorry. *Have you prayed about it?*

Daughter: No. I'm not sure what to say.

Mom: Well, Heavenly Father can help you if you'll let Him. Can we pray together? First I'll pray and then you pray, okay? Then we'll see what you feel you should do about it.

Enduring and valuable lessons come from experiences such as this when Mom doesn't immediately step in to resolve it by calling the teacher or the other girl's parents. In addition, the daughter gets to hear, by listening to her mother, how to pray and seek answers.

As children learn to pray and get answers, they will learn to follow feelings and impressions. *They will also learn that their impressions do not always yield immediate solutions.* Sometimes a problem persists or takes an unexpected turn. Later, we can point out the hand of the Lord in providing a better answer than the one they anticipated.

Picture a child's problems as a bright red beach ball they hold in their hands. Eventually, they will learn what to do with the ball [problem], but until then, it dominates their life. When we solve their problems for them, we snatch the ball out of their hands. We take care of it for them. Because we will probably take care of the problem successfully, we teach them to solve problems by having us do it for them. Then, each time another ball shows up, they learn to throw it to us.

Obviously, there are some serious problems that require parental intervention. At those moments we do step in and help solve it. But, we do need to make it our goal to keep the "ball" in their hands as much as possible. As a parent, we can then help them generate solutions rather than taking over and increasing their dependence on us. By continually asking, *What have you tried?* or *What else have you thought about doing?* we do not rescue, but we do not abandon, either. We can help them examine all sides of a situation before taking a decision to the Lord.

Example #2:

Your fourteen-year-old son comes home one day with a problem. A group of four or five boys in his geometry class have been cheating on quizzes. Your son has resisted their invitations to join them. The result is that their scores consistently end up higher than his. And he has found out that they are preparing to cheat on the big final exam next week. He wants to know what he should do:

> Son: So, Dad, what do I do? If they go ahead and all cheat it could really hurt my final grade!
>
> Dad: Well, I'm proud of you for not cheating. *What have you thought about doing?*
>
> Son: I could go tell the teacher about them. Then they would all be mad at me. Nobody likes a snitch!

Dad: That's a pretty big bind. *What did you feel when you prayed about it?*

Son: I didn't. Heavenly Father doesn't care about my geometry score!

Dad: But He does love you and cares about you being honest.

Son: Okay.

Dad: Pray about it tonight and listen for what you feel.

Son: But what if the answer is that I'm supposed to tell the teacher?

Dad: If the Lord tells you to tell the teacher, don't you think He knows everything will be for your good if you do?

Son: I guess so.

Dad: And if that is the answer, I can't promise they won't be mad—just that it will be okay. You just have to be willing to do whatever He tells you to do.

Son: Alright, Dad. I'll try it.

How We Praise

How we praise our children has a major impact on their problem solving skills. For the past ten years, psychologists have been studying the effect of praise on a large group of students in four New York City schools. Researchers administered a simple test made of puzzles to fourth graders—puzzles easy enough that any of them would do well. When they completed the test successfully, some children were praised for their *effort*, others for their *intelligence*.

The impact of this seemingly minor difference was seen when they were asked to choose the next test to be given:

One choice was a test that would be more difficult than the first, but the researchers told the kids that they'd learn a lot from attempting the puzzles. The other choice . . . was an easy test, just like the first. Of those praised for their effort, 90 percent chose the harder set of puzzles. Of those praised for their intelligence, a majority chose the easy test. The "smart" kids took the cop-out (Po Bronson, "How Not to Talk to Your Kids: The Inverse Power of Praise," *New York Magazine*, Feb. 19, 2007).

What the researchers learned was when children were told they were intelligent, they began to take fewer risks, academically. I was thinking about this, not long ago, when I found myself standing in line behind a mother who was talking on her cell phone. Her nine-year-old son stood by her side. The conversation was centered on her son's intelligence. "The school psychologist says that his intelligence is 'off the charts,'" she said, excitedly. "Probably close to 180."

As I listened, I watched her son intently listening to his mom and wondered what effect this well-intentioned mother was having on her son's future choices.

We live in a culture that praises innate "natural" ability over effort. The natural athlete is worshiped over the less talented athlete who accomplishes more by hard work. Stories are legendary about students who didn't study but scored higher on the test than the one who studied all night. These children are held up as role models for youth. Why would we do that?

We need only to recall Lucifer's seductive marketing pitch in the premortal council. The great plan of happiness called for our sacrifice through a broken heart and contrite spirit and our Redeemer's infinite sacrifice in our behalf. Lucifer wanted neither. He rallied his brothers and sisters into his rebellion with promises of ease and lack of accountability. He promised the impossible to spirit children looking for an easier way. And he continues to preach that seductive message to each succeeding generation of young people today.

When we praise and focus on intelligence or talent over effort we tell our children that their hard work is less valued. Each time they take an exam where that "intelligence" will be proved, they have to put that intelligence to the test. Educators can tell story after story of "smart" children who will not subject their "natural" ability to scrutiny. They do not try; they discount effort. "I am smart," the kid's reasoning goes: "I don't need to put out effort." Expending effort becomes stigmatized—it's public proof you can't cut it on your natural gifts.

In our well-intentioned rush to be supportive, we can actually be doing the same thing we do when we overindulge: we are sabotaging the very children we are trying to help. Children praised constantly "just because you're you" or for "the cutest smile" begin to see the emptiness of that praise as they enter their teen years. Many teens begin to see a teacher's praise, for instance, as proof they are less intelligent and need the encouragement!

The other side of the spectrum can also be a concern. One mother at church, with her teenage son standing next to her nodding, explained how her son was unable to do many things "because of his ADD." I knew this boy. I knew his life-long struggle with attention-deficit disorder. I knew the decision-making struggles his parents had gone through before deciding to use medication to help him. There was no question about the legitimacy of this very real disorder in the young man's life and his daily battles to focus his attention.

Over time, however, this boy began to use his "ADD" as a

label to excuse his lack of effort or to justify manipulative behaviors. His label was used as a "get out of jail free" card, something he thought should excuse his destructive choices and shelter him from consequences.

As we have said repeatedly, when we keep our long-term goals for our children foremost in our mind, we make better parental decisions. If we stay focused on our prime directive, molding responsible adults with strong testimonies, they will learn why we do what we do. If, in our "heart of hearts," we are more anxious to have them compliant or reflect well on us, they will know that, too.

With this in mind, let's now begin to look at how we enforce the "unenforceable": discipline and the use of parental authority.

Eight

Almost Painless Discipline

Chasten thy son while there is hope, and let not thy soul spare for his crying. —Proverbs 19:18

In 1831, the Prophet Joseph Smith directed the Brethren to publish the revelations that had been received to that point. That collection, called the Book of Commandments, was printed to provide guidance and direction to the growing Church. As they were preparing those revelations for printing, the Prophet received an additional revelation that would be known as Section 1 of the Doctrine and Covenants, sometimes called the Lord's Preface. In it, the Lord explains that "knowing the calamity which should come upon the inhabitants of the earth, [I] called upon my servant Joseph Smith, Jun., and spake unto him from heaven, and gave him commandments" (D&C 1:17).

Throughout history, our Heavenly Parent has blessed us by giving us commandments. These commandments are given to help us to avoid disastrous behavior that would put our salvation in jeopardy and to help us achieve all He has in mind for our eternal destiny. In order to receive those blessings, we promise to obey. With each "rule" there are consequences, clearly laid out, that will result from our obedience or lack thereof. There are no secrets, no surprises. The God of Heaven has clearly laid out His plan and made it abundantly clear what we have to do to inherit eternal life.

The idea that commandments are given to us to bless our lives is confusing to those wanting to rebel. Seduced by Satan's lies, "rules" are seen as a roadblock on their highway to freedom. Over time the rebellious become more irritated by anything—or anyone—that restricts their desire to do what they want. They cannot view any restriction as a blessing.

Youthful rebellions begin at the crossroad where rules and parental authority intersect with a child's desire to exercise his agency. How rules are written and authority administered is critical. Again, *how* we do it is as important as *what* we do. No aspect of our parental style is more on display than when we exercise parental authority. Parental authority is the power we use to make decisions for the family. It is the veto a parent wields over a child's choices. The more extensively we use it, the less children are empowered. How it is used, and when, is a function of our parental style.

Controlling parents, for instance, lean heavily on their authority, imposing their will in most decisions relative to the family. Because the rules are very "top down," in a controlling home, children who break family rules are also challenging parental authority. Discipline is used as a consequence of disregarding that authority. In a similar vein, overprotective parents also use a lot of parental authority. For these parents, however, rule-breaking is viewed as dangerous and unsafe. They exert the parental sword constantly, with the intent that they are protecting their kids from danger.

As we've discussed, effective parents develop a balance

between warmth, structure, and a calm demeanor. As they parent, they need to determine what role discipline will play and then evaluate how much authority to apply and when. They also must decide how much input their children will have in deciding what the discipline will be—and why.

Stephen Covey has suggested:

> In a discussion of discipline, the practical question often focuses around forms of discipline that many equate with punishment.
>
> Let us first ask, What is the purpose of discipline? Would we not all agree that the purpose of disciplining is to teach, and to teach in such a way that the children learn a correct principle?
>
> Let us further ask, What is the purpose of teaching a correct principle? Wouldn't we agree that the purpose is that the children, or individuals involved, learn to apply that principle in their own lives? Isn't that really what learning means?
>
> If this reasoning is sound, we must conclude that the purpose of parental discipline is to build *internal* discipline (*The Spiritual Roots of Human Relations* [Salt Lake City: Deseret Book Company, 1970], 232).

Let's suppose we have a teenage driver in the house with a curfew of 10:00 P.M. on a school night. What is the purpose of the curfew? We might respond: to make sure he gets to bed at a decent time or to prevent him from getting into trouble or a difficult situation. If he violates that curfew, will there be some type of consequence? If so, why?

Asking *why* we discipline may sound like a silly question, but our intent, the reason we apply consequences, is much more complicated than we may want to believe. When our teen comes in past curfew, are we more concerned about his lack of sleep, or are we angry that we have been sitting in the living room for hours, wondering when our child, and our car, is coming home? Our intent drives our emotions, a concept that is well-documented in the scriptures. Our emotions then dictate our behavior. If we are angry because we feel he willingly disregarded our rules, our response may lead us to impose heavy consequences, which we dream up at the spur of the moment.

On the other hand, if our intent is that our teen learns internal discipline, then consequences for breaking curfew have probably already been discussed and agreed upon. The only parental authority we have to exercise is to calmly remind him of his agreements and help him with his follow-through.

I had a missionary companion who was raised with an interesting set of dynamics in his home. All through his high school years he would stay up, well into the early morning hours. Not surprisingly, he always had a hard time waking up. Mornings consisted of his father shaking him and roughly pulling him out of bed. My companion would generally respond by fighting off his father's attempts to rouse him. Apparently, this was the regular morning pattern all during his teen years.

The first night we were together as new companions, he tried to explain how *I* was to get him up. "In the morning," he said, "I'll sleep through the alarm because I'm a really deep sleeper. You'll have to shake me and yell at me to wake me up. When you do, you'd better stand back because I'll probably take a swing at you! But, it's okay because if you'll keep shaking me I'll finally get up."

Now, I should point out that my new companion was

almost a foot taller than me and outweighed me by seventy-five pounds. I ran track in high school; he was an all-district linebacker for his football team. His fist was larger than my head. I knew that if he swung at me, one solid hit would disconnect my head from my shoulders.

"I have another idea," I responded. "When the alarm clock goes off, get up. I'm not going to shout and duck every morning. It's your job to get you up, not mine!" The next morning, to his surprise, he got up when the alarm sounded. And he continued to do so the entire time we were together. We became good friends, and I never had to duck to get out of the way, other than at the dinner table.

Again, if we approach discipline as parent/teachers, then our purpose should be to help each child instill their own checks and balances not just impose punishment. Our goal is to teach them to police themselves. Granted, other concerns are no less valid: lack of sleep, flaunting of family rules, etc. But, any discipline applied for breaking rules should lead toward the ultimate goal, not merely serve to vent our anger over being ignored or disobeyed.

It should be noted that some forms of discipline administered *without this goal* in mind can also be effective—extremely effective—but at what cost? As we've said before, *beware of what works.* Parents can exercise their authority and force compliance through constant, heavy-handed punishment and obedience will be achieved. The long-term cost, however, is a child with little self-confidence who becomes either compliant and withdrawn or rebellious. Worse, they may end up submissive, not to the Lord, but to a destructive peer group. What works in the short-run can easily result in a long-term disaster.

What Are the Rules?

As Heavenly Father's children, we are not required to covenant or obey without an understanding of the rules—both what is expected and the consequences for disobedience. In the premortal council, we did not agree to earth life until we knew the plan and were assured a Savior would be provided. In the Garden of Eden, Adam and Eve were taught their responsibilities as well as the consequences of their actions. Only then did they exercise their free agency and move the plan of salvation forward.

Children need a clear understanding of what is expected of them before they can learn to be obedient for the right reasons—not out of fear but because they *want* to be obedient. To ensure family discipline is designed to help the children and not merely to gratify the parents' need to exercise control, moms and dads might ask themselves:

- How many rules do we have?
- Are those rules clear?
- How often do they change?
- How much input do the children have in making rules?
- How do we change a rule?
- What are the consequences if someone breaks a rule?
- Are the consequences predetermined and well-understood, or are they decided on the spot?

These are questions best asked in a family council, as soon as the children are old enough to participate. Remember, homes, like nature, abhor a vacuum. If we don't outline the rules, they will create themselves—seemingly out of thin air!

Night #1:
Jan: Mom, I've got some friends coming over tonight.
Mom: Oh, how many?
Jan: Just three or four.
Mom: We always love seeing your friends, dear.

Night #2:
Jan: Mom, I've got some friends coming over tonight.
Mom: Oh, how many?
Jan: Just five or six.
Mom: Haven't you got homework?
Jan: No, I'm all done.
Mom: And your room is a mess! Maybe you should
tell them another night.

There is no established rule, at Jan's house, on how many friends she can have over at one time. Mom always says she "loves to see her friends." But Jan has learned that Mom prefers three or four friends rather than five or six. Jan has also learned that anytime she invites more than four she ends up having to justify it; less than four and there is no discussion. Mom would tell you there is no rule about the number of friends over at one time, but her behavior says otherwise. Children learn, from us, what our unwritten limits are.

Thirteen-year-old daughter: Mom, can I go to the mall?
Mom: Not on a school night. That's the rule!
Daughter: Please?
Mom: No.
Daughter: Please?
Mom: No.
Daughter: Pleeeeeease?
Mom: Oh, alright. Just quit whining! Be home by
nine . . .

What is the rule in this case? To the mother, it is: "No going to the mall on school nights." To the daughter, it is: "Ask three times and whine a lot to go to the mall on school nights." The rules are very clear—to the daughter. Mom just doesn't recognize them yet, though she lives by them. Many unwritten rules evolve over time, and children learn quickly how to work within them and around them.

The difficulty comes when "lived by" rules are different than stated rules. Parental authority is compromised when what we say ("These are the rules!") is different from what happens in reality. Any rule that cannot or will not be enforced is not a rule, just a wish. The more rules that are ignored the less children will take parents seriously when parents attempt to exercise authority.

Establishment of well-understood family rules, along with well-understood consequences, is critical in rearing children. The number of rules will be a function of parental style, but when establishing these rules, we need to keep three main ideas in mind.

Parental Example

In outlining family structure, parental responsibilities should also be well understood. The role we play in implementing those rules helps to prepare children for adulthood. By watching us, children can learn how righteous authority should be exercised. If we are arbitrary or inconsistent, they can also learn, by observing us, to disrespect authority as well.

During the turbulent decade of the sixties, a researcher by the name of Kenneth Keniston set about to discover exactly who was rebelling on college campuses. Along with his conclusions, he also learned a lot about how children form opinions.

As he studied Vietnam war protestors, he found that many of these youth were "uncommitted to our system of laws and government: they had developed a pessimism about America."

> Keniston at first assumed that youth were troubled primarily because of conditions existing in schools and in government. Further investigation, however revealed that the attitudes of young people were virtually identical to attitudes expressed by their parents. *Keniston was able, therefore, to find a strong relationship between parental attitudes about laws, police, society, and community* (see A. Lynn Scoresby, *Bringing Up Moral Children* [Salt Lake City: Deseret Book Company, 1989, 185; emphasis added).

An acquaintance of mine retired from the FBI where he had run a gang task force. He explains that members of his task force were very accurate in predicting youth behavior simply by walking through a home and talking to the parents. For instance, they found that if a father was physically abusing his wife, the task unit immediately needed to identify the son's girlfriend as "at risk" for domestic violence. Gang members also often heavily reflected their parents' attitude toward authority. The difference was that the youth would act out those attitudes while their parents usually didn't.

Parenthood requires us to look closely at ourselves and our attitudes. This need to constantly scrutinize ourselves and our behavior is one of the great blessings that comes from raising a family. We have constant reminders that we are being watched and that our behavior is being critiqued or copied. This fact forces us to see ourselves through "outside" eyes. Just what do they see and hear?

A good friend of mine has been an active member of the Church all of his life. He has served in many callings, including assignments in the temple. He loves the Church completely. Even when a Church leader hurt his feelings, his commitment never wavered.

Unfortunately, my friend has always been openly very critical of local Church leaders. When he disapproved of their decisions, he was quick to point out their shortcomings, even in the presence of his children. As they have grown older, his children have adopted his critical attitude. Over time, as each of his children developed serious personal problems, I encouraged them to see their bishop. They responded with a description of the bishop's faults and asked, "Why would I tell that man anything that's going on with me?" The sad result was that my friend's kids never received the help they might have gotten, and they've all left the Church.

Do our children hear us supporting those in authority or do they listen as we complain? It is difficult to instill trust and obedience, let alone household rules, in the face of daily skepticism. This antipathy extends to elected officials as well. Children growing into their teen years need to critically evaluate those in government as they prepare to vote. Do they hear honest evaluation from us or antipathy toward all government officers?

As parents, we make a mistake when we compromise the standards we hope to teach our children. Do we strain at and break commandments "just a little." We try to keep the Sabbath day holy, but occasionally run out to the store to get something. We watch inappropriate movies, ignoring the one bad scene and the foul language. Unfortunately, while we've determined how far we will go, our children are more likely to come along behind us and watch the entire movie or disregard

Sabbath day observance on a regular basis. We have opened a hole in the fence, and they have slipped through it.

A Regular Family Schedule

Establishing and observing a regular schedule, especially with regard to getting up and going to bed, helps build discipline and order in a child's life. Regardless of a child's individual style, they still have a need to function during the day. Some children, especially teens, will claim they do their best work at 3 A.M. Others may want to focus on a project around the clock until it is completed. However, these children can easily become the college students who wait until the last week to write their term papers then write day and night while existing on energy drinks and NoDoz. They may complete their assignments, but health and scholarship both suffer.

Family rules establish a routine the family can live with. Stephen Covey explains:

> I found in the mission field how tremendously powerful a daily schedule is. It is a form of external discipline, but gradually this becomes a habit, and once it is a habit it tends to become internalized. When missionaries learn to work and study according to this very rigorous schedule until it becomes part of them, they find themselves capable of applying that kind of self-control to many other fields of endeavor both on their mission and after it (*Spiritual Roots of Human Relations*, 235).

Contrast this kind of schedule with the teen who plays video games around the clock or spends her entire weekend chatting online. Neither develops the discipline necessary to work through less agreeable tasks. Family rules help establish limits that not only keep this kind of behavior in check but also instill a discipline that will govern the child's life after he or she is grown.

Rules Connected to Consequences

Maturity is our ability to recognize the connection between our actions and the resulting consequences. As we mature, we begin to understand better the effect our behavior has on those around us. And though we do not always see that effect of our behavior, it is there.

One of the goals of establishing family rules—and discipline—is helping growing children learn that what they do has an impact on others. They also need to understand how another's behavior impacts them. Essential to their growth is beginning to anticipate others' reactions (see below). Those reactions can be positive or negative, immediate or delayed. But when kids later evaluate their behavior, they are in a position to understand why the world reacted as it had.

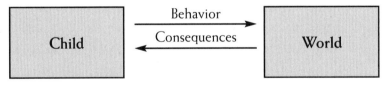

Figure 9

When children break a stated rule, it is our opportunity to help them learn this law. Some behavior produces *natural consequences*. Natural consequences are the ones that occur with little or no parental intervention. If a child decides to play with a beehive, he soon learns that bees don't find him very amusing. And, he probably doesn't have to be told twice! If our child leaves his coat at home on a winter's day, nature will teach him, before he gets to school, that it was a poor choice. The more he shivers, the less likely he is to do it again.

One problem is that much of our children's behavior has no natural consequence. The world doesn't automatically respond with negative effects when they do a lot of things. Therefore, we have to create consequences. Non-natural consequences are called *punishment.* Nature has no immediate consequences for a child refusing to do her chores. Teachers and parents and leaders have to establish the kinds of consequences that help a child acquire *internal* discipline. These imposed consequences help children to clearly see the link between their actions and the world's response to them. Without consequences, negative behavior has no reason to end, so it continues.

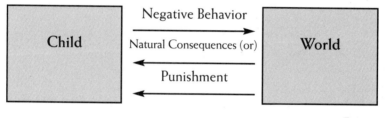

Figure 10

It is this lack of consequences that is so damaging to the children of overindulgent or the proverbial "helicopter" parents. When Mom intervenes at every turn, to rescue the child, the child learns that Mom will handle everything. They know that others suffer consequences for their behavior; but they do not. Thus, for whatever reason, they see themselves as "special" and begin to expect it at every level. It is similar to a charming child who learns to avoid punishment through insincere sweetness, believing that their rule is "manipulate others in order to avoid the rules."

Individualized Discipline

We have been considering structuring rules and punishment in a way that fosters internal and self-directed control. How do we do that? We know that experiencing consequences is critical, but how do we help children move to the point where they begin to discipline themselves? Part of the answer is that we individualize rules based on our child's personality.

Someone once said that if you treat three children exactly the same, you are probably mistreating two of them. As any parent can attest, each child is unique with a different temperament, motivation, and personality. As soon as we figure out how to parent our first child, we have a second one, and our learning starts over completely. Much of what "worked" for the oldest does not always translate to the next.

In chapter 6, we talked about individual differences in our children: Talkers, Doers, Thinkers, and Planners. In the illustration below, we see how teaching to their styles helps them

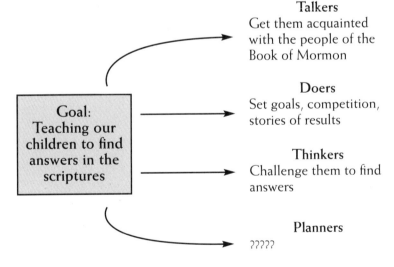

Talkers
Get them acquainted with the people of the Book of Mormon

Doers
Set goals, competition, stories of results

Thinkers
Challenge them to find answers

Planners
?????

Goal: Teaching our children to find answers in the scriptures

Figure 11

gather new information their way. For instance, if we are looking for ways to help them draw answers from the scriptures,
each will relate best when he or she does it *their* way, for *their* reasons, using *their* style. As parents and teachers, we will succeed
to the extent that we individualize our approaches. (You will
notice that I have left the Planner suggestion unanswered. I have
my ideas about what would help a "planner" child find answers
in the scriptures—but I think that you, as the reader, also have
ideas—especially if you are a planner or know one. Please take a
moment and see what kind of ideas you can put together.)

When we establish consequences for a child, we tend
toward setting up consequences we, ourselves, would learn
from. If the child's personality is similar to ours, that will likely
work. But if not, our chosen discipline, the one that would have
the most effect *on us*, may have little effect *on them*. Again, they
are motivated to change for their own reason.

Because of this individuality, it is critical to involve the child,
as much as possible, in establishing consequences for given behaviors. This means that in the same family, different children will
have different consequences, based on their input as to what they
need to help them. This is not an exact science, but I take comfort in my belief that if we seek the guidance of the Holy Ghost,
we can know, together, what will be best for the individual child.

> Dad: So, Mike, your job is to mow the lawn on
>   Saturday mornings and clean your bathroom.
> Mike: Right.
> Dad: And what happens if you forget?
> Mike: I don't know.
> Dad: Well, is there anything we know doesn't work?
> Mike: Grounding, I guess. We tried that before and it
>   was no big deal.

> Dad: I remember that. You're right. So what should it be?
>
> Mike: (shrugs) (Note: I promise they will be less than quick to point out the consequences they dislike the most!)
>
> Dad: Well, please pray about it tonight and let me know in the morning if you have an answer. Okay?
>
> Mike: Pray about a punishment?
>
> Dad: Right. Ask what will help you follow through with what you agree to do. I'll do it, too, and we'll see what we come up with.

Once rules are agreed upon and in place, the more we are in a position to use our authority to help them follow through.

> Mom: Julie, I noticed that the dishes weren't done last night.
>
> Julie: I know, Mom.
>
> Mom: Wasn't it your night?
>
> Julie: I got busy reading and forgot!
>
> Mom: That can be easy to do. What did we decide would happen if a chore wasn't done?
>
> Julie: I don't remember.
>
> Mom: I do. You decided you'd do an extra chore the next night as well as finish the one you missed.
>
> Julie: Mom! We're going over to Lisa's tonight to watch a movie! I can't do it tonight!
>
> Mom: Julie, it's *your* rule we agreed to. And I love you enough to help you keep your commitments.
>
> Julie: That's mean!
>
> Mom: No, helping you follow through is my job as your mom.

Individualized discipline simply means that children become part of the process where they help establish the rules they need to keep. When we come across situations for which there is no agreed upon rule or established consequence, it is helpful to use a four-step approach, similar to the one we used to help them problem solve. These steps help them evaluate their actions and prevent it from happening again. They are:

1. Can you tell me what happened?
2. What were you thinking about?
3. What needs to happen now?
4. What did you learn?

A father comes home to find his son sitting on the porch, eyes red. A baseball mitt and bat are lying on the front lawn and a large hole can be seen in the picture window of the house:

> Father, sitting down beside his son: *Do you want to tell me what happened?*
>
> Son: Mike and I were playing baseball in the front yard and the ball just happened to hit the window!
>
> Father: Since we talked about not playing ball in the front yard, *can you tell me what it is you were thinking?*
>
> Son: Well, we decided we could only hit left-handed, so we wouldn't hit the ball very hard. Then Mike hit it hard and it broke the window.
>
> Dad: I'll bet that scared you pretty bad.
>
> Son nods, but doesn't say anything.
>
> Dad: *Well, can you tell me what you need to do?*
>
> Son: I guess I need to pay for it. But, Dad, I don't have any money right now!
>
> Dad: What have you thought about doing then?
>
> Son: Uh, I guess I could do some extra jobs to earn the money.
>
> Dad: Good idea. Shall we go in the house and write up a list of jobs?

Son: Okay. But, aren't you going to ask me what I
learned?

Dad, smiling: You knew what was coming, didn't you?
Okay, *what did you learn?*

Son: Only use tennis balls in the front yard?

Dad: Nice try . . .

Son: No playing baseball in the front yard.

Dad: I think so. It's a hard lesson, Son, but I hope you
learned it this time.

When something like this happens, responsibility and consequences belong firmly on our children's shoulders. These four
steps help them evaluate their actions and make better choices
in the future. As a parent, the hardest part is resisting stepping
in too fast, providing advice, or lecturing. Keep putting the
focus back on them.

These four steps are the same we use as adults. When we
do something we wish we hadn't, we react to what has
occurred, go back through our thinking, and start planning
how to fix it. When children are ready to hear it, we need to
explain that we are helping them prepare for the future by
using the same evaluation plan as we use on a daily basis.

When I was about ten years old, my friends and I were playing in a creek bed near our house. A friend brought some
matches and before long we had a little fire going. Suddenly the
fire spread to some nearby weeds and was quickly out of our
control. In horror, we didn't know what else to do, so we each
ran home. It was with a sickening feeling that I heard the sirens
of the fire department coming up our street to put out the fire.
Luckily, no homes were damaged and the fire was soon out.

Later that night, I sheepishly confessed to my dad my part
in the incident. I then steeled myself for the worst. Without

saying much, my dad had me get into the car with him. To my surprise, he drove to a nearby drive-in and bought each of us an ice cream cone. While we ate, he told me how proud he was of me for my honesty. He also explained that our bishop was the town's fire chief and that we'd talk to him on Sunday.

How grateful I am for a father who saw the need for consequences, but also recognized a larger picture, one in which a boy had mustered up the courage to tell the truth.

Learning to Sacrifice

The third step, deciding what to do, will not always be obvious or pleasant. There may be multiple options with no apparent "right" answer. Since this step often involves restitution, the child is consciously choosing to do something painful or uncomfortable. This is a vital, powerful step toward living a life of sacrifice and service. *Children who learn to face this step begin to move toward a surrendered life.* Children who avoid this, or who have parents who consistently intervene (no matter how well-intentioned), miss a valuable opportunity to grow and develop.

"We must begin to think about our obligation rather than our convenience," taught President Spencer W. Kimball. Then he added, "The time, I think, is here when sacrifice must become an even more important element in the Church" ("Are We Doing All We Can?" *Ensign*, Feb. 1983, 4).

Many would think there is plenty of sacrifice. Certainly, our youth, perhaps with early morning seminary to attend and looming missions to serve, might think they have sacrificed enough.

True sacrifice, as in restitution, occurs when our children are called upon to sacrifice their pride. The result is that they can be at peace with themselves and others. The prophet Mormon taught: "I would speak unto you that are of the

church, that are the peaceable followers of Christ, and that
have obtained a sufficient hope by which ye can enter into the
rest of the Lord, from this time henceforth until ye shall rest
with him in heaven. And now my brethren, I judge these things
of you because of your peaceable walk with the children of
men" (Moroni 7:3–4).

Even the Prophet Joseph Smith was rebuked for failing to
implement this principle of sacrifice in his own home: "Your
family must needs repent and forsake some things, and give
more earnest heed unto your sayings" (D&C 93:48). Teaching
children to sacrifice and "forsake" is a large part of the gospel
plan and can be developed in part by learning to live by rules
and consequences.

A man I know reaped the benefit of just such teachings. He
was between jobs, and his family was hurting financially.
Money was tight, the future uncertain, and they were struggling to acquire the simple necessities of life. At the same time,
their oldest daughter was preparing to graduate from high
school. As part of graduation, she was invited to participate in
a senior trip—a once-in-a-lifetime opportunity to visit many
Church history sites as well as New York City and Washington,
D.C. The cost for this trip was well out of the range of this
family at that moment, and it appeared the daughter would
have to forgo the trip.

The week the money was due, the young woman's younger
brother stepped forward. He had been watching the drama
play out with his sister. Secretly, he had been saving money for
another purpose—something he really wanted. But without
talking to anyone, he quietly emptied his account and put the
money for her trip in her hand. Because of his sacrifice, she was
able to go. Even today, the father cannot speak of his son's
selfless generosity without experiencing emotion and gratitude.

Nine

Peers:
Dealing with Friends' Swords

There's one advantage to being 102. There's no peer pressure.
—Dennis Wolfberg

During my daughter's junior year in high school, we moved to another state. She had been doing well in school, was on the tennis team, and was surrounded by good friends. The idea of moving away from her friends was a very painful one. She and I moved ahead of the rest of the family so she could get started in school sooner. As I dropped her off at her new high school, I silently petitioned Heavenly Father to help her find a new set of good friends who would help her during this difficult and critical transition in her life.

To my joy, kids from the seminary council found her and invited her to an activity. They loved her into their group and set her at ease. They also won our eternal gratitude. The rest of the move was easy now that she had solid friends in her corner.

Parents and kids are acutely aware of the power of peer groups. Friends with strong morals and values can support a struggling child and help keep him or her on the right path.

Conversely, parents of rebellious teens can tell story after story of the damage caused by "bad friends."

"I Will Call You Friends"

In the course of restoring the Church, the Lord established three different relationships with His young prophet. In a revelation given in 1841, the Lord refers to Joseph in this way: "Verily, thus saith the Lord unto you, *my servant* Joseph Smith" (D&C 124:1; emphasis added). However, during times of trial, the Lord chose to address Joseph in a more intimate manner. For instance, at the time of his imprisonment in Liberty Jail, Joseph heard himself referred to by the Lord as "*My son,*" and was comforted, "peace be unto thy soul" (D&C 121:7; emphasis added). At that moment of great need, the Prophet was being reminded that he had the support of a loving Parent, One who would not abandon him. The assurance of a Father-to-son relationship must have been very sustaining in that trying circumstance.

The third characteristic of the relationship was declared in a revelation about the temple: "Verily, I say unto my servant Joseph Smith, Jun., or in other words, I will call you friends, for you are my friends, and ye shall have an inheritance with me." Then the Lord makes a distinction: "I called you servants for the world's sake, and ye are their servants for my sake" (D&C 93:45–46).

The idea that the Lord would consider His servants to be friends was not new. For instance:

"The Lord spake unto Moses face to face, as a man speaketh unto his friend" (Exodus 33:11).

"But thou, Israel, art my servant, Jacob whom I have chosen, the seed of Abraham my friend" (Isaiah 41:8).

Finally, in speaking to those early disciples in Kirtland, the Lord declared, "Ye are they whom my Father hath given me; ye are my friends" (D&C 84:63). What an honor it would be to have the Lord refer to us in that way.

Pondering the concept of friendship, consider this: We *hire* servants and *love* our children, but we *choose* our friends. We spend time with a friend because we want to. True, we love the members of our families, but we may not always like them much. However, we surround ourselves with people we enjoy being with. Those people, who may also be family members, are our friends.

Though we are grateful to work as servants in the kingdom and we are awed by the atoning power that makes it possible for us to become sons and daughters of Christ (see Mosiah 5:7), literally to become heirs with Him of "all [the] Father hath" (D&C 84:38), how impressive is it that the Lord has reserved the title of *friend* for those who make sacred covenants to become like Him. For the Lord to refer to us as a friend is to have Him acknowledge we are the type of individual that He would be happy to have close by—one who shares the same values and holds the same things sacred.

The powerful influence of friends can be manifest in negative ways as well. When I was in high school, my fellow students were identified by the peer group with which they associated. We all knew the athletes, or "Jocks," as well as the "Cowboys" and the "Brains," and so forth. Each group was governed by an unwritten set of laws, dictating who could join their group, the kind of clothes they wore, and even where in the cafeteria they would sit to eat lunch.

One of these groups met every morning before school in a little grove of trees, directly across from campus. This group

distinguished itself from all others in that it was *not* exclusive—
they accepted anyone. No one was ever turned away. They
accepted the lonely and socially awkward, the overweight and
the economically disadvantaged. Dress and social status didn't
matter. Many kids who were excluded from the other groups
eventually ended up crossing the street in the mornings in
search of the friendship they found in the grove.

We called members of the group "stoners" or "druggies"
because of their penchant for drug abuse. They gathered before
school to smoke, use drugs, and make plans on how they would
get more. In essence, they became expert at avoiding life and
responsibility.

Kids I knew, who found their way to the grove, were never
quite the same afterward. Their appearance would gradually
suffer and they would begin skipping classes. Then their grades
would drop. When they were in class, their mood would cycle
from high to low, depending on the drug they had taken that
morning. But, as chaotic as their lives became, they took great
comfort in the fact that they had "friends," people who would
accept them, no matter what.

Friends and Exclusion

If we are to help our children live a more surrendered life,
we must do all we can to prevent them from looking in "the
grove" for a friend. Helping prepare them to find good friends
as well as teaching them to be a good friend are important in
helping prevent rebelliousness.

In chapter 3, we explored the importance of helping children develop divine-esteem rather than self-esteem. The more
closely a child's sense of self is tied to the Lord, the less likely

he is to let his friends define who he is. Elder Marvin J. Ashton explained:

> Pure religion is having the courage to do what is right and let the consequences follow. It is doing the right things for the right reasons. To be righteous or serving or loving or obedient to God's laws just to earn praise or recognition is not pure religion. It is being able to withstand ridicule and even temporary unpopularity with some peer groups when you know who you are and for what goals you are reaching. So many of our young people, and older ones also, have developed just such inner strength. They have a great influence for good on others with whom they associate (*Be of Good Cheer* [Salt Lake City: Deseret Book Company, 1987], 14).

Youth who do the right things for the right reasons have come to understand who they really are. These kids stand out in a crowd. I listened, not long ago, to a group of priests and laurels who had traveled long distances to participate in a spiritual weekend. At their testimony meeting on Saturday night, teen after teen stood to proclaim their love for the gospel of Jesus Christ. Some went on to describe the difficult situations they faced daily. One beautiful young woman stood to say, "After the divorce, I went to live with my father. I love my father. We love to debate everything and anything and have fun doing it. But it's been much harder since he left the Church. Now he always wants to debate with me on why Joseph Smith was wrong."

She then testified of the love she felt for the Prophet Joseph Smith and declared she knew him to be the prophet of the Restoration. No one, she concluded, not even her dad, could take that from her. Powerful! Once that testimony had settled into her heart, she wasn't about to be swayed by her apostate father, let alone kids in the small high school where she was the only Latter-day Saint. Without the gospel support of her father, she was now alone at home and at school—but remaining strong. I found myself praying that she would one day find a faithful priesthood holder who could match her deep faith and go with her to the temple.

Other testimonies were similar. Most chose to limit friendships rather than abandon their faith. These stalwart youth expressed gratitude for activities such as youth conferences, saying they were a welcome oasis of living water in an otherwise arid school year.

As I listened to them, I became aware, as never before, that the Church organization, Church activities, and Church members were not merely a helpful support for these young people. For them, the gospel structure was a critical lifeline back to their Heavenly Father. These teens were clinging tightly to that lifeline and refusing to let go.

In his book, *Uncommon Sense for Parents of Teenagers*, author Michael Riera says:

> The main consequence of saying no to negative peer pressure is not just withstanding "the heat of the moment," as most adults think. Rather, it is coping with a sense of exclusion as others engage in the behavior and leave the adolescent increasingly alone. It is the loss of the shared experience. Further, the sense of exclusion remains whenever the group later recounts what happened. This feeling of loneliness then becomes pervasive but carries an easy solution—go along with the crowd (San Francisco: Celestial Press, 1995, 22).

"A disciple of Christ will be tolerant," wrote Elder Neal A. Maxwell, "but he will also be constant and consistent. A few years ago, student peer groups practiced a kind of fashionable tolerance that was really one-sided. Some students simply were not tolerating the returned missionary as much as the swinger, and some were much less understanding of the believer than the agnostic" (*Be of Good Cheer* [Salt Lake City: Deseret Book Company, 1972], 25).

Our youth are growing up in a world that is increasingly less tolerant of those who believe in clear rights and wrongs. Those with a clear moral compass are frequently characterized as narrow-minded and judgmental. They will often have to rely on their own internal compass to negotiate difficult situations. The very last thing our kids need is to compound that difficulty by surrounding themselves with associates who devalue their faith.

Children and youth do need to be prepared to make social sacrifices. Choosing good friends and refusing to go along with the crowd may mean fewer friends and activities. Are your children aware this can happen? Do they understand that holding tightly to their values will be seen as "odd" or worthy of ridicule by teens with different values?

Recently, a national radio personality from New York was invited to speak at BYU-Idaho. As he was driving into Rexburg from the airport, he described being surprised by a billboard advertising prom dresses. He said that one word on the billboard just leapt out at him: *Modesty!* He was floored. Coming from New York, he had never seen anyone try to sell any product based on the idea it was "modest." He said he was gratified that there were enough people looking for unrevealing prom dresses that the company felt a billboard promoting modesty would be their most effective sales pitch.

For all these reasons, the value of good friends with similar standards cannot be overestimated. To find such friends, our youth must first know what constitutes a good friend. They must understand that someone you "hang out with" may or may not be a friend!

Speaking of friends, Elder Marvin J. Ashton said: "There seems to be a misunderstanding of some men today as to what it means to be a friend. Acts of a friend should result in self-improvement, better attitudes, self-reliance, comfort, consolation, self-respect, and better welfare. Certainly the word *friend* is misused if it is identified with a person who contributes to our delinquency, misery, and heartaches" (in Conference Report, Oct. 1972, 32).

LDS author Allan K. Burgess offers the following checklist in evaluating friendship:

1. If I slept over at my friend's house, I would feel comfortable kneeling down and saying my prayers.
2. My friend doesn't ask me to do things that are wrong.
3. I usually feel happy and positive when I'm with my friend.
4. My friend uses good language and helps me want to do the same.
5. My friend would return change if given too much at the store.
6. I notice that I act better when I'm with my friend.

[OR]

7. My friend sneaks around and does things that his parents don't want him to.

8. My friend thinks everything is stupid and puts everyone down.
9. My friend never goes to church and makes fun of my religious feelings.
10. I usually don't feel comfortable inside when I'm with my friend (*Helping Your Child Stay Morally Clean* [Salt Lake City: Deseret Book Company, 1984], 50).

This is a good list to start with. Consider going through this list with your child, or make up one of your own. Have your son or daughter consider their friends in the context of the list. Then, as situations come up, you can have a conversation similar to this:

Dad: The other night, I heard your friend Mike saying his teacher was stupid. Is he a little like the kid listed in number eight of that list?

Chad: Yeah, that's pretty much him. Everything is stupid. Teachers are stupid.

Dad: I know you don't think that way.

Chad: Nope. But, that's just Mike, Dad.

Dad: What would cause Mike to think that way?

Chad: I don't know. He's always been like that.

Dad: I understand. What would you guess would make someone think the whole world is stupid?

Chad: I don't know. I haven't really thought about it.

Dad: Well, does Mike think *he's* stupid?

Chad: He says he's the dumbest kid in school!

Dad: Right. So, what are the chances he thinks everything is stupid because he feels stupid himself?

Chad: Oh, I see. Pretty high, I guess.

Dad: I'd think so, too. I've found that people who don't like themselves much tend to see the rest of

the world that way. The result is that they sometimes do dumb things because they just don't
care.

Chad: Yeah, they might.

Dad: That's the only reason I bring it up. We're fine
with Mike being here. We love having him. But, I
think you're going to have to be careful when you
are around him. People who think everything is
stupid tend, sometimes, to do dumb things. It
wouldn't surprise me if sometime you'll have to
stand up and say, "That's not a good idea," or "If
that's what you're going to do, I'm going home."
Because you know the difference between right
and wrong, you may have to stand strong.

Chad: I get it, Dad.

Dad: I know you do, Son. You're doing just fine.
Learning to anticipate what might lie ahead is
part of being an adult. You'll find that out soon
enough!

What else are kids hearing from successful parents? Here
are some actual comments:

- *"They tell me that I should select friends who have the same
  standards as mine so there will be no temptation."*

(I like this one; not just because they should pick
friends with high standards but because it reminds children that *they* have high standards. It is a subtle way of
reminding them they are different and need friends who
mirror that uniqueness.)

- *"They put great emphasis on my friends and like to know what
  they are like and what their influence is on me. They express
  their feelings about them, but they don't choose them for me."*

(Beautiful! Do we ask kids to consider what effect a

friend has on them, good and bad? It helps them learn to analyze, for themselves, how friends are impacting their lives. As they recognize, they will learn the extent to which having good people around us can bring about healthy changes.)

- *"They tell me to choose good friends because my friends will be like my future spouse."*

(That puts it in perspective, doesn't it? If a future spouse is to be our best friend, then what kinds of friends do we have now? What kind of choices are we currently making?)

- *"My parents have told me of their experiences with their friends when they were my age and usually let me know how they feel about my friends."*

(We do have firsthand knowledge of good friends and bad ones—at their age. They need to hear that.)

- *"If they feel that I'm associating with the wrong people, they ask me to spend less time with those people and more time with others that are more suitable. They let me know that they trust me but don't always trust my friends."*

(We mustn't be afraid to give counsel and make our feelings known, for fear of offending our child. Would you rather appear a little too concerned now or try to pick up the pieces after some unfortunate or tragic event that might have been avoided? And, as a young person learns to trust the Spirit more, they should also learn not to trust some "friends.")

- *"They ask me if I feel good with the friends that I have. They ask me if I want to be like the friends that I have."*

(This is another reminder that friends can change us. We may become like them; do we like what we see?) [The comments quoted above are from Allan K. Burgess, *Helping Your Child Stay Morally Clean* [Salt Lake City: Deseret Book Company, 1984], 53–54).

In the examples listed above, it goes without saying (so we'll say it!) that these youth are referring to actual conversations they've had with their parents about their friends. As parents, we need to be talking to our kids about their friends. We know we should meet them, meet their parents, know who they are. We also know that we should be concerned when our child doesn't want to talk about his friends or he never brings them to the house. For our part, we must go out of our way to welcome their friends, spend time visiting with them, and help them feel this is a place they can come.

Friends As an Indicator

Our children's choice of friends can help us understand how they see themselves. In *You and Your Adolescent*, author and researcher Laurence Steinberg asserts: "Peer pressure is not a monolithic force that presses adolescents into the same mold. . . . Adolescents generally choose friends whose values, attitudes, tastes, and families are similar to their own. In short, good kids rarely go bad because of their friends" ([New York: Harper Collins, 1991], Introduction).

If I could say it differently, I would say that kids seek out other kids they are comfortable with. When "good kids" begin seeking out friends who appear to have different values, parents should question what values their child is developing.

"Tom" was in my Sunday School class when he was young. His family was always active in the ward. As Tom entered high school, he began to distance himself from the other youth in the ward. He remained active but seemed to be emotionally withdrawn. Soon, the other kids reported that Tom was running around with peers who were clearly antagonistic toward religion.

On a campout, I had an opportunity to have an extended visit with Tom. After a few moments, he turned and stated, "Brother Hinckley, I just don't see why one man was supposed to die for everyone else's sins. That doesn't make any sense to me. I believe we're all responsible for what we do." I was stunned. At some point in his growing up, Tom had undergone a dramatic shift in his faith without any of us knowing it. As he began to question the Atonement, the rest of his faith was also called into question.

In the short time we had together, I tried to patch up some of the cracks in his foundation. Unfortunately, he had already found a new set of friends who were busy encouraging his doubts. They supported his new "intellectual" approach to life, which he saw as more enlightened than that of his "simplistic" parents. Tom simply found others who would reinforce what he had already been thinking. While this was occurring, his parents, like me and others, had failed to notice that this monumental shift had occurred.

In cases like Tom's, friends can be an indicator of our child's internal struggles or doubts. The phrase "all behavior is purposive" was coined to suggest the child's behavior may reveal things about that child he or she cannot or will not talk about. Usually, what a child *does* tells us more than what he *says*. Their choice of friends tells us much about what they value.

Who Is Leading Whom?

> Mom: Lisa, I didn't recognize the girl who dropped
> you off after school. Who was that?

Lisa: Her name is Marcie, and she's just getting active in the Church again.

Mom: I guess I don't know Marcie.

Lisa: Oh, she's had a really hard life. She gave a baby up for adoption when she was fourteen. Since that time, she's had a lot of bad friends. She's been going to parties all the time where there's a lot of drinking and stuff. Now, her mom wants her to find some better friends so she's coming back to church. We might go do something on Friday night.

Ah, the great parental dilemma. Kids who have made mistakes need good friends to associate with. They need a major upgrade in their peer group. We encourage good kids to reach out for the lost, to befriend those who need to come back to the Church. For this reason, good kids should befriend those with problems if they love and serve.

From the standpoint of the teen who needs to change, better friends may indeed prove to be their salvation. On the other side of the ledger—the child is now spending more time with a kid with a past—the question is a much different one: Who is leading whom?

We want our children to be concerned and outgoing, to develop an impulse to help others. And as our youth mature in the Spirit, there will be a natural pull to reach out to others. It is part of being filled with the love of the Savior. The prophet Mormon explained: "If a man be meek and lowly in heart, and confesses by the power of the Holy Ghost that Jesus is the Christ, he must needs have charity; for if he have not charity he is nothing; wherefore he must needs have charity. . . .

Wherefore, cleave unto charity, which is the greatest of all" (Moroni 7:44–46).

Reaching out to help others is what we desire of our kids; it is an essential step in their spiritual growth. And, there is no greater work than the rescuing of struggling peers.

On the other hand, I share the concerns of parents who worry about their own children's values being compromised while trying to help. How, then, do we encourage our youth to reach out to those who need it, while preserving their own growth and testimony?

That is why we ask *"Who is leading whom?"* Youth in a service mode must know that this relationship has some inherent differences from other friendships. They chose to enter this relationship because they wanted to help someone who has had different experiences than they have. It remains their job to be strong, to be leading out, to be the one suggesting things to do and deciding what not to do. Their values and morals must be the deciding factor in the things they do and say. It may be well for us to remind our youth of President Harold B. Lee's counsel:

> You must be on higher ground to lift another. You cannot lift another soul until you are standing on higher ground than he is. You must be sure, if you would rescue the man, that you yourself are setting the example of what you would have him be. You cannot light a fire in another soul unless it is burning in your own soul. You teachers [and youth], the testimony that you bear, the spirit with which you teach and with which you lead, is one of the most important assets that you can have, as you help to strengthen those who need so much, wherein you have so

much to give (*The Teachings of Harold B. Lee*, edited by Clyde J. Williams [Salt Lake City: Bookcraft, 1996], 462).

In the process of trying to help, these youth helpers have the opportunity to learn to pray for someone else. The prophet Enos is a good example. After his titanic effort to have his sins forgiven, the Lord reveals to him that his sins are "swept away." Enos explains "that when I had heard these words I began to feel a desire for the welfare of my brethren" (Enos 1:6, 9).

As they strive to help others, children will be blessed to know what they should do to help as they pray for their friends. Remembering their struggling friends in their prayers will help keep the relationship in proper perspective. It will also give them inspiration on how to help their friends maintain the necessary changes. Also, children should be hearing their parents, in family prayer, asking for help for their children involved in the work of spiritual reclamation.

Finally, as we will discuss in greater detail in the next chapter, only God changes hearts. Friends don't do it. Bishops don't do it. Parents cannot do it. The scriptures are full of instance after instance where a loving Father in Heaven "delivered their souls from hell . . . Behold, he . . . changed their hearts; . . . and they awoke unto God" (Alma 5:6–7).

In reaching to help another, we can easily get caught up in trying to "fix" or "change" another. Without recognizing it, we take on responsibilities that are not ours. The Lord heals and changes hearts, not us.

One young woman I know tried valiantly to help a friend who had been raised in a dysfunctional family. Her friend's mom had been divorced and then remarried, to a solid, active priesthood holder. However, the chaos of their earlier life seemed to constantly stalk her friend. Wild mood swings and inappropriate male relationships were a weekly battle. There was constant drama in her friend's life; there was always a secret or a crisis.

In trying to help, this young woman was forever attempting to smooth out the daily demons and spending inordinate amounts of time propping up her friend's fragile ego. Eventually, this courageous young woman realized her friend had emotional issues far beyond her capacity to be her sole support. With some encouragement, her friend began receiving professional help. This enabled the would-be rescuer to step back somewhat and reduce the intensity and constant emotional drain this friendship created in her own life.

Only after stepping back and looking at the friendship from some distance, did this young woman realize she could not prevent her struggling friend from using her agency to make poor decisions. She could not fix her, she could only love and support her.

While facilitating a therapy group one night, I listened to a discussion among several women who were struggling with depression. They began talking about how they struggled not just with their own problems but with their children's problems, their husbands' problems, and the problems of all those who constantly called them, looking for advice. Each of them found they were doing the same thing—spending much of their time trying to advise and fix the problems of people close to them while their own issues were left unresolved. Finally, I stopped them and wrote, in large letters, on the board, "FIXING IS NOT LOVING!"

The room went silent. When you try to "fix" someone else, I explained, you rob them of their chance to grow. You enable them to remain weak. Your intervention, however well-intentioned, is not a loving act. The result of love is a stronger individual. The result of your "help" is that they are weaker and you are emotionally exhausted. No one is being loved here! You must love them enough to support them while they solve their own problems.

Teens, and adults, can become confused about what a friend is. A friend who rescues us from all our problems is not a friend. They are, instead, what I call "a broken wing specialist," someone who is looking for someone to fix. Friends help each other grow stronger, stand straighter. Friends do not assist while another does things that are destructive or wrong. Friends do not keep secrets when it prevents another from getting the help they need. Friends love enough to make hard decisions, to say no, to challenge someone's false assumptions. No wonder, then, that we learn about friendship by watching the Savior, who sees those who keep His commandments as friends.

Finally, as children grow older, the greater the role friends play in their lives. Their ability to find good friends depends, to a large extent, on the emotional foundation established at home. This search is also driven by the extent that gospel values have taken root in their souls. They will seek out like-minded friends and avoid those who are different.

We need to remind our youth that holding tightly to their standards may come at a high cost; they may experience exclusion, teasing, and ridicule when they do not submit to peer pressure. To successfully withstand such things, they will need to hear constantly from their parents that their standards will make them stand out. They will be seen as a little "odd," but that is alright. If we can inoculate them against the coming pressures while they are still young, children will be less likely to be taken by surprise when it occurs as teens.

We can encourage the acquisition of good friends by teaching them how to recognize healthy relationships. As parents, we need to stay alert and pay close attention to their friendships. Those choices may provide the most accurate indicator of how they are doing, emotionally and spiritually.

Ten

Rebellion and Strong-Willed Children

Children aren't happy with nothing to ignore,
and that's what parents were created for.—Ogden Nash

O ne of the blessings of the restored gospel is our knowledge of the premortal life. We believe that our existence does not begin at birth, but "trailing clouds of glory do we come/From God who is our home" (William Wordsworth, "Ode on the Intimations of Immortality," *Best-Loved Poems of the LDS People* [Salt Lake City: Deseret Book Company, 1996], 62). In that spiritual sphere we had eternities to grow and develop, learn and rebel, sin and repent. Within each of us is a spirit who's "been around the block," so to speak.

Experts of child development theory, speculating without this restored knowledge, engage in endless debate as to whether a child's personality is determined by nature or nurture; were we born this way or do we develop as a result of our environment? With our knowledge of our premortal life, most of us would agree that the answer is some combination of the two. Certainly we are heavily impacted by our family and our surroundings. For most of us, our attitudes and values mirror those we grew up with. In addition, our emotional temperament also tends to mirror the example of our parents.

And then there are those who don't.

No discussion about discipline and rebellion would be complete without a short look at some of the emerging research concerning Strong-Willed Children (SWC). We should begin by saying that the parents of an SWC probably doesn't need much of a description because they already know they have one! This is the child who from his or her earliest moments has a temperament completely different from—and at odds with—his or her siblings. SWCs are born defiant, headstrong, and oppositional. They generally have difficulty bonding with others and are unusually focused on getting what they want. Many lie for no reason and see everything around them as a battle of wills. Their dominant personality may be the strongest evidence yet for a premortal life!

Cynthia Tobias, who has researched SWCs extensively, suggests the following checklist. SWCs:

- almost never accept words like *impossible* or phrases such as "it can't be done"
- can move with lightning speed from a warm, loving presence to a cold, immovable force
- may argue the point into the ground, sometimes just to see how far into the ground the point will go
- when bored, would rather create a crisis than have a day go by without incident
- consider rules to be more like guidelines (i.e. "As long as I'm abiding by the 'spirit of the law,' why are you being so picky?")
- show great creativity and resourcefulness—seem to always find a way to accomplish a goal, good and bad

- can turn what seems to be the smallest issue into a grand crusade or a raging controversy
- doesn't do things just because "you're supposed to"—it needs to matter personally
- refuse to obey unconditionally—seem to always have a few terms of negotiation before complying
- is not afraid to try the unknown; to conquer the unfamiliar (although each SWC chooses his or her own risks)
- can take what was meant to be the simplest request and interpret it as an offensive ultimatum
- may not actually apologize, but almost always makes things right (www.cantmakeme.com/swctest.htm).

All children have moments of defiance as part of normal growth. They have periods of insolence or being uncooperative. For SWCs, this behavior is not restricted to a particular age. It does not exist as a phase nor will it relent next week. No amount of discipline or punishment seems to deter or to slow them down. Instead, they tend to push others away and draw close to those who will help them get what they want.

We should also note who SWCs are not. They are not children with unmedicated ADD. They are not antisocial personalities with little or no conscience. They cannot be "cured" simply by modifying their nutrition, keeping them sugar free, or increasing their B vitamins. That said, some SWCs will have some ADD symptoms; others do have sensitivities to sugar or caffeine, etc.

Parents of an SWC child need to be careful about searching for a single cause in hope of finding a quick cure. This is important because the beleaguered parents of these children receive volumes of well-meaning but conflicting advice from all quarters. Family, friends, ward members, MDs, your CPA, will all believe they have the answers about what these children lack or need.

Dr. James Dobson, who coined the phrase, *strong-willed child,* provides the following research based on a study involving 35,000 parents.

> Male SWCs outnumber females only by about 5 percent, though there is a false tendency to see this as a male-dominated personality trait.
>
> An SWC has nothing to do with birth order.
>
> Most parents know they have an SWC very early. One-third can tell it at birth. Two-thirds know by the first birthday, and 92 percent are certain by the third birthday.
>
> 74 percent of SWCs rebel significantly during adolescence.
>
> SWCs have significant grade and behavior problems in school, especially during the last two years of high school.
>
> 35 percent of SWCs describe disliking themselves, and 8 percent experience strong self-hatred.
>
> Now, the good news: most SWCs' rebelliousness rapidly declines in their early twenties (*Parenting Isn't for Cowards* [Portland, Ore.: Multnomah Books, 2004], 23).

One SWC I knew, a sophomore in high school, continued to let his grades drop, despite Mom sitting beside him every night while he did his homework. His only real love was baseball. His coach told him he had to improve his grades or he would be dropped from the team. He ended up quitting the team just to prove he was in charge.

The SWC's Impact on the Family

Not long ago, a severe thunderstorm raged through our neighborhood. Hurricane-force winds and heavy rain battered us all evening. The next morning, we went out to survey the damage. Many trees had been toppled, their exposed roots poking out at all angles, though the tree next to them remained undamaged. A quick look at the roots of the fallen trees told the story. Trees blown over by the storm had developed a shallow root system, running close to the surface of the ground. From all outward appearances, these trees were large and strong. When the winds came, however, those with shallow root systems were the first to fall.

One result of raising an SWC is the disruption it can have on parents and siblings. The SWC's behavior batters everyone around with hurricane-force intensity. If the roots of a marriage relationship are shallow or strained, this force can and will batter and tear at those weaknesses. Since an SWC constantly struggles for control, he or she will spot inconsistencies or hypocrisies in our behavior or values, trying to use them to their advantage. Parents with unresolved guilt or a poor self-image, for instance, will have those weaknesses exposed.

Siblings, especially those who are younger, are directly in the storm track. In the desire for control, the SWC may be physically aggressive. They will overreact when challenged. We should also assume that many of their actions against siblings will stay unreported due to threats or fear of retaliation.

It is also not unusual for younger siblings to respond to their SWC sibling's behavior by becoming the *white sheep* of the family. They watch the constant trouble caused by their SWC brother or sister and overcompensate by becoming the "good child," the one who makes parents proud. Besides the pressure this imposes on the "good child" to never make a mistake or never cause a ripple, such a child may also bottle up concerns or issues that go unreported due to their louder sibling.

Failure by the SWC to follow family rules can also easily cause serious family dysfunction. Other children may become resentful or rebellious themselves when they see rules being flaunted and witness inconsistent responses by parents. They may learn quickly from their sibling's outrageous behavior and exploit the chaos to get what they want as well. Children often resort to what works; if an SWC shows the way, they can lead others down a destructive path.

One family I know had three sons. The middle son, a classic SWC, raged in all directions within the home. His oldest brother, a good son and worthy priesthood holder, eventually grew resentful living under two sets of rules—one for him and the permissive set for his destructive brother. Eventually the oldest son threw up his hands, left the Church, and has yet to return. The youngest son eventually did the same. Meanwhile, the middle son, now in his late twenties, looks back over the wreckage he caused in amazement and sadness. He also regrets many of the poor decisions he made being shortsighted and rebellious.

What Do We Do?

Some parents I have talked to, who struggled with a rebellious child, accurately describe living with an SWC, though they did not realize it at the time. Again, given their innate nature and active constitution, there is no magic formula for changing an SWC's personality. Research tells us that the storm blows itself out during their mid-twenties. However, the way in which we parent and discipline can have a profound effect on dampening the storm's damage until they become the productive adults they are capable of becoming.

A client, who has a black belt in judo, once described to me judo's overall mind-set: "If someone is rushing to attack you," he said, "the goal is to use their weight and force against them. You never try to meet them force on force. If you do, you will both get hurt. Instead, you *redirect* their momentum in the direction *you* want them to go." In essence, the key is to learn not to attempt to stop an attacker in his tracks but to help use his energy to move him where you want him to go.

The same principle applies in dealing with an SWC. If we try standing directly in the way of such a child and meet him force on force, we will be run over. Remember, *they have more drive than we have resolve!* Trying to exercise complete dominance and control will also meet with disaster *because they are better at manipulating than we are at monitoring.* If we turn our relationship with them into a competition—who will win and who will lose—both parent and child will end up losers. A battle for control has no winners.

In the long run, we still have the same goals for them as we would for any other child: we want to help them learn internal discipline that they may surrender to the Lord. Helping them adhere to house rules is still vital (for them and for their siblings). Teaching them to reach out and spiritually connect with their Heavenly Father is still the key to their obtaining a strong testimony. That said, let us look at some basic guidelines for helping SWCs (and us) survive childhood on their way to becoming responsible adults.

Establish a Clear Understanding of What Is Acceptable and What Is Not

SWCs are infinitely curious. These kids not only need to understand *what* behavior is acceptable, they also need to know *why*. Answers such as "because I told you" and "because I'm your mom" will be seen as a challenge to see who can win. They need to constantly be reminded of the long-term goal of becoming a responsible adult and what it will mean to them. They still will not agree with every rule and consequence but will be more likely to accept our reasoning. In addition, teaching them the connection between behavior and consequence needs to begin as early as possible.

Target behavior needs to be explained as a way to get their wants and needs met. They will obey for their reasons, not ours. In setting up rules and consequences, begin with their goals as much as possible. By helping them work toward their ultimate goals, we join their team rather than being seen as a roadblock.

Some parents worry that their SWC has no real goals. They just want to sleep or play video games or hang out with their friends. But they are driven when there is something they want or are curious about. Projects and activities, based on their interests, will help channel their natural energy.

One teenaged SWC I worked with was causing his single mother endless heartache. His rebellious nature was made worse during the divorce, which became angry and contentious. This teen emotionally withdrew, stopping only to torment his sisters. In our discussions, he finally admitted what he really wanted was his own car. As we examined his mother's limited finances, he determined that in order to get a car, he would need to get a job to pay for the car, insurance, gas, and so forth.

. And that's what he did. He needed to have a job to pour his energy into and learn to socialize better. But he did it for his reasons, not his mother's. The result was the same. Predictably, he kept his first job for only two weeks. He refused to follow the manager's rules and walked out. Only then did he realize he didn't have the money for the car he wanted. So he went out and found another job. He actually went through several jobs before deciding, on his own, to "shut up and do what they tell me." SWCs learn quickly; they just need to make their own mistakes along the way.

Give Them Choices

For the SWC, daily life is about trying to control and regulate their world. To do that, they try to impose their will on everyone and everything. In order to channel that tendency, they need to have multiple options for everything they do. Our job, as parents, is to help establish an acceptable list of options.

Warning: Frazzled parents sometimes see "choices" as allowing the difficult child to do almost whatever the child wants. When the child chooses destructively, these parents respond with harsh punishment. Giving them choices doesn't mean opening up every option to them. As a parent, our leverage exists in the choices presented. For young SWCs, these choices can be pretty limited. For older teens, the range of choices will be much greater.

> "So, honey, do you want to do your homework right after school or at 7:00?"
>
> "Do you want to clean your room tonight or Saturday morning?"

"Do you want to finish your chores this afternoon or be grounded this weekend?"

"The backyard needs to be raked. What night do you want to do it?"

Letting the child choose works well when combined with a firm approach called "Broken Record" to help keep them focused on the task at hand. The term "broken record" has been around for a long time. It originally described what happened when a vinyl record would become chipped and the needle would get stuck, causing the music to keep repeating itself until the needle was physically moved forward. We use the Broken Record technique by simply repeating the core idea, over and over, so that we are not drawn into irrelevant side distractions.

> Mom: The backyard needs to be raked. *What night* do you want to do it?
>
> Son: Why do I always have to rake the leaves?
>
> Mom: Because that's the job you agreed to during family home evening. *What night* is best for you?
>
> Son: Why can't Lyle do it?
>
> Mom: Because this is your job. *What night* do you want to do it?
>
> Son: None of my friends have to rake the lawn!
>
> Mom: Probably not. *What night* is best?
>
> Son: You guys just want free labor around here!
>
> Mom: I'm sure it feels that way sometimes. *Which night?*
>
> Son: I've got a big paper due in history.
>
> Mom: Wow. Sounds like earlier in the week might be better for you then. So that would be *which night?*
>
> Son: OK. Tuesday.

Techniques such as "Choicing" and "Broken Record" can be effective and helpful. They allow a parent to be firm and consistent in helping a child obey. Conversely, when these techniques are used by parents or adults as simply an attempt to control, they can also be seen as manipulative.

Help Structure the SWC's Independence and Individuality

SWCs are creative and full of ideas. They are also impulsive and spontaneous, often choosing to act on those ideas at the last minute or with little thought. If we can avoid advice-giving or immediately interjecting our own conclusions, we can keep the lines of communication open while teaching them to think completely through their options.

Example #1:

> Dad: Hi, looks like you're hard at work on the computer.
>
> Mike: Dad! I'm going to make a ton of money fixing computers.
>
> Dad: Do you know how to fix computers?
>
> Mike: Hey, they're easy. Bill, at school, does it all the time. He said he'd teach me.
>
> Dad: Have you checked to see how many computer fix-it stores are out there?
>
> Mike: No.
>
> Dad: Well, they are all out of business! Everyone just buys a new one.
>
> Mike: Not everyone! Bill says he knows three guys who need their computer fixed.
>
> Dad: Mike, focus on your homework instead. You're behind as it is. The computer thing will take up your time just like the last three things you said you were going to do.

> Mike: You watch me. I can keep up and fix computers
> at the same time!

Now, it may be true that Mike knows nothing about computers nor has the time to start a business. However, in trying to point that out, Dad has actually created a situation where Mike will try harder and longer just to prove his dad wrong. Let's try again.

Example #2:

> Dad: Hi, looks like you're hard at work on the computer.
> Mike: Dad! I'm going to make a ton of money fixing
> computers.
> Dad: Really, what got you thinking about that?
> Mike: I was talking to Bill at school. He said he'd
> teach me.
> Dad: Fixing computers is a pretty good thing to
> know. Whose computers would you fix?
> Mike: Bill says he knows two or three guys who need
> their computers fixed.
> Dad: Well, that would be one way to start. How did
> Bill learn to fix computers?
> Mike: I don't know. I think his dad has some old computers he's been learning on.
> Dad: Great. So is he practicing on some other computers before he begins working on someone
> else's? (Suggestion without telling)
> Mike: I think so.
> Dad: I'm guessing that's probably what you were
> going to do as well, wasn't it? (Soft suggestion)
> Mike: Yup. I'm going over to Mike's tomorrow and
> he's going to show me what he's been doing.
> Dad: I'll be interested to hear what you find out.

A week later, it's hard to know if Mike will even remember he was going to start the next great computer repair service. But, he heard his dad being supportive. Dad was also able to make useful suggestions without telling Mike what to do. "I'm guessing that's probably what you were going to do . . ." really means: "Before you go tear up someone's computer without knowing how to fix it, you might want to work on some old ones first. That would teach you and help you know if this is something you enjoy doing."

The key here is that Dad phrased his suggestions in such a way that Mike simply confirms them. Mike didn't hear criticism because Dad redirected his energy. Again, he successfully avoided that force against force scenario.

Remain Calm and Consistent

When our SWC storm comes blowing in, we might be drawn to overreact. When a child is yelling, we might be tempted to yell back. If they are pushing hard against a rule, we might decide to change the rule in order to avoid the storm. *Anytime we react with anger or anxiety, they have gained control.* When their behavior escalates our emotions, they have effectively taken over. Once emotions escalate, we then try to reassert our control by restricting in a coercive manner the things they are permitted to do. Nothing stirs up an SWC's defiant behavior like a yelling parent. Any reaction on their part will be the opposite of what we wanted to see happen—guaranteed.

When we respond in the heat of the moment, we also tend to contradict rules we agreed to earlier. Or we might go counter to something our spouse has said or done. SWCs are champions at "splitting"—playing one parent against the other. For some, it is a game designed to test the fences, to see what they can get away with. Remember, SWCs focus on getting what they want and will frequently do or say whatever is necessary to do that.

Learn Good Pacing

One of the most helpful skills a parent can learn is called "pacing." Studies into human behavior reveal a natural tendency, on the part of all of us, to "match" or "mirror" the emotional state of someone we're talking to. For instance, if you are talking to someone who begins whispering, you automatically lower your voice. If you are talking excitedly, others around you tend to become excited as well.

Pacing is helpful when attempting to calm an angry or upset child. This means pitching our voice *just below* their voice. Each time we respond to a loud voice with a calmer voice, it will tend to calm the situation. We then gradually keep lowering our voice and allowing them to follow us.

Conversely, if we react to their actions by becoming angry or demonstrating our anxiety, we can escalate a situation in a hurry. Whether they will admit it or not, children expect parents and adults to act more mature and settled than the child is acting. That maturity is best shown in our tone of voice and our overall demeanor. Nowhere is this more true than with an SWC. Angry voices and threats play into their natural tendency of defiance. If we are emotionally reactive, they will feel the need to control the situation. Our reactions will feel unsafe to them.

Our ability to discipline is further compromised when Mom and Dad disagree about what discipline is appropriate. As punishment after punishment fails, it is easy to differ on what needs to happen next. When the parents appear to be at odds, the SWC will play to the parent most likely to give them what they want, thus effectively pitting the parents against each other.

Splitting is not limited to parents only! In addition, well-meaning but enabling grandparents can jump in (or be pulled in), further complicating attempts to structure life for an SWC. The same is true for youth leaders, coaches, teachers, and other adults who are part of their lives. We remedy that by making sure that anyone who will spend time with these kids knows the overall plan and is committed to its implementation.

Avoid Under-Disciplining

Under-discipline is just as destructive as overreaction. As one therapist put it, "Swearing at Mom deserves more than a 'Watch your language, Son.'" We may think, "I'm tired. I just don't have the energy to battle him again tonight." We might threaten consequences endlessly without ever following through. In essence, parents can become all bark, no bite. SWCs in these homes will tell you that the unwritten family rule is: "Act like you heard the threats and the lectures then do what you want."

Under-discipline can be avoided by involving the SWC in choosing the consequences to broken rules. No yelling or guessing is necessary. The punishment is clearly established, and the parents' responsibility becomes helping the child obey what they agreed to do. But, again, any discipline that is decided must be enforceable.

Fifteen-year-old Alex has been in constant trouble most of his life. The youngest of four children, he is the only child still at home. A true SWC, he rarely thinks of consequences before impulsively doing what it is he wants. After violating a ten o'clock school-night curfew, his parents grounded him for a week. However, since Dad travels extensively and Mom has heavy church commitments on many evenings, Alex is often left without supervision at nights. Since being grounded, he still spends most evenings with friends, then lies to his mom about being home.

The problem is that the punishment was unenforceable, and Alex knew that when he agreed to it. Mom, who feels overwhelmed already, knows he is probably sneaking out, but she does not know how to stop him. So, she does nothing but refer Alex to a rule she cannot enforce.

Kids such as Alex stand the greatest risk of rebelling. They challenge authority and chafe at restrictions. What helps is that SWCs are creative problem solvers. They learn quickly to assess a situation and figure out how to solve it.

Because of this skill, the four-step process we discussed earlier works well with SWCs. This is referred to as "Reality Therapy," and it was developed in the 1970s to help delinquent teens recognize the consequences of their behavior.

> **What happened?**
> **Is it what you wanted? (Does it help you reach what you really want?)**
> **If not, what are you going to do differently?**
> **Did it work? (evaluate, evaluate, evaluate)**

The simplicity of this approach with SWCs is that they are constantly being asked to tie in their behavior with its consequences. They have to match what they're doing against what they really want. Again, it also establishes the parent as an advocate, helping them get the things they really need.

A true SWC can severely challenge a family. As they move

along their destructive course, they can put a strain on marriages, negatively impact their siblings, and make poor decisions that put their eternal lives in peril. There will be some rebellion of some kind. How we parent them limits the extent. If we find ourselves in a battle of wills, there will be no winners.

We just need to continually remind ourselves that the research suggests that most of these kids actually grow into creative, driven adults once they achieve some maturity. Parenting is a matter of directing their energy in a way that will cause the least damage and keep them as close to the path as possible. As we try to do that, our relationship with them may be the most stable thing in their lives.

Protect that relationship at all costs.

Eleven

Rebels and Prodigals: What Do We Do Now?

When my kids become wild and unruly, I use a nice, safe playpen. When they're finished, I climb out.—Erma Bombeck

Robert L. Millet has observed:

> If the greatest joys in life are family joys, then surely
> the greatest sorrows in life are family sorrows. If no other
> success in life can compensate for failure in the home,
> then what can be more painful than having wandering
> children? If the most important work we will ever do in
> the Church is that which we do within the walls of our
> own home, then nothing causes deeper turmoil and soul-
> searching than having children who stray from the path
> of truth and righteousness (*When a Child Wanders* [Salt Lake
> City: Deseret Book Company, 1996], 31).

How true this is. The rebellion of a child could be likened
to living through a slow-motion car wreck. You see the crash
coming, hear the screeching of the tires, and feel the impact,
but seemingly can do nothing to stop it.

During the past few years I've been polling parents who
have experienced the pain of a wayward child; asking them, in

retrospect, what they feel they did right and what they might have changed. Their answers were as poignant and painful as they were honest.

For instance, one mother responded:

My sons really did not click with the sports and Scout type of boys. So when it came to Church programs they really did not fit in . . . The oldest got his Eagle [but] I think I would deemphasize Scouting even though it is a good program . . . I'm not sure what I would put in its place.

Said another:

I could see the signs for my boys' rebellions way before the serious stuff. I think I would have gotten my oldest son into therapy as early as second grade.

One father wrote:

I was blindsided by my daughter's 180-degree change in behavior when she was seventeen. I am still confused by it. She was a model of a good young woman, but I think that somewhere along the line her outward behavior was for show. I am saddened by that because I thought I had an honest relationship with her.

Says one mother:

I ended up getting a part-time job in a law firm when their dad was laid off from his job. Their father would not take any work unless it met his standards, so for two years he did not work. Since I was working I could not be at home all the time when the kids got home from school, so sometimes the boys would go off with friends and get into trouble. If I could do it over, I would not have gotten a job, and I would have taken and picked up my kids from school each day.

Looking back, many parents still search for what they could have done differently. And they still have few answers.

I also asked, "What helped and what made the situation worse?" In responding to "what helped," one mother answered with a list:

> My husband and I kept our relationship strong, talking through the situation and being unified in our response to the child.
>
> Despite the problems we had, we kept the communication channels open with our daughter, and she still wanted to talk with us.
>
> Extended family and Church family were able to get through when we were not able.
>
> Having a forgiving heart.

An intended insult was taken as a positive comment by one set of beleaguered parents. As they were attempting to hold their daughter to the consequences of her actions, her frustrated boyfriend told her, "Your parents won't do anything unless the prophet says it!" Needless to say her mom and dad were pleased with that.

Concerning what made matters worse, a father explained:

> Two things. One, getting angry broke down communication channels and drove our daughter away and back to the environment that we were trying to avoid. Second, despite good intentions, there was no follow-up by priesthood leaders on disciplinary council actions: No weekly interviews, no meetings, no straight counsel.

Other comments included:

> Maybe I would have gotten some counseling for myself earlier.
>
> I would never let my daughter single date at sixteen. I just didn't know better even though we are told to let them group date and double date. . . . I got to find out the hard way.
>
> Spend more individual time with our kids.
>
> Loved more, lectured less.
>
> Followed up on those feelings from the Holy Ghost.
>
> Should have probed more as to where our child was going and with whom.
>
> Should have moved sooner.

Each of these parents, now looking back over the years, remembers the struggles with their rebellious kids with a mixture of regret, resignation, and hope. Elder John K. Carmack reminds us that these emotions are the "typical parental reactions [which] include sorrow, despair, desperation, depression, feelings of guilt and unworthiness, and a sense of failure. In these circumstances, parents may also experience anger and withdrawal and may feel like simply giving up. *These reactions usually make matters worse,* deepening the problems they face" ("When Our Children Go Astray," *Ensign,* Feb. 1997, 29; emphasis added).

President Gordon B. Hinckley had this to say in support of discouraged parents:

> It is very easy to say that if we will do this or that, all will go well. But, I have seen conscientious men and women, people who are faithful and true, people who try to observe the teachings of the church, who still experience broken hearts over the conduct of their children . . .

To any who may have such sons and daughters, may I suggest that you never quit trying. They are never lost until you have given up. Remember that it is love, more than any other thing, that will bring them back. Punishment is not likely to do it. Reprimands without love will not accomplish it. Patience, expressions of appreciation, and that strange and remarkable power which comes with prayer will eventually win through (*Faith: The Essence of True Religion,* [Salt Lake City: Deseret Book Company, 1989], 66–67).

With President Hinckley's counsel in mind, let us now look at several important guidelines for those who have children currently rebelling.

Take Care of Yourselves First

Parents undergoing trials have the opportunity, and the need, to draw closer to the Lord. They are driven to their knees, to the temple, to the scriptures, in search of answers and solace. If we are spiritually listening, the experience may humble us in a way that invites an outpouring of the Spirit and teaches us some things about ourselves and a loving God that we might not otherwise discover.

Marriages will be subjected to powerful forces. Wayward children, like the SWCs described in the last chapter, often attempt to "split" or seize on any marital differences as a way to get what they want.

For the wayward, "the problem," as they see it, is that they aren't allowed to do whatever they want. In truth, parents are the ones with "the problem"; they are the ones who fear the long-term consequences of their child's shortsightedness. They are the ones who can picture the future unhappiness that is coming. And that is why many parents are the ones who, at first, would benefit the most by seeking inspired counsel, ecclesiastical and/or professional, in seeking how to parent and to keep a marriage strong throughout the crisis.

Inspired Church leaders and trained professional counselors can provide direction on how to keep our emotional boat from capsizing in the midst of the storm. They supply perspective as we ride out the highs and lows, contributing encouragement and valuable suggestions, ideas, and experience.

We also have at our disposal a loving Father in Heaven, whose Son "descended below all things" (D&C 88:6) and is our "Guardian, Guide, and Stay" (*Hymns*, no. 78). There is nothing the Savior has not experienced, no pain He does not know. It is no wonder that in our time of need He sends the Comforter, to bring much welcome comfort—if we are listening. We must not let the great deceiver, the source of all lies, persuade us that our child is beyond rescue, that we have failed in our parenthood, or that God loves us less. Satan has a storehouse of falsehoods he unleashes when we are discouraged and down. It is the same set of lies he whispers to our wandering child when he or she realizes the futility of their decisions.

As we mentioned earlier, many parents with kids who struggle are "guilt waiting to happen." They look around at other good kids, other good parents, other successful students or achievers and become immediately depressed at the announcement of an awards ceremony. If you are one who feels guilty at the first opportunity, I congratulate you for reading to this point! Like the rest of us, you probably haven't mastered all we've talked about, but we can begin to look at what we do have control over.

Maintain a Spiritual Environment in the Home

Prodigals see only the restrictions of a commandment. They push to do whatever it is they want. But if they have been exposed to the light of the gospel, deep inside they will know that they are selling their birthright for worthless GSB pottage (great and spacious building). Their wickedness will prevent them from knowing happiness (see Alma 41:10). As destructive experiences pile up, second thoughts may arise and doubts enter in when no one is around to see them. And, at some point, some children will begin to reevaluate the home and the faith they have spurned. If he is to be saved, when our prodigal finally comes "to himself," he must feel home is a haven to which he can return. Regardless of what is going on with him, we must ensure that our home is a place where the Spirit dwells and is a safe harbor in which a battered heart can find refuge from the storms of life.

President Hinckley described the travail of personal friends who had a son leave home, much like the prodigal son. His mother continued to love him and feed him whenever he came around. President Hinckley noted: "The love of his mother finally began to touch his heart. He came back occasionally to sleep. . . . He came to realize that there was no place as comfortable, no place as secure, no place as happy as that home he had left earlier. He finally got his life under control" (*Faith: The Essence of True Religion*, 66).

Many parents will say that their rebellious child, still living at home, is the exact reason that the atmosphere in their home is anything but peaceful and spiritual. Their child is actively sowing contention and discord. Such children flaunt family rules. He or she may be violating the Word of Wisdom or disobeying laws of morality. In short, they are doing everything they can to disrupt the spirit of the Holy Ghost. What are parents to do?

There are circumstances when an older teen or young adult must obey some basic rules of the house or temporarily find another place to live. Is that the absolute last resort? Of course. I also recognize that some parents say they would never consider it. But, having worked with conflicted families for years, I have repeatedly witnessed the damaging *collateral effect* a rampaging rebellious teen has on the other children in the home. Too often I have watched as parents labor vainly to save one child only to lose others in the process—or live for years in a home with such a level of contention that the Spirit is unable to dwell there.

Other siblings, especially younger ones, watch closely to see if family rules are being followed. They become resentful if good behavior is required of them but not of their rebellious older brother. Sometimes they will say something about the inequity, many times they won't. If that is the case, they will discover that the way to avoid following the rules is to rebel themselves. A willful, disruptive, rebellious child therefore puts his or her siblings at risk as well.

Home must be a place where the Spirit is welcome. It must be the safe harbor in the storm, not the epicenter. To ensure that, after all other options have been exhausted, sometimes that older child is gently but firmly invited to find another place to live—until he or she is ready to abide by family rules. To avoid creating permanent alienation or closing doors forever, this conversation must take place in an atmosphere of love and concern, not anger or rancor.

Dad: Rick, I need to talk to you.
Rick: Yeah, Dad?

Dad: Son, I could smell the tobacco smoke coming from your room again tonight.

Rick: Okay. I'm busted.

Dad: Do you remember our agreement?

Rick: The one about "Rick, you have to follow the rules."

Dad: I mean the one about respecting the family enough to follow the rules we live by.

Rick: Oh, those rules. Well, I didn't kill anybody. I don't know what the big deal is.

Dad: The deal is that you agreed to live by those rules the last time you did this. And each time you promised to follow through.

Rick: Hey, a little cigarette isn't that big a problem. You and Mom are the ones who freak out all the time.

Dad: Look, Son, you know how important it is to follow the Lord's commandments. And, you promised me you wouldn't do it again, and then you've kept doing it. I love you enough to hold you to your commitments. After the last time, you agreed to keep the Word of Wisdom or make some other living arrangements.

Rick: Fine. Maybe I will move in with one of my friends.

Dad: That's probably best for now. It will be painful for me to have you move out, but I need you to respect yourself and us by following through with the responsibilities you agreed to do. You will always have a place here; you just need to follow some simple rules. I also need you to respect your little brothers.

We never "kick" a child out of the house; we are anxious to hold them close to us as long as possible, especially when they are swimming in doubts. We do not abandon them or write them off. However, there are times we need to invite them to stay elsewhere until they are ready to abide by some basic rules of decency. Those rules cannot and should not require things such as scripture study and family prayer when they are not yet ready to do that. But we must require an acceptable level of behavior, especially toward the rest of the family. The child must know that behavior such as physical violence and drug use will not be tolerated nor excused and will result in being reported to the proper authorities.

Enforcing this kind of standard has a precedent in the Lord's ancient dealings with the children of Israel. He bestowed upon them a wonderful land of inheritance. But their disobedience resulted in their having to leave that place, and they were taken into captivity. But the Lord restored them as quickly as possible. And as they repented and turned again to Him, they were restored to their lands, and the Lord graciously put a "ring on [their] hand and shoes on [their] feet" (see Luke 15:22).

For the rest of the family, maintaining prayer, church attendance, family home evening, and other righteous practices provides a conducive setting for the Spirit to dwell in the home. It helps protect the rest of the family against the forces that would tear them apart. This structure also enables inspired parents to closely watch other children for the ill effects of their wayward sibling.

Keep in Mind That Rebellion, by Its Nature, Is Rebellion against Something

One researcher informs us:

> An important step in dealing with rebellious children is to understand that rebellion is *always* a power struggle, whether the child is two, fifteen, or forty. They are

rebelling against something or someone. Understandably, then, authoritarian and coercive behavior on our part only alienates and offends them. Coercion is not part of the gospel plan, and it plays no useful role in teaching the gospel to our children (R. Wayne and Leslee S. Boss, *Are My Children Going to Make It?* [Salt Lake City: Deseret Book Company, 1991], 194–95; emphasis in the original).

If the child can understand what it is they are rebelling against, he or she is more likely to see that their destructive behavior leaves them the greatest loser. For instance, a daughter who sees herself as rebelling against the Church may, in time, come to see that she was rebelling against parents or a youth leader she had a clash with but not rebelling against the gospel or God. She may also come to understand that, in her blind rebellion, she painted the entire Church with an angry brush when, in truth, she was only mad at a few select people or her parents.

In those rare moments when they will talk about their behavior, we should look for opportunities to help them clarify who or what they are really rebelling against.

Unfortunately, out of a sense of frustration, coercion and force are often our first weapons of attack as we strive to squelch the rebellion. One thing we should quickly learn is that children are better at rebelling than we are at coercing. If we use enough control, we may find their rebellion becomes more secretive. If it becomes a battle of wills, an angry teenager is more stubborn than we are and infinitely more creative!

As with the SWCs we discussed, we avoid the power struggle by not engaging in it. Once family rules are decided upon and agreed to, they are not up for daily renegotiation.

They do not have to be defended each time there is a breech. They simply have to be obeyed.

One young mother complained of constant stress caused by her disagreeable thirteen-year-old daughter. She was weary of her daughter's endless arguments over dress standards, phones, friends, and anything she was asked to do. It seemed to this mother that her daughter was pre-wired, from the pre-existence, to automatically oppose any suggestion or request Mom might make.

As Mom explained this to me, she began to describe another long-running dispute she'd been having with her daughter over something very inconsequential. I stopped her and asked:

"Do you see what you are doing?"

"What?" she responded, giving me that "tired mother" look.

"You are arguing with a thirteen-year-old."

She looked at me, still not comprehending.

"You are an adult and a mother," I reminded her. "You have years of experiences she doesn't. And you're arguing with a thirteen-year-old."

After a moment, a smile crept across her face. "I am, aren't I?" she concluded.

Over time, she began to recognize that her daughter was better at dragging her into quarrels than she was at resisting them. Once she began responding to her daughter's arguments with a little humor, most of the "nothing" arguments came to a stop.

Responding to rebellious children, without anger and resentment, is a delicate balancing act. When they hurt us, as they sometimes mean to do, it is natural to react out to the pain. We may say things we don't mean. We threaten even when we've promised ourselves we wouldn't. We label their friends and demean their choices. The result is that we end up building roadblocks where we were hoping to construct bridges.

At the same time, meekness does not mean allowing a child to be verbally abusive to other members of their family. There must be consequences for unacceptable behavior. When established rules are broken, our response must be firm, but filled with love. "How oft will I gather you," the Savior said to the Nephites, "as a hen gathereth her chickens under her wings." Then the expectation: " . . . if ye will repent and return unto me with full purpose of heart" (3 Nephi 10:6). This becomes our approach as well. As often and as quickly as they return, we will draw them as close as they will allow.

Remember, Rebellion Will Not Bring Them the Happiness They Seek

Satan's plan of misery is a classic bait and switch scheme: it brings short-term gratification and long-term misery. At the time children begin to waver, they chafe under rules and resent being told what to do. They dismiss Alma's warning that "wickedness never was happiness" (Alma 41:10). They know only that their worldly peers have fewer restrictions and seem to be having more fun.

As it did in the premortal council, pride ferments the soul. These rebellious ones gratify their pride, (see D&C 121:37), believing they are wiser than those who "blindly" follow outdated rules. By their decisions, however, they cut themselves off from the real sources of peace and joy. Ultimately, they are left to pursue a daily escape in an attempt to replace the emptiness they feel or mask the guilt they experience. Month by month, their new freedom becomes less and less fulfilling.

Of course, pride prevents them from admitting they are not happy—especially to parents and Church leaders. It will be pride that binds them to the dubious path and pride that will keep them from admitting their mistakes. Eventually, that pride combines with the guilt they feel as a consequence of disobeying commandments they were taught to honor. Thus, they are carefully bound with "a flaxen cord" (2 Nephi 26:22); a soft rope, which Satan hopes to replace, someday, with the chains of hell.

Yet, there are revealed reasons why we should not despair. In the April 1929 general conference, Elder Orson F. Whitney gave one of the great addresses in recorded writ on rebellious children. His comments are oft repeated in the Church and bear repeating here because they have given hope to parents for generations.

> The prophet Joseph Smith declared—and he never taught a more comforting doctrine—that the eternal sealings of faithful parents and the divine promises made to them for valiant service in the Cause of Truth, would save not only themselves, but likewise their posterity. Though some of the sheep may wander, *the eye of the Shepherd is upon them, and sooner or later they will feel the tentacles of Divine Providence reaching out after them and drawing them back to the fold.* Either in this life or the life to come, they will return. They will have to pay their debt to justice; they will suffer for their sins; and may tread a thorny path; but if it leads them at last, like the penitent Prodigal, to a loving and forgiving father's heart and home, the painful experience will not have been in vain. Pray for your careless and

disobedient children; hold on to them with your faith. *Hope on, trust on, till you see the salvation of God.*

Then this encouraging reminder:

You parents of the willful and the wayward! Don't give them up. Don't cast them off. They are not utterly lost. The Shepherd will find his sheep. They were his before they were yours—long before he entrusted them to your care; and you cannot begin to love them as he loves them.

They have but strayed in ignorance from the Path of Right, and God is merciful to ignorance. . . . Our Heavenly Father is far more merciful, infinitely more charitable, than even the best of his servants, and the Everlasting Gospel is mightier in power to save than our narrow finite minds can comprehend (in Conference Report, Apr. 1929, 110; emphasis added).

Brigham Young taught the same thing:

Let the father and mother, who are members of this Church and Kingdom, take a righteous course, and strive with all their might never to do a wrong, but to do good all their lives; if they have one child or one hundred children, if they conduct themselves towards them as they should, binding them to the Lord by their faith and prayers, I care not where those children go, they are bound up to their parents by an everlasting tie, and no power of earth or hell can separate them from their parents in eternity; they will return again to the fountain from whence they sprang (*Discourses of Brigham Young*, sel. John A. Widtsoe [Salt Lake City: Deseret Book Company, 1941], 208).

I wholeheartedly agree with these sentiments: I also do not know if the Prophet Joseph ever taught a more comforting doctrine, one more overflowing with love and mercy. I admit I do not understand how this is done, but the spirit and peace of this doctrine confirms its truthfulness to me each time I read those words.

The Lord, through His Spirit, Changes Hearts

As one parent told me, "Never, never, never, never give up. You can't pray away free agency but you can soften hearts by praying."

As parents, we naturally want to take on the role of repairman. From his earliest moment, we bandage a child's skinned knee, we kiss an "owee," we soothe and comfort when things go wrong. Seeing to their safety, growth, and development is our most important project. Then, when they begin to rebel, we want to fix that as well.

For a small number of rebellious souls, there seems to be little that can be done to fix the problem. Once it has established a successful beachhead, pride effectively turns back any loving attempts to soften a hardening heart. Pride is usually progressive; it does not stagnate nor stay motionless. It builds and strengthens; it spins rationale and twists the truth. It grows when it is reinforced by the pride in others and ridicules submissiveness as weakness whenever it is found.

Worse yet, as pride sours a rebellious child's soul, it changes their motives. They may outwardly demonstrate appropriate behavior, but at their core, the reasons are strictly selfish. At a moment's notice, this behavior is quickly discarded in favor of actions more likely to get what they want.

At its most basic, any rebellion is a "heart condition"; it

testifies as to the state of our humility and submissiveness. Whether we are adults or teens, rebellion puts us at odds with our Heavenly Father, making us an "enemy to God" (Mosiah 3:19). Until our hearts are changed, any behavioral change will be superficial or temporary.

Nephi understood this when he prayed: "O Lord, wilt thou redeem my soul? . . . Wilt thou make me that I may shake at the appearance of sin? . . . because that my heart is broken and my spirit is contrite" (2 Nephi 4:31–32). We also have the record of King Benjamin's people who reported to him that:

> We believe all the words which thou hast spoken unto us; and also, we know of their surety and truth, because of the Spirit of the Lord Omnipotent, which has wrought a mighty change in us, or in our hearts, that we have no more disposition to do evil, but to do good continually (Mosiah 5:2).

These Book of Mormon prophets recognized that the change of heart we seek is done *for* us, not *by* us. This powerful transformation is beyond our capacity to achieve but is done by virtue of the Lamb of God.

Our wandering children need this change of heart. But, as it is with us, it is beyond their capacity to do it on their own. We cannot do it for them as parents any more than we can do it for ourselves. As hearts change, behaviors change. When the time comes, for whatever reason, that they begin to exercise different choices, the Spirit takes over. Elder Henry B. Eyring has counseled that, "A choice to be good—even with the trials that come—will allow the Atonement to change your heart. In time and after persistence, your wants and even your needs will change" (*To Draw Closer to God* [Salt Lake City: Deseret Book Company, 1997], 70–71).

This is why both our parental approach and our home environment must be conducive to the Spirit. Our prayers will avail us nothing if our conduct and home life are contrary to the love of the Savior.

We Hold Parental Keys and Are Entitled to Heavenly Guidance in Our Stewardship

I will never forget the day the mantle of bishop descended upon me. My wife and I were sitting in a restaurant, discussing the fact that our bishop had announced he was moving. We wondered, aloud, who the successor might be. Suddenly, in a powerful way, I knew that the next bishop would be me. The sensation shook me from my head to my feet. And though it was a month before the actual call came, I was grateful that I had several weeks to prepare myself for this new challenge.

During that time, though the call had not yet been extended, I found myself with new insights into ward members and their difficulties. I had received a new and immediate source of guidance that had not been there previously.

I also felt the same mantle descend with the birth of each of my four children. As I looked at the new child before me, I felt the additional responsibility resting upon my shoulders. I was very aware of my new role as their parent, protector, provider, and teacher.

The intensity of the pain we feel when a child rebels comes from our deep love for them. Whenever I have watched kids rebel, even though they were not mine, I have been filled with a deep sense of pain and sorrow. Their destructive choices seem to tear a hole in me. I have since learned that any stewardship—be it parent, youth leader, or friend—produces deep spiritual connections to those we love. These associations produce the greatest joy as we watch them grow. That affection also fills us with the greatest sorrow when they struggle.

With each stewardship, the Lord extends spiritual keys—a mantle if you will—to help us with our assignment. These keys entitle us to seek and receive heavenly guidance for those under our care. They give us the right to insight and knowledge about how to serve them. I also believe these keys increase our capacity to love them. Stewardships give us a small sampling of just how much their Heavenly Father loves them.

Some parents, finding themselves in the midst of a parenting stewardship that appears to have gone horribly wrong, plead with heaven for answers and despair when they receive none. They want answers. They want peace. Most of all, they want their child back.

We need to remember that we hold heavenly keys that entitle us, as parents, to guidance from above. If those answers are not there, we need to begin by examining what it is we are asking for. It could be we are receiving answers, but rejecting them because they are contrary to what we feel needs to happen.

For example, when there are problems, do we want the rebellion to be strictly about our child? Are we also willing to follow the Spirit even if it whispers that we are the ones needing the help first? Are we anxious to see our children change so long as it doesn't require any changes in us?

We pray, but those prayers may be conditional. Do we counsel the Lord rather than wait on His direction? It is true that by the help of the Spirit "ye may know the truth of all things" (Moroni 10:5). But, we then have to be willing to follow any guidance that comes.

Also, divine answers will not come when we are filled with

anger. One of the most damaging effects of a wayward child is the long-term effect it can have on us. Constant arguing and contention can leave you angry and ill at ease. The continual stress of waiting to see "what's next?!" drains us of energy and hope. At those moments, heaven—and answers—may seem far away.

We must never forget that the Lord loves these children, whatever their rebellion has led them to do. He knows them; He knows their hearts and their potential. He desires for them all the same things He desires for us. Because He does, He is anxious to provide answers to parents who are listening and willing to obey. These answers may come immediately or they may be years in coming. But come they will. When the Lord knows our prodigals are ready, He will begin the work of reclamation. He will place individuals and circumstances in their path that provide them with the opportunity to make different decisions. That work will go much easier if we have prayerfully prepared ourselves as stewards by leaving lines of communication open and have maintained a home of peace.

Doing all we can, then trusting the Lord's timetable may be as difficult a task as we can have as a parent. We will be unable to see all the circumstances or the road ahead. But we need to trust that Heavenly Father loves them more than we do, knows them better than we do, sees what they need and can change them in a way we cannot.

"Be still, and know that I am God" (Psalm 46:10).

Twelve

Turning the Hearts
of the Children:
Help from Beyond the Veil

Peer pressure is nothing compared to ancestor pressure!—Pickles

Earlier, we discussed how only the Lord has the power to change a heart. By virtue of our fallen condition, we all need to become new creatures in Christ and to have our very natures changed. We sing:

> Here's my heart, O take and seal it;
> Seal it for thy courts above
> ("Come, Thou Fount of Every Blessing,"
> *Hymns*, 1948, no. 24).

To strengthen our children against wandering, we seek to put them into situations where the Spirit is present so that the Lord can go about His work of softening their hearts. As the Spirit bears witness, children will begin to comprehend the wonderful blessings promised to their parents by virtue of the sealing ordinances of the temple.

It also has been suggested that we never learn anything new spiritually in this life; it is all a "re-membering" of things we learned in the premortal life. When children are placed in situations where the Holy Ghost can bear witness, they can be reminded of things they already know, things stored behind the veil. If this is the case, the Spirit is the key to reminding them of covenants made long ago, for it is a familiar spirit to which they learned to respond during eons before their birth here.

These eternal covenants are also brought to mind by the aid of a powerful facilitator, the Spirit of Elijah. As we will discuss, exposing children to this spirit, as often as possible, (1) strengthens them in this life and (2) helps return them to us should they wander.

Strength in This Life

In September of 1823, Joseph Smith was seventeen years old. It had been three years since the First Vision, and he began to question his standing before God. He was fearful, given his prophetic calling, that some of his teenage behavior had not been appropriate. He also wanted to know what the Lord expected of him now.

As we know, the heavens again were parted and Joseph met, for the first time, the prophet Moroni, the resurrected being who would be his tutor for the next few years. In multiple subsequent visits, Moroni explained that Joseph's sins had been forgiven and that the Lord still had a work for him to do. The young prophet also learned he was to translate records containing thousands of years of Nephite history. The long-buried story of these ancient people would whisper "out of the dust" through him (Isaiah 29:4).

To prepare Joseph for that task, Moroni began to teach him. That night, he quoted several scriptures that would help Joseph better understand the importance of the sacred records he would translate. The first scripture Moroni quoted, though familiar to us, may seem a little out of context when talking about the Book of Mormon. Moroni recited verses from Malachi, though Joseph recognized they were being quoted differently than they appeared in the Old Testament.

> Behold, I will reveal unto you the Priesthood, by the hand of Elijah the prophet, before the coming of the great and dreadful day of the Lord.
> . . . *And he shall plant in the hearts of the children the promises made to the fathers, and the hearts of the children shall turn to their fathers.* If it were not so, the whole earth would be utterly wasted at his coming (JS—H 1:38–39; emphasis added).

The two emphasized phrases should leap out at any LDS parent. In conjunction with the coming of the Book of Mormon, Moroni is saying that sacred promises will not just be taught but they will be *planted* and cultivated in the hearts of children. The result is that those hearts will be turned toward their fathers and those promises.

Mormon expounded on this idea when he wrote the title page of the Book of Mormon. His abridgment of Nephite history had been carefully prepared and preserved to:

> Show unto the remnant of the House of Israel what great things the Lord hath done for their fathers; *and that they may know the covenants of the Lord,* that they are not cast off forever—And also to the convincing of the Jew and Gentile that Jesus is the Christ, the Eternal God (emphasis added).

The prophets of the Book of Mormon recorded their words and experiences so that modern-day Jews, Gentiles, and remnants of the House of Israel (Lamanites)—indeed, modern-day sons and daughters—would all know the great blessings and covenants made with their forefathers. Moroni's rephrasing of Malachi's verses, in relating the location of the plates, was an affirmation that the Book of Mormon would assist in planting promises deep into the hearts of its readers.

Millions of Latter-day Saints can testify to the Book of Mormon's unique and powerful spirit. It has a distinctive voice, touching us as no other book can. But we rarely associate that feeling with the Spirit of Elijah, when, in fact, this spirit permeates every page.

Is it any wonder, then, that when President Gordon B. Hinckley challenged members of the Church to read the Book of Mormon by the end of 2006, he commented that "those who read the Book of Mormon will be blessed with 1) an added measure of the Spirit of the Lord, 2) a greater resolve to obey His commandments, and 3) a stronger testimony of the living reality of the Son of God" (see "The Power of the Book of Mormon," *Ensign*, June 1988, 6).

For parents seeking to fortify their youth against future rebellions, teaching a child to love and use the Book of Mormon is a key part of the plan. Problems experienced by young people ought to be a catalyst to send them scouring through the book, searching for an answer. And, again, shame on the parent who circumvents that search by being too quick to provide solutions to a child's problems. Their growth comes in their struggle and in finding answers to prayers. And many answers can be found in the Book of Mormon.

Some of my earliest memories involve sitting at the kitchen table while my mother fixed dinner. This inspired woman, seeing her young son sitting there, often chose to talk about stories from the Book of Mormon as she stood cooking at the stove. One particularly fond memory is of her wondering aloud why it was that the Nephites would let themselves get to the point where they were being slaughtered at Cumorah. As she stood and stirred her cooking and wondered aloud, she made those ancient prophets come alive for me.

Reading and studying the Book of Mormon is one powerful way to invite the Spirit of Elijah to help turn the hearts of our children.

The Spirit of Elijah and Our Pioneer Heritage

The Church of Jesus Christ of Latter-day Saints has a unique heritage. During the process of the Restoration, the Church established and was forced from settlements in New York, Ohio, Missouri, Illinois, and Iowa. In many of these places, as well as along the Mormon Trail and at Winter Quarters, the remains of our faithful dead lie in quiet cemeteries.

Beginning in the early 1900s, the Church began looking for opportunities to purchase historical sites. The Carthage Jail, the Joseph Smith farm, and the Hill Cumorah were among the first to be acquired. In recent years, more extensive purchases and renovations have been made at sites such as Nauvoo, Martin's Cove, and Kirtland, creating desirable destinations for thousands of Latter-day Saints.

Why does the Church spend so much time and money to purchase and develop these historical sites? The answer is simple: because the spirit of our forebears still broods over those locations. Their blood and sacrifice sanctified the ground. Only the most hardened can visit these places and not be touched by the feelings that overcome them while contemplating the events that transpired there. More specifically, what heart *is not turned* toward them while we visit?

The Church improves and dedicates Church history locations in hope that members will come and have their faith fortified. While many nonmembers also come and learn something about the Church as well, these renovations are for us. As most missionaries called to serve at these locations will attest, the vast majority of visitors are LDS. We are drawn to see and connect with our sacred past.

Not long ago I visited the historic Liberty Jail. The original jail is long gone. A house has been built on the location, keeping only the original floor from that cold winter of 1838–39. After the Church purchased the home, a beautiful visitor's center was constructed over the original site, along with a replica of the old jail beneath it.

And yet, as countless visitors will testify, the spirit that exists there is moving and unmistakable. It is a sobering experience, a reminder of the sacrifice and revelations that occurred in that "temple/prison." I can only compare the feeling there to the one I feel in the temple. It is sweet and tangible and moving, and it reaches out to the hearts of those who are feeling for it.

In our rush to provide entertainment and vacations for our children, shouldn't we also be motivated to provide them with experiences such as the Liberty Jail? If the Lord uses the Spirit of Elijah to change hearts and plant promises, why not have our children stand on the very ground where those promises were made?

What a wonderful opportunity it is to take our children to Liberty, to Martin's Cove, to Palmyra. Have we visited with them at the top of Ensign Peak and talked of Brigham Young's vision of the future city to come? Have we paused in the cemetery at Winter Quarters, gazed at the temple there, and discussed the sacrifice of those who perished there? Or did we spend the week water-skiing instead?

Recently a young girl rose to bear her testimony in our ward. She began by saying that her family had gone to the Hill Cumorah over the summer. In a simple manner she described the spirit she felt and said that she knew that Joseph Smith had seen Heavenly Father and Jesus in the Sacred Grove. She then bore a powerful testimony. As I listened, I felt sure that this young sister was already developing spiritual sensitivities that would help insulate her from Lucifer's blasts later in her life.

My family knows me as an amateur Church historian. I agree with Sister Susan Easton Black who told a class, "I think you can be exalted without visiting Nauvoo—but, then again, I'm not sure." I made a promise to my three sons to take them to Nauvoo in conjunction with their mission calls. I wanted them to connect with the Prophet Joseph Smith before they went out to testify of his work. I hoped that a visit to the City of Joseph would help with that connection. Two experiences stand out from those visits.

My second son and I traveled to Nauvoo in early February just before his departure. We attended the Nauvoo Temple the evening we arrived, then went back to our hotel and planned our visit to Nauvoo and Carthage the next day. During the night a heavy winter storm blanketed the area with snow. The next day, we waited for the storm to let up and for the city to dig out. Shortly after noon, we learned that there would be a brief lull in the storm, followed by more snow that evening. My son and I took the opportunity to venture out that afternoon and drive directly to Carthage.

When we arrived, the old jail appeared to be closed. Heavy snow made parking impossible and no one else was around. I slowly drove around the jail, describing the events of that June 1844 day to my son. Suddenly, a senior sister flagged us down and asked us if we wanted to see the jail. We assured her we did, as my son would soon be leaving on his mission. She then told us to leave our car parked in the middle of the snow-covered street and come in.

For the next hour, we had the jail and her well-versed husband to ourselves. This unique experience deeply touched my son as well as me. We quietly sat in each room and talked about the events that had occurred there. Without the summertime crowds, we had time to prayerfully ponder and feel the Spirit there.

The next morning, as we prepared to drive home to Texas, we took time to stare out at the frozen streams and snowy landscape. We watched chunks of ice float down the Mississippi River. Only then did we realize that we were leaving on the exact same day Brigham Young and our pioneer ancestors had crossed the river for the last time and begun their great migration west. My son was so moved by that experience that he took the time to write up his account of that day. His story was later published in the *New Era* magazine (McKay Hinckley, "A Snowy Day in February, May 2005, 26).

Second, just before my youngest son left on his mission, I took him and his friend, who also had his mission call, to Nauvoo. We had a wonderful time visiting the sites and later watching a football game together on TV in our hotel room. The next morning, before we left, I took them to the place that is, for me, the highlight of any trip to Nauvoo—the old Pioneer Burial Ground, far up on Parley Street. In this cemetery Joseph preached numerous funeral sermons and revealed many new doctrines. The small graves and worn headstones are scattered randomly among the trees in a peaceful setting. To me, it is as sacred a ground as exists anywhere on earth. And the spirit of peace in that place is unmatched. It is the last resting place of many of my heroes.

When I took my son and his friend to the burial ground, we quietly wandered around in different directions, each lost in our own thoughts. After a while, I noticed my son, head down, sitting near the headstone of Edward Partridge. As I approached, he looked up at me, eyes moist, and said, "I think this is my favorite place of all." More powerful than sightseeing and football games, this experience touched his heart more than any other. In that way, those Saints of long ago were still bearing testimony to the truthfulness of the work. They impressed on him the importance of sacrifice and love. Both my son and his friend went on to serve effective missions.

This spirit is also present at our temples. The grounds are well-kept and impressive. When we are on a family vacation, do we stop and find the temple in town? Do we go out of our way to find any excuse to place our children on holy ground and allow them to feel the Spirit of Elijah?

The Spirit of Elijah and the Spirit World

There is another source of spiritual guidance, another transforming presence we may not be aware of. The prophet Nephi, speaking to his future readers, explains the Lord's blessings to those who follow Him:

> I know that if ye shall follow the Son, with full purpose of heart, acting no hypocrisy and no deception before God, but with real intent, repenting of your sins, witnessing unto the Father that ye are willing to take upon you the name of Christ, by baptism—yea, by

following your Lord and your Savior down into the water,
according to his word, behold, then shall ye receive the
Holy Ghost; yea, then cometh the baptism of fire and of
the Holy Ghost; *and then can ye speak with the tongue of angels*
(2 Nephi 31:13; emphasis added).

What does it mean to "speak with the tongue of angels"?
Robert L. Millet suggests that when anyone speaks under the
inspiration of the Spirit,

> they convey not merely their own will and desires but the
> mind and will of Christ. Stated more simply, [whenever]
> President Gordon B. Hinckley [has spoken] with the
> tongue of angels . . . [h]e spoke with the power and per-
> suasion of the Holy Spirit. He spoke what angels would
> have spoken. He delivered what Christ wanted delivered.
> It was as though angels had come and delivered the mes-
> sage, or, more powerfully, as though our blessed
> Redeemer himself had been present and had spoken to his
> people (*Alive in Christ: The Miracle of Spiritual Rebirth* [Salt
> Lake City: Deseret Book Company, 1997], 133).

Nephi provides additional insight to this concept: "Do ye
not remember that I said unto you that after ye had received
the Holy Ghost ye could speak with the tongue of angels?" he
asks. "[And] how could ye speak with the tongue of angels save
it were by the Holy Ghost?" Nephi then provides this explanation: "Angels speak by the power of the Holy Ghost; wherefore, they speak the words of Christ. Wherefore, I said unto
you, feast upon the words of Christ; for behold, the words of
Christ will tell you all things what ye should do" (2 Nephi
32:2–3).

As followers of Christ, the words of Christ are our guiding
light; they do tell us the things we should be doing. When we

are feasting upon those words, when they tell us the things we should be doing and we are feeling the Holy Ghost, could we also be hearing, from the other side of the veil, the voice of angels?

In this dispensation, the Lord has promised His servants: "I will be on your right hand and on your left, and my Spirit shall be in your hearts, and mine angels round about you, to bear you up" (D&C 84:88). One way He does that is by the ministering of angels. If we were to ask most members of the Church if they have ever heard the voices of angels, they would likely say no. Have they ever seen an angel? No. Have they been blessed, or ministered to, by an angel? The answer is yes.

The prophet Mormon tells us that even prior to Christ's earthly advent:

> There were divers ways that he did manifest things unto the children of men, which were good; . . .
>
> Wherefore, *by the ministering of angels,* and by every word which proceeded forth out of the mouth of God, *men began to exercise faith in Christ;* and thus by faith, they did lay hold upon every good thing; and thus it was until the coming of Christ (Moroni 7:24–25; emphasis added).

Obviously, men could not learn to exercise faith if these ministrations were actual visual visits by angels. Is there another way that we, and our children, could be blessed by angels *we don't see?* Alma seems to confirm this in his great discourse on faith. "And now, *he imparteth his word by angels unto men,* yea, not only men but women also. Now this is not all; little children do have words given unto them many times, which confound the wise and the learned" (Alma 32:23; emphasis added).

What active member of the Church has not had the wonderful experience of giving a talk or teaching a class or talking to an investigator and having words form, unbidden, in our mind and mouth? At those moments, we hear the "words of Christ" being spoken; we feel the power of the Holy Ghost speaking words that can "confound the wise and the learned." What we may be hearing, at that moment, are the tongues of angels, ministering to us and to those we are teaching. As the Prophet Joseph taught: "If you live up to your privileges, the angels cannot be restrained from being your associates" (*History of the Church*, 4:605).

If the Lord did indeed send angels, unaware to us, to enlighten our minds, whom would He send? President Joseph F. Smith helped us understand who, from beyond the veil, might be involved in this work of love.

In early 1916, President Smith struggled with a double tragedy: the loss of a beloved wife and the untimely death of Hyrum M. Smith, his son and a member of the Quorum of the Twelve Apostles. These two events sapped his strength, leading him to be something of a recluse the final two years of his life. This two-year period culminated with his vision of the redemption of the dead (D&C 138) and his death a few weeks later.

However, on April 6, 1916, he stood in general conference and gave a powerful witness to the active influence of those beyond the veil. In his talk, which he entitled "In the Presence of the Divine," President Smith observed:

> I feel sure that the Prophet Joseph Smith and his associates, who, under the guidance and inspiration of the Almighty, and by his power, began this latter-day work, would rejoice and do rejoice—I was going to say if they were permitted to look down upon the scene that I behold in this tabernacle, but I believe *they do have the*

privilege of looking down upon us just as the all-seeing eye of
God beholds every part of His handiwork. For I believe
that those who have been chosen in this dispensation and
in former dispensations, to lay the foundation of God's
work in the midst of the children of men, for their salvation and exaltation, will not be deprived in the spirit
world from looking down upon the results of their own
labors, efforts and mission assigned them by the wisdom
and purpose of God, to help to redeem and to reclaim the
children of the Father from their sins.

So I feel quite confident that the eyes of Joseph, the
Prophet, and of the martyrs of this dispensation, and of
Brigham and John and Wilford, and those faithful men
who were associated with them in their ministry upon the
earth, are carefully guarding the interests of the Kingdom
of God in which they labored and for which they strove
during their mortal lives. I believe they are as deeply
interested in our welfare today, if not with greater capacity, with far more interest behind the veil, than they were
in the flesh. I believe they know more: I believe their
minds have expanded beyond their comprehension in
mortal life, and their interests are enlarged and expanded
in the work of the Lord to which they gave their lives and
their best service. . . . I stand in the presence not only of
the Father and of the Son, but in the presence of those
whom God commissioned, raised up and inspired to lay
the foundations of the work in which we are engaged.
Accompanying that sense or feeling, I am impressed with
the thought that I would not this moment say or do one
thing that would be taken as unwise or imprudent, or that
would give offense to any of my former associates and
co-laborers in the work of the Lord.

I would not like to say one thing or express a

thought, that would grieve the heart of Joseph, or of Brigham, or of John, or of Wilford, or Lorenzo, or any of their faithful associates in the ministry. Sometimes the Lord expands our vision from this point of view and this side of the veil, that we feel and seem to realize that we can look beyond the thin veil which separates us from that other sphere. If we can see by the enlightening influence of the Spirit of God and through the words that have been spoken by the holy prophets of God, beyond the veil that separates us from the spirit world, surely those who have passed beyond, can see more clearly through the veil back here to us than it is possible for us to see to them from our sphere of action. I believe we move and have our being in the presence of heavenly messengers and of heavenly beings. We are not separate from them. We begin to realize more and more fully, as we become acquainted with the principles of the Gospel, as they have been revealed anew in this dispensation, that we are closely related to our kindred, to our ancestors, to our friends and associates and co-laborers who have preceded us into the spirit world. We can not forget them; we do not cease to love them; we always hold them in our hearts, in memory, and thus we are associated and united to them by ties that we can not break, and we can not dissolve or free ourselves from.

If this is the case with us in our finite condition, surrounded by our mortal weaknesses, short-sightedness, lack of inspiration and wisdom from time to time, how much more certain it is and reasonable and consistent to believe that those who have been faithful who have gone beyond and are still engaged in the work for the salvation of the souls of men, the opening of the prison doors to them that are bound and proclaiming liberty to the captives who can see us better than we can see them; that they know us better than we know them. They have advanced; we are advancing; we are growing as they have grown; we are reaching the goal that they have attained unto; and therefore, I claim that we live in their presence, they see us, they are solicitous for our welfare, they love us now more than ever. *For now they see the dangers that beset us; they can comprehend, better than ever before, the weaknesses that are liable to mislead us into dark and forbidden paths. They see the temptations and the evils that beset us in life and the proneness of mortal beings to yield to temptation and to wrong doing; hence their solicitude for us and their love for us and their desire for our well being must be greater than that which we feel for ourselves* (Robert L. Millet and Joseph Fielding McConkie, *The Life Beyond* [Salt Lake City: Bookcraft, 1986], 82–84; emphasis added).

Is it possible that our kindred dead are more involved in our lives and the lives of our children than we perceive? Do those who have learned to love, with great intensity, brush up against the veil to minister to our needs? And, if they do, would we not sense that intense love, though we do not see them? If so, wouldn't we be filled with their warmth, their excitement, their joy?

One day, we may find that the spirit we call the Spirit of Elijah was, in actuality, loving, deceased members of our own extended family, motivating us forward from the world of spirits.

Elder Melvin J. Ballard asked, "Why is it that sometimes only one of a city or household receives the Gospel?" In response, he explained, "It was made known to me that it is because the righteous dead who have received the Gospel in the spirit world are exercising themselves, and in answer to their prayers elders of the Church are sent to the homes of their posterity so that the Gospel might be taught to them, and that descendant is then privileged to do the work for his dead kindred." Elder Ballard then added this insight, "It is with greater intensity that the hearts of the fathers and mothers in the spirit world are turned to their children now in the flesh than that our hearts are turned to them" (ibid., 85).

This concept was reinforced by Elder Bruce R. McConkie. In a talk given to the Joseph F. Smith family reunion, Elder McConkie told the group that President Joseph F. Smith had attended the funeral of his son Joseph Fielding Smith. He went on to teach that when a righteous man or woman dies, they do not cease to love their family in the flesh. They continue to pray for them and do not cease to labor in their behalf. In the same way their family was the primary concern in this life, it continues to be their primary concern on the other side of the veil (ibid., 85).

The Spirit of Elijah and Family History

Our kindred dead remain interested in us, blessing us and giving us unseen direction from time to time. A child who is exposed to genealogy, will, by its very nature, come to know and love his or her ancestors. They will be touched by the spirit of that great work. Teens who take family names to the temple to do baptisms for the dead are being put into spiritual situations where Elijah's binding influence can help soften and change their hearts.

Family home evenings that focus on family history can also help children feel the power of their lineages. When our children were small, we took occasion to spend some family home evenings talking about their ancestors. One evening, I told them about *our* "Father Lehi," Arza Hinckley. I explained that after the dedication of the Kirtland Temple, Joseph Smith called John E. Page on a mission to upper Canada. Days later, seeing that Brother Page had not yet left, the Prophet asked him why he had not yet gone. Brother Page responded by saying he had been delayed because he did not have a coat to take with him. Joseph responded by immediately removing his own coat, giving it to him, and then again instructing him to be on his way.

I explained to my children that as a result of that act, Brother Page would find Arza Judd Sr. in Bastard County, Canada, along with Arza Judd Sr.'s young grandson, Arza E. Hinckley, and that shortly afterward (in 1836) John E. Page and John Blakesly also converted Arza Hinckley's mother and his younger brother Ira, who was President Gordon B. Hinckley's grandfather. I told them that, as a boy of eight, Arza would tend the sheep and read the Book of Mormon and would cry, feeling its truthfulness.

Other stories, such as Arza Hinckley's marching with the Mormon Battalion or assisting in the rescue of the Martin Handcart Company, also helped my children come to understand their pioneer heritage. We would then bring out the crayons and have them draw pictures of the handcart rescue. I believe that all these stories helped fill them with the Spirit of Elijah, helping turn their hearts. When taking my children to Nauvoo, they have seen Arza's workmanship on the Nauvoo house or stones he might have quarried for the temple. He left behind an inspiring trail of faith and sacrifice that touches my spirit and inspires my children's as well. Having and loving such a heritage has no doubt served to help our children resist any temptation to rebel.

Conversion Lineage

Because they are recent converts, the vast majority of the members of the Church have no direct pioneer connections. Though the history of the Church belongs to all members, regardless of when they were converted, still, the personal connection helps Church history live in the hearts of children. May I suggest that each member of the Church can trace their conversion lineage back to those early Church members and to the pioneers? How is that? It is possible through the lineage of those who helped bring them into the Church.

How helpful are these stories in buttressing a child's faith? When Nephi and his brothers were sent back to Jerusalem to get the brass plates, Laban, the plates' caretaker, kept refusing to give them up. Nephi's brothers, knowing that Laban had tried to kill them, wanted to immediately return to their father, without the plates. Young Nephi responded by recalling the faith-filled stories of their ancestors as a reason to trust the Lord. "Let us be strong like unto Moses; for he truly spake unto the waters of the Red Sea and they divided" (1 Nephi 4:2). For Nephi, part of the source of his faithfulness was that he remembered "what great things the Lord [had] done for their fathers" (see Title Page of Book of Mormon) and believed he would be similarly blessed.

Building faith in children by remembrance is the exact purpose of the Jewish Passover. "Why is this night different from all others?" the youngest child asks. What then follows is an evening of stories: bricks without straw; unleavened bread; bitter herbs, and so forth. During the Passover Seder, or meal, one chair sits empty, its setting never used. Who is it for? Jewish tradition teaches that someday, during Passover, Elijah the prophet will come to fulfill his promises. At most Seders, the outside door is ceremoniously opened and shut in order to symbolize inviting Elijah in. The silent presence of Elijah is part of the retelling and faith-building traditions of Passover.

Latter-day Saints understand that Elijah did come during Passover in 1836. Following the dedication of the Kirtland Temple, Joseph Smith and Oliver Cowdery retired behind the massive curtains that separated the far end of the temple from the rest of the building. This effectively created the Holy of Holies in the temple, the place where the Lord could come and dwell. In that place, the visions were opened to Joseph and Oliver, and the Savior came to His house and accepted the sacrifice of the Saints. Other prophets came, bearing priesthood keys essential to the complete restoration of the gospel. Finally, came the moment foretold for millennia:

> After this vision had closed, another great and glorious vision burst upon us; for Elijah the prophet, who was taken to heaven without tasting death, stood before us, and said:
>
> Behold, *the time has fully come*, which was spoken of by the mouth of Malachi—testifying that he [Elijah] should be sent, before the great and dreadful day of the Lord come—
>
> To turn the hearts of the fathers to the children, and the children to the fathers, lest the whole earth be smitten with a curse—
>
> Therefore, the keys of this dispensation are committed into your hands (D&C 110:13–16; emphasis added).

Whether we are intent on preventing future rebellion in our children or trying to reclaim the wandering teen, the sweet Spirit of Elijah exists to remind them of the "great things" the Lord has done for their fathers and their fathers and their fathers. We have a history full of the Lord's interventions and blessings toward those who trusted in His promises. In addition, those fathers who have passed on feel a great connection to us who are still in mortality, attempting to work out our own salvation. They share our love and concern for our children. They weep after the prodigal as do we.

Alma fasted and prayed that God would intervene with his wicked son, Alma the Younger, and bring him back to the fold. In response, the Lord sent an angel, who told the rebellious young man, "The Lord hath heard the prayers of his people, and also the prayers of his servant, Alma, who is thy father; for he has prayed with much faith concerning thee that thou mightest be brought to the knowledge of the truth; therefore, for this purpose have I come to convince thee of the power and authority of God, *that the prayers of his servants might be answered according to their faith*" (Mosiah 27:14; emphasis added).

Many parents in the Church hope such a miraculous intervention could occur for their child. "If only," the grieving parents opine. Who is to say that these visitations do not occur, when hearts are sufficiently humble to rehear the message of the gospel—especially for those exposed to the Spirit of Elijah in their early years. Do not discount the possibility that, like Alma, angels will minister to our children, in answer to faithful prayers. Unseen, they wait for the right moment to teach principles and soften hearts.

Thirteen

Secondhand Afflictions

In spite of the seven thousand books of expert advice, the right way to discipline a child is still a mystery to most fathers and . . . mothers. Only your grandmother and Genghis Khan know how to do it.—Bill Cosby

Parents are people.

We did not begin to exist when our first child was born. We grew up, went to school, skinned our knees, got good grades, got bad grades, made our parents proud, did stupid things, made friends, lost friends, had good days, did more stupid things, survived junior high school, stood around at the school dance, went on that horrible date, despaired, fell in love, survived the engagement, and the reception, and swallowed hard when the pregnancy test came back positive.

Parents are people. Our premortal existence, our life experiences, our family, our friends, have all contributed to who we are. They helped prepare us to become people-adults and they have had a large bearing on the things we do as people-parents.

Our people-ness—who we are—is the single largest determinant of how we parent. Parenting, when all is said and done, is a relationship with added responsibilities. Look at our friendships and we see an outline of how we will relate to our children. We cannot disconnect our people-ness from our parent-ness. It is exactly that people-ness our children learn to trust.

When we look at our people-ness, most of us cringe a little. We see our "warts" and wish we had a way to remove them. "If men [and women] come unto me," the Lord told Moroni, "I will show unto them their weakness" (Ether 12:27). And He does. Those weaknesses are there in all their glory, shining out like a neon sign on a dark night. We know because we see them more clearly than anyone else does.

We've also worked on changing those weaknesses with mixed success. Each year, our "thorn in the flesh" still remains; it doesn't seem to be going anywhere, anytime soon. As parents, we might begin to wonder just how much our weaknesses impact our children. We ask: Are my children as "resilient" as some people say? (Children *are* pretty resilient, you know!) Or are they learning things from me I wish they weren't?

Children do have incredible resiliency. They are quick to forgive and move on. Their love for us and our love for them helps us overcome a laundry list full of parental miscues. We dust ourselves off, give each other a hug, and keep going.

Sometimes, however, our people-ness—our foibles and dysfunctions—can become a major stumbling block to how we parent and the examples we set. There is no softening the fact that children are impacted by some of our weaknesses more than others. Because we are not finished products, we deal with our unresolved personal ills in the family arena, with our children sitting on the front row.

Some weaknesses do not become obvious until after we have children. The act of dealing with a colicky baby or a two-year-old with a four-hour tantrum may activate a side of us we didn't know existed or thought we'd forgotten or hoped we'd lost. A defiant or rebellious child will bring us face to face with our own rebellious nature (or rebellious past). In short, the act of parenting draws on our people-ness, whatever shape that may be in.

Our individual "thorns in the flesh" can come from a wide variety of sources. For instance, statistics tell us that approximately one-third of the sisters in the Church experienced some type of abuse while growing up. Others were subjected to physical violence or had a parent with an addiction, an eating disorder, or untreated depression. The list goes on.

Whatever the source or reason, we battle our personal demons at the same time we parent. As we do, we begin to understand, more clearly than ever before, the long-term effect our parent's dysfunction has had on us. This may fill us with fear that we will emotionally handicap our children in the same way. Please, Lord, we pray, let them be resilient!

The good news is that the Lord didn't require or expect perfection from us before sending us a family. There wouldn't be any parents, if that were the case. However, if we (and our children) are being impacted by any of the issues listed below, it is critical we attentively work to heal those wounds.

Let us first look at some examples of weaknesses I call Secondhand Afflictions. We will then review some of the ways the Lord has provided to help us heal from them. Secondhand Afflictions affect us in a way similar to secondhand smoke from tobacco users. We, and our children, are impacted negatively simply by being in close proximity to someone else's problem. We inhale, if you will, some of their toxins.

Most such afflictions are the result of the environment we grew up in; others are a product of our individual genetic inheritance. *We wouldn't have chosen any of these,* but, over time, they have become part of our regular behavior.

Destructive Coping Skills

In an effort to cope with the world, we resort to patterns of behavior that can be helpful or they can be destructive. Let me give an example.

I have a good friend whom I'll call Brother Jones. He and Sister Jones are a retired couple in their mid-60s. Recently, they inherited a large sum of money. I was asked by their grown children to come and present several options on how they might preserve that inheritance in such a way that they could live comfortably the rest of their lives. Sister Jones was clearly anxious to protect their windfall, given that their own retirement savings were virtually nonexistent. Brother Jones, on the other hand, had immediately begun spending and had drawn up a long list of places in the world he wanted to visit.

Each time we met, Sister Jones listened attentively. She gathered information, carefully weighing one option against the other. Brother Jones, on the other hand, began reacting the moment he realized that any investment program I might recommend would dramatically curtail the amount of money he could spend in a given year. From that time on, he would make a pretense of listening for a short period of time, then complain of a headache and excuse himself to go lie down. For days afterward, he would lapse into a moody and distant silence. His lack of cooperation made it impossible to complete any further planning. The final result was that no decision was ever made, and the inheritance was soon depleted.

Later, other members of the family explained that this was a long-term pattern for Brother Jones. He had always kept a sword of sullen silence at the ready, swinging it with impunity anytime it appeared he might not get what he wanted. He was never outwardly angry or abusive. He had served wonderfully in a wide variety of callings in the ward. He was well-respected in his profession. But his sullenness continually hung over the family's personal life whenever he disapproved of what was going on.

Now, though Brother Jones's avoidance may be a little extreme, we all have developed ways of coping that may or may not be helpful to us. We cannot *not* cope because we always deal—in some way—with our challenges.

Obsessive and/or Compulsive Behavior

A few years ago, I had a client who was the perfect perfectionist. She described her house as "filthy," complaining that she had not vacuumed the living room in months. When I asked why, she replied she didn't have time.

"Why wouldn't you have time?" I asked. "It would take only fifteen minutes!"

"Well, I cannot vacuum the living room without doing the dining room as well," she replied.

"Okay," I said, "maybe twenty-five minutes?"

"If I vacuum the living room and the dining room, I also have to mop the kitchen floor."

"Forty minutes?"

"And I cannot do the floors without cleaning the drapes and the windows. The whole job would take four hours! And I just don't have four hours right now . . ."

In her head lived a set of rules entirely of her making. She couldn't break them without becoming anxious and irritable. Other rules, also of her own making, extended to her husband and kids as well. Rather than face her wrath, her family learned to live with those rules, regardless of how odd they thought them to be.

For her, the entire situation was depressing. She knew that her endless rule-making made everyone's life more miserable. But when she would try to relax those rules, her anxieties would rise to levels she couldn't tolerate. Ultimately, she was driven to get psychiatric help because she feared the effect her anxieties were having on her children.

Another client was subject to panic attacks whenever he was stuck in a large crowd. Being a sports fan, he had season tickets to all his college's football and basketball games. In order to avoid being caught in a crowd, he would always come early and then leave well before the game was over. Regardless of the score, he and his family were on their way to the car before the game was over. He too had learned to live with his anxieties but worried about how they would impact his kids.

Anxieties and obsessions can make us miserable. If unchecked, they also determine how we parent. We can easily become overly controlling, trying to keep our children away from irrational situations *we* fear. Parents with untreated anxieties can also overreact during discipline, yelling or crying while trying to curtail a child's behavior.

Excessive Focus on Appearance

In speaking to the young women of the Church and their mothers, Elder Jeffrey R. Holland wisely said:

> I plead with you young women to please be more accepting of yourselves, including your body shape and style, with a little less longing to look like someone else. We are all different. Some are tall, and some are short. Some are

round, and some are thin. And almost everyone at some time or other wants to be something they are not! . . .

Every young woman is a child of destiny and every adult woman a powerful force for good. I mention adult women because, sisters, you are our greatest examples and resource for these young women. *And if you are obsessing over being a size 2, you won't be very surprised when your daughter or the Mia Maid in your class does the same and makes herself physically ill trying to accomplish it. . . .*

In terms of preoccupation with self and a fixation on the physical, this is more than social insanity; it is spiritually destructive, and it accounts for much of the unhappiness women, including young women, face in the modern world. *And if adults are preoccupied with appearance—tucking and nipping and implanting and remodeling everything that can be remodeled—those pressures and anxieties will certainly seep through to children.* At some point the problem becomes what the Book of Mormon called "vain imaginations" (1 Nephi 12:18) (*Modesty, Makeovers, and the Pursuit of Physical Beauty* [Salt Lake City: Deseret Book Company, 2006], 17–20; emphasis added).

Generally, an over-preoccupation with appearance can be a symptom of deeper emotional unrest and dissatisfaction. It is seeking to heal the emptiness inside by remodeling the outside. It is also a method of coping, easily copied by children, especially image-conscious teens. They see us doing it and recognize it for what it is. Unfortunately, it is only a mirage; it does not heal the source of the unrest. In the end, it provides only a temporary fix. Children learn that image is more important than substance—a destructive conclusion actively promoted in worldly settings.

Excessive Focus on Weight

Not long ago, a national television news program featured a ten-year-old girl with an eating disorder. During the program, the little girl looked directly at the camera and described all the reasons she did it—she was too fat, too ugly, etc. Then, incredibly, her mother followed up those comments with, "Now, I also have an eating disorder, but that isn't why she does it." The total disconnect on the part of the mother was astonishing to the interviewer and to me. She had fooled herself into believing that her own anorexia had no effect on her child, when, in fact, it had everything to do with her.

During most of their early years, children learn about coping with life by watching us. They watch what works and doesn't work. If a parent needs to lose weight and begins to lose that weight through eating less and exercising more, the child sees the results of hard work, discipline, and persistence. However, if they watch us cycle through a never-ending series of fad diets and quick fixes, they learn to solve problems through gimmicks and shortcuts. In addition, if weight and diets are the focus of constant conversation and consternation in a family, then what do the children learn about life's priorities?

Adult Children of Alcoholics

Alcoholism is a disease that affects multiple generations. Children who grow up in an alcoholic home have to learn to deal with the unexpected. A child coming home from school, for instance, does not know if the evening will be tranquil or explosive. They don't know if they should bring friends around or just play outside. Everything is a mystery up to the moment they open the door.

Because of this chaos, these children grow into adults who live by three simple rules:

Don't talk
Don't trust
Don't feel

These three rules, born out of a sense of survival, deeply impact the quality of their relationships, including their inter-actions with their children. Such persons are less likely to share inner feelings with a spouse or kids. When they do, they uncover feelings such as anger, loss, and inadequacy. Rather than expose those feelings, many adult children choose to simply keep those emotions under wraps. The result is they may have inner turmoil they feel they can never express.

Other children are placed in the caregiver role for an addicted parent. They end up with the responsibility of getting a drunk parent to bed or lying to a parent's boss about a hang-over. When this happens, they may grow into adulthood with an excessive need to nurture to the point of overindulgence. Or, they may struggle with low self-esteem and end up being dominated or abused by a spouse.

Whatever the result, it is easy to see how a parent's unhealthy coping skills can be passed along to their kids. Alcoholics, like smokers, leave their successive generations dealing with secondhand afflictions not of their choice. If these successive generations can recognize their need to heal, they can prevent these afflictions from continuing to spread.

Adult Survivors of Abuse

Childhood trauma, such as sexual or physical abuse, also has a lasting effect on its victims. A child who is being sexually abused by a loved one develops a complicated set of rationales for the abuse. Being young, they have no control over the abuse. They know only that they dread it and want it to stop. It causes feelings they don't understand and are unprepared to deal with.

In order to gain some control over their abuse, a child often sees themselves as the cause of the abusive behavior. While some might see this as illogical, taking the blame for the abuse is actually a means of self-defense. The logic (which is generally unconscious) goes something like this: "If I caused it, I can stop it. I may not know what I'm doing that's causing me to be hurt, but if I can figure out what I'm doing and change it, the abuse will stop. Otherwise, I'm being hurt and there's nothing I can do to stop it. I would rather be responsible and be able to stop it than not be responsible and have it all out of my control."

This thought process, sometimes called a "locus of control" shift, helps the child deal with abuse when they are young. As they mature into adulthood, however, this self-blame has a devastating effect on the adult victim's self-concept. They view themselves with contempt because they believe they are guilty of some unknown flaw or sin. In their minds, they must have done something to deserve the punishment, they just haven't identified it yet.

In the same way an alcoholic's behavior negatively affects future generations, so does childhood abuse. Left unresolved, a parent's past abuse will play a role, of some type, in the way the child eventually parents. At one extreme, parents who were abused are more at risk to abuse their own children. At the other extreme, a parent's low self-esteem may cause them to try to buy their children's love through overspending and lax discipline.

Addictions

When Lucifer was cast down to this earth, he brought his war in heaven tactics with him. He continues to lie and to deceive as a way to capture the souls of men. To do that, he must entice us to surrender the agency we fought so hard to obtain.

Elder Dallin H. Oaks warns:

> We should avoid any practices in which one person attempts to surrender even part of his will to another person or in which another person attempts it. Whether the means are chemical, behavioral, electronic, or others not yet dreamed of . . . we should avoid any behavior that is addictive. Whatever is addictive compromises our will ("Free Agency and Freedom," BYU Fireside, Oct. 11, 1987).

Why would any of us allow ourselves to become addicted to a substance or practice that "compromises our will"? C. S. Lewis suggests that "An ever increasing craving for an ever diminishing pleasure is the formula . . . to get the man's soul and give him nothing in return" (*The Screwtape Letters* [New York: Bantam, 1995], 26).

I've never talked to anyone who started out with the intent to become addicted. Most people are simply looking for a way to cope. Some, like many of our prodigals, want to find a way to escape whatever tyranny they envision. They use addictive substances to escape stress or prove they are free or in defiance of their parents.

> The invitation to yield our will to God's appears at first to restrict our freedom, yet acceptance of the invitation eventually blesses us with the full-blown liberty of eternal life. . . . Because of the law of gravity, we can walk; the rules of grammar make coherent communication possible; . . .

In contrast, Satan always offers early freedom, as if freedom requires no price. Yet that seductive beginning ultimately ends with his ensnaring his victims in the full-blown bondage of eternal slavery. As both a literal and symbolic example of this enslavement, drug addiction—like other addictions—begins with the promise of a mind-expanding adventure; then it ends in mind-destroying tragedy (Bruce C. and Marie K. Hafen, *The Belonging Heart: The Atonement and Relationships with God and Family* [Salt Lake City: Deseret Book Company, 1994], 138).

The difficulty of parenting while being addicted to anything, speaks for itself. Whether our addiction is food or pornography, we know, intuitively that what we are doing is destructive. We know that it robs us of the Holy Spirit and it interferes in our relationships. What we don't know is how to quit. We've tried and failed. We then beat ourselves up for lack of willpower. "I should be able to do this," we sigh. "What's wrong with me?" In answer, many decide they are too weak in character to climb this mountain. When this happens, lack of confidence in personal issues further erodes effectiveness as a parent.

The possibility of our overcoming some addictions can seem even more remote when we read of recent research into the brain biology of an addict. The National Institute on Drug Abuse (NIDA) has proven, through brain-imaging studies, that some substances, such as nicotine, actually alter brain chemistry. Nicotine has been found to reduce the number of dopamine (pleasure) receptor sites in the front part of our brain. As these sites decrease, there is a need for more and more nicotine to give the user the same pleasurable feeling. Work is underway to determine what other foods and chemicals have the same effect (see "Pay Attention to This," *Psychology Today*, November/December 2004, 84).

So, what do we do?

The Really Good News

This list of secondhand afflictions is far from complete. These are examples of the personal weaknesses we battle as we parent. Again, the Lord still grants parenting stewardships to those of us who are weak and imperfect.

Overcoming serious weaknesses is a difficult task. At times those defects seem insurmountable. When we feel like giving up, we look at our spouse and our children and know we must keep trying.

In working with families, I constantly look for ways to help my clients make the changes they know they need. In reality, there is only one true way to heal from these weaknesses and dependencies and that is through the Atonement of Jesus Christ.

To his son Helaman, Alma declared:

> I would that ye should do as I have done, in remembering the captivity of our fathers; *for they were in bondage,* and none could deliver them except it was the God of Abraham, and the God of Isaac, and the God of Jacob; *and he surely did deliver them in their afflictions* (Alma 36:2; emphasis added).

Alma also described how the Savior would "go forth, suffering pains and afflictions and temptations of every kind; and this that the word might be fulfilled which saith he will take upon him the pains and the sicknesses of his people. . . . and he will take upon him their infirmities, that his bowels may be filled with mercy, according to the flesh, that he may know according to the flesh how to succor his people according to their infirmities" (Alma 7:11–12).

This is the good news. Certainly the Lord took upon Himself our sins to redeem us from our fallen condition. But, He also experienced our pains, our sicknesses, our infirmities, so that He would know, exactly, how to succor us, to strengthen us, and to heal us. Only He knows, because He felt it all, what we will need to be freed from the weaknesses that bind us.

When we struggle with addiction or dysfunction we are in bondage. Our agency is under attack. Our choices decline steadily over time. We try repeatedly to make the necessary changes and it seems we always seem to find a way to fail.

The good news is that the Savior never intended for us to do it on our own. We can't. We are filled with people-ness, fallen people-ness! We fail then promise we will try harder. Before long, we fail again. What is worse, we become very aware of our inability to "fix" ourselves. It is only when we let the Savior take over that the nature of the battle changes; only when we turn our life and will over to Him does change become possible.

Our Church leaders understand this concept perfectly. In order to aid all of us with weaknesses we cannot change, they've developed the Addiction Recovery Program of the Church, which relies solely on the power of the Atonement to effect change.

The Addiction Recovery Program

Thus far, we have looked at many issues related to preventing rebellion in our children. In this chapter, we'll explore ways to help them by helping ourselves. We begin that process by taking a fearless moral inventory of ourselves (look for that phrase later!) so we can be more effective parents.

In the Addiction Recovery Program group (ARP) my wife, Cindy, and I facilitate, we have members who visit and do not return; assuming this program is not for them because they are not alcoholic or don't view pornography. They feel they must have a classic addiction in order to benefit from the program's twelve steps. Nothing could be further from the truth.

True, ARP is adapted from the Alcoholics Anonymous twelve-step program. The AA program is an inspired way for alcoholics to progress toward sobriety. When one reads what they have done, it is easy to see its inspired foundations.

When I first reviewed the AA program, I found the experience similar to the one I have when I attend meetings at other churches—I find I agree with most of what they are saying. I also find myself frustrated, wanting to jump up and tell them "the rest of the story!" Participating with earnest people in their endeavors is like watching a good movie and having it end before the final climatic scene. The restored gospel of Jesus Christ provides the rest of the story; completing the truth others have. President Gordon B. Hinckley has frequently said: "I believe with all my heart that all churches do good. We say to those [of other faiths], you bring all the good you have and let us see if we can add to it" (*LDS Church News*, "South Pacific Visit: President Hinckley Completes Eight-day Tour," May 24, 1997).

In a similar way, in seeking to help the addict, the Church has said to AA, "Bring all the good you have and let us see if we can add to it." The result was the Addiction Recovery Program of the Church, a twelve-step program based on the Atonement. As you read through these steps, watch how the principle of surrender fills the participant with greater power, freeing him or her to parent more effectively.

The ARP Twelve Steps

Step 1: Admit that you, of yourself, are powerless to overcome your addictions [and weaknesses] and that your life has become unmanageable.

After being introduced to this concept, I struggled for a long time with the idea that people were "powerless." Most of what I had been trained to understand was that the remedy for serious weaknesses was empowerment and strength. When people struggled with self-doubt, it was my job as a therapist to help them become stronger by building up their self-esteem. And the idea of sending them off to a program that taught powerlessness as its first principle struck me as self-defeating at best.

In hindsight, I was 180 degrees off. As we discussed earlier, we do not have the power to change our children's hearts— only the Lord can do that. In the same way, we do not have the power to heal our *own* hearts. In the psalm of Ammon, we read, "Yea, I know that I am nothing; as to my strength I am weak; therefore I will not boast of myself, but I will boast of my God, *for in his strength I can do all things*" (Alma 26:12; emphasis added).

When we become tired of failing in our attempts to rid ourselves of destructive behaviors and quit trying to "cure" ourselves, we learn that only the healing power of the Savior can do for us what we cannot do for ourselves. That then leads us to Step 2.

Step 2: Come to believe that the power of God can restore you to complete spiritual health.

Colleen Harrison, who was instrumental in helping the Church develop the Addiction Recovery Program, writes:

> I . . . wept as I realized that while I had been so very active in the Church, like the "good son" in the parable of

the prodigal son, I had not come to know the Father or His Son, Jesus Christ. I began to realize the term "agnostic"—which applies to someone who only hopes God exists, but doesn't feel they can know—was actually true of me. I had to stop denying the fact that I had serious doubts about God's capacity to love and help someone as "messed up" as I was (*He Did Deliver Me from Bondage* [Pleasant Grove, Utah: Windhaven Publishing, 2002], 7).

When we believe we are a special case (I am beyond healing; He can't love me; He loves others more than me) our faith wavers. Conversely, you "cannot have faith and hope, [unless you are] meek, and lowly of heart" (Moroni 7:43). That meekness comes as we admit we are powerless and concede that only Christ can heal hearts. One of my students pictured it this way:

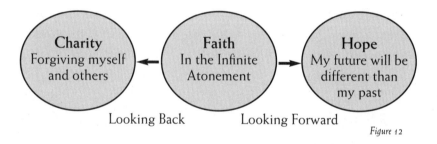

Looking Back   Looking Forward

Figure 12

The power of the Atonement enables us to heal our past mistakes and look forward with a "perfect brightness of hope" to a better life (2 Nephi 31:20).

Step 3: Decide to turn your will and your life over to the care of God the Eternal Father and His Son, Jesus Christ.

As we come to know that He loves us and will succor and strengthen us, we voluntarily turn our will over to Him. Elder Neal A. Maxwell has pointed out:

The submission of one's will is really the only uniquely personal thing we have to place on God's altar. It is a hard doctrine, but it is true. The many other things we give to God, however nice that may be of us, are actually things He has already given us, and He has loaned them to us. But when we begin to submit ourselves by letting our wills be swallowed up in God's will, then we are really giving something to Him ("Insights from My Life," *Ensign*, August 2000, 9).

The more we understand the Savior, the more we find it a joy to place our lives in His hands.

When we turn our will over to Him—He who is the source of our eternal joy—we cease trying to counsel Him. We are more willing to receive needed spiritual guidance. We are then more willing to follow the commandments; not out of moral obligation but out of a deep sense of love and gratitude for "tender mercies" (1 Nephi 1:20) extended to us every step of the way.

Prior to His crucifixion, the Savior told His disciples that when He returned, He would "separate them one from another, as a shepherd divideth his sheep from the goats" (Matthew 25:32). In conjunction with that scripture, I once asked a Gospel Doctrine Sunday School class to characterize the difference between "goat thinking" and "sheep thinking." They did a good job describing the differences between the two. I then asked: "Given the goat's stubborn nature, who does the goat trust?"

"Only itself," replied several people.

"And the sheep?" I asked. "Who does he trust?"

From the back of the class, a sister answered quietly, "the Shepherd."

Step 4: Make a searching and fearless written moral inventory of yourself.

As we come to more completely understand and trust God, we are ready to begin the process of clearing out those weaknesses that afflict us and others. We begin a spiritual spring cleaning. We open up the closets; we look under the bed. We open the windows and let the light in. In short, we begin to make a list of all those things we've tried to keep hidden, even from ourselves. Since the Lord knows they're there, we admit we're not fooling anyone.

Step 4 is the step universally dreaded in most recovery groups. Because it requires complete honesty, it is not confronted without pain or regret. I've known individuals to spend a year or longer working on this inventory. It is a *searching* inventory because we are masters at hiding things, even from ourselves. When we doubt our ability to be whole, we effectively bury those weaknesses we've failed to change. We try to pretend they don't exist. When we come to trust the Lord, however, we finally place those weaknesses on the altar as well.

Step 5: Admit to yourself, to your Heavenly Father in the name of Jesus Christ, to proper priesthood authority, and to another person the exact nature of your wrongs.

Depending on the nature of our weakness, we may or may not need to involve priesthood authority. Always, though, we admit them to our Maker, with full purpose of heart and deep humility. The idea of involving another, a confidant, is also a difficult step. Who else needs to know? we ask. Confiding our intent in a spouse or a good friend is an indication of our sincerity and can strengthen us in our determination to be honest and not give up. The confidant can also help monitor our growth while providing vital perspective as we change.

Step 6: Become entirely ready to have God remove all your character weaknesses.

Step 6 is about becoming ready. Notice that this step comes halfway through a twelve-step program. Some might think this should be the first step. "I'm ready to change," they'll explain, "that's why I'm here!" In reality, the first five steps prepare us to ask the Lord to make the necessary changes in us. It takes time and preparation to really decide we want to change and even longer to truly understand the powerful Being who will execute that transformation. And only after we've made a thoughtful inventory will we really understand what changes need to be made.

Preparing also involves spiritually and emotionally surrendering to Him. It involves reminding ourselves that we cannot, in a thousand years of trying, make the necessary changes that will finally heal us. If we have prepared properly, the next step should come with some excitement and anticipation!

Step 7: Humbly ask Heavenly Father to remove your shortcomings.

After we've learned to trust God and fully disclosed our weakness, we come to the moment of change. We have acknowledged those habits we've been unable to remove, the ones that demean us and interfere in our parenting. The process of change begins. Will it happen overnight? Of course not. But, as the Lord is going about His work we will be inspired to change routines, friends, things we eat, places we go, our entertainment. We will know what we need to change as we become "new creatures."

Don't assume you know what the new creature will look like. When Joseph Smith went into the grove to pray, he went as a farm boy who just wanted to know where he needed to go to have his sins remitted. But the Lord had in mind turning him into a "polished shaft" in His quiver (see Isaiah 49:2). Joseph's humility and obedience allowed the Master Potter to form the rough clay into a thing of beauty. He promises no less with us.

Step 8: Make a written list of all the persons you have harmed and become willing to make restitution to them.

This step requires a great deal of humility and is further evidence of the person's sincerity. To make such an admission of guilt is also therapeutic. More important, the meekness thus demonstrated invites the Holy Ghost to minister comfort and peace to the repentant soul.

Step 9: Whenever possible, make direct restitution to all persons you have harmed.

The Book of Mormon is filled with stories such as those of Alma, Enos, Lamoni, and Nephi who sought forgiveness from the Lord. When forgiveness was freely given, their hearts immediately turned to those around them. The "turning of the heart" is a natural part of the process. After their conversion, Alma and the sons of Mosiah went about the countryside "zealously striving to repair all the injuries which they had done" (Mosiah 27:35). Hearts that are full of gratitude seek to restore, as much as is possible, any secondhand afflictions we might have caused. The morning after the storm we start up our chain saws and go to work.

As our hearts are changing, we begin to see everything in a different light. This change will ultimately allow us to see others as God sees them. When we do, we will seek to heal any damage we might have caused. Restitution without the attending change of heart is a mere check mark on our repentance checklist. But true restitution is driven by love and gratitude and a genuine concern for those around us.

Step 10: Continue to take personal inventory, and when you are wrong promptly admit it.

A favorite movie of mine is called *The Straight Story*. It is the true story of seventy-three-year-old Alvin Straight, a man who learns that his brother, to whom he has not spoken for ten years, has had a stroke. Alvin decides it is time to heal the relationship. He cannot drive, so he attaches a trailer to his riding lawn mower and drives three hundred miles to reconcile with his brother. At one point, after his mower breaks down and needs to be repaired, a man approaches Alvin about taking him the rest of the distance to his brother's house. Alvin thanks him but declines. "You're a good man," he tells his new friend, "talkin' to a stubborn man."

Pride makes stubborn men and women of us all. It leads us to continue to do things we know are wrong. We do them rather than admit we need to change. When we become new creatures in Christ we begin to take a daily accounting of what we are doing. Our new heart will "shake at the appearance of sin" (2 Nephi 4:31) and will help us move quickly to admit our error and move on.

The prophet Moroni makes a poignant observation about the Book of Mormon. Looking back over the things his father has written, he writes:

> Condemn me not because of mine imperfection, neither my father, because of his imperfection, neither them who have written before him; but rather give thanks unto

God that he hath made manifest unto you our imperfections, that ye may learn to be more wise than we have
been (Mormon 9:31).

In other words, he is humble enough to write of his weaknesses, with the hope it will help us not to repeat their mistakes. At the right time and in the right place, being open with
some of our weaknesses may turn out to be a great blessing to
those we're seeking to help.

When children see their parents admit mistakes, they are
more likely to admit their own. It establishes an environment
of honesty and forgiveness. When we stubbornly hold to our
prideful decisions, long after we understand they were wrong,
we teach our children that how we look is more important than
the truth.

**Step 11: Seek through prayer and meditation to know the
Lord's will and to have the power to carry it out.**

One lady approached me, wanting to know what it means
to really turn our life over to God. "How will I know when I'm
doing it?" she asked.

After thinking about it for a minute, I told her that during
those times I feel I have really placed my life in Heavenly
Father's hands I am more solicitous of His advice; I constantly
want to know what He wants me to do. On those days, I feel
I'm on His errand, not mine. On those days my prayers change;
they become more specific and more solicitous for others. I'm
also more likely to find myself with a prayer in my heart at
many points during the day. My will is joyfully swallowed up
in His, if only for a while.

Alma clearly understood this principle when he directed a
missionary effort to the Zoramites. As he prepared to go into a

hostile situation, he did not pray, "and bless that no harm or accident will befall me," as most of us probably would have done. Instead, he prays, "O Lord, wilt thou grant unto me *that I may have strength*, that I may suffer with patience these afflictions which shall come upon me, because of the iniquity of this people" (Alma 31:31; emphasis added).

Following the Lord's will doesn't mean He will exempt us from difficult times. Rather, because He seeks our growth, He will not shield us. He will, however, sustain us, lending His strength to carry out His purposes.

Step 12: Having had a spiritual awakening as a result of the Atonement of Jesus Christ, share this message with others and practice these principles in all you do.

It was President Ezra Taft Benson who declared:

> Men and women who turn their lives over to God will discover that He can make a lot more out of their lives than they can. He will deepen their joys, expand their vision, quicken their minds, strengthen their muscles, lift their spirits, multiply their blessings, increase their opportunities, comfort their souls, raise up friends, and pour out peace. Whoever will lose his life in the service of God will find eternal life ("Jesus Christ—Gifts and Expectations," *Ensign*, Dec. 1988, 4).

In chapter 3, we talked about the Divine Paradox. To remind us, here are some examples:

To find ourselves
We lose ourselves
To be forgiven
We forgive
To be filled with joy

We endure tribulation

To be "raised up"

He descended below all things

To receive an endowment of power

We make covenants

To achieve Exaltation

We first become a servant

To gain power over our weaknesses

We become meek and submissive

The Lord uses our moments of fear or pain or anxiety to teach us what we need to know. We love more clearly as we serve than when we are being served. This is the path of true humility. It is the example we hope our children see and follow. As Elder Neal A. Maxwell once quipped, "It means that eagles meekly serve under sparrows—without worrying over comparative wingspans or plumage" (*The Collected Works of Neal A. Maxwell*, vol. 4: *A Wonderful Flood of Light* [Salt Lake City: Eagle Gate, 2001], 99).

The principles of the Addiction Recovery Program show us how the Atonement works. We all have weaknesses we need removed. True change occurs when we stop trying to fix ourselves and begin submitting more completely to the Lord.

Earlier we said that pride is the driving force behind rebellion. This is true of adults and children. *If pride is the cause, submission is the cure.* As parents, the sooner we learn to submit to the Lord's will the sooner we can demonstrate and teach that redeeming principle to our children.

Finally, in looking at how we handle our imperfections, Elder Jeffrey R. Holland has plainly said:

If there is one lament I cannot abide, it is the poor, pitiful, withered cry, "Well, that's just the way I am." If you want to talk about discouragement, that is one that discourages me. I've heard it from too many people who want to sin and call it psychology. And I use the word *sin* to cover a vast range of habits, some seemingly innocent enough, that nevertheless bring discouragement and doubt and despair.

The difficulty in making those changes sometimes seems too great. Elder Holland goes on to explain:

You can change anything you want to change, and you can do it very fast. *Another satanic suckerpunch is that it takes years and years and eons of eternity to repent. That's just not true.* It takes exactly as long to repent as it takes you to say, "I'll change"—and mean it. Of course there will be problems to work out and restitutions to make. You may well spend—indeed, you had better spend—the rest of your life proving your repentance by its permanence. But change, growth, renewal, and repentance can come for you as instantaneously as they did for Alma and the sons of Mosiah. Even if you have serious amends to make, it is not likely that you would qualify for the term "the vilest of sinners," which is the phrase Mormon used in describing these young men. Yet as Alma recounts his own experience, it appears to have been as instantaneous as it was stunning. (See Alma 36) (*However Long and Hard the Road* [Salt Lake City: Deseret Book Company, 1985], 6; emphasis added).

Fourteen

Spiritual Maturity and the Hard Questions

You've got the brain of a four-year-old boy, and I bet he was glad to get rid of it.—Groucho Marx

Tony never intended to leave the Church. Between semesters at college, he was spending some time on the Internet. In doing so, he came across a Web site that was very critical of a former President of the Church, listing a number of conflicting things he had supposedly said. The more Tony read, the more confused he became. *Surely, this can't be true, can it?* he thought. While he knew this was a Web site designed to attack the Church, what he read still bewildered him, especially after checking some references. By the time he went to bed, he was sick and concerned.

He didn't tell anyone of his research but spent the next two weeks trying to resolve his confusion by consulting Web sites focused on exposing Mormon "secrets." As he studied, he felt doubts beginning to grow, which left him feeling more miserable. Sleep began to be difficult. Finally, he went to his dad with a long list of questions he couldn't answer.

After listening to Tony's concerns, his dad responded, "Son, why are you delving into junk like that?"

Tony looked down. "Because I want to know if these things are true or not."

"Look," warned his dad, now alarmed, "just quit reading that garbage. It's all nonsense in the first place. All lies. You start reading it, the next thing you know you're out of the Church on a rocket. None of it has anything to do with your salvation, okay? Just drop it and leave it alone."

But Tony couldn't "leave it alone." The more he read, the more questions he had and the more uneasy he felt. What added to his uneasiness was the way his father had sounded defensive about the entire topic. He eventually talked to his mother and the bishop, both of whom repeated the same thing his father had: "Let it alone and don't worry about it."

When fall came, Tony went back to school, but he stopped attending church. Six months later he announced to his parents he had "taken a break" from the Church while he was "sorting some things out."

Some rebellions occur later in a child's life. Every week, LDS wards average about 50 percent attendance, meaning that half of the members on their records are not in church, most of those choosing not to attend. Some simply become less active because they'd rather not go through the demanding rigors of being active. For others—far too many others—lack of attendance is a deliberate act of separating themselves from the Church. Some choose to leave the Church completely and have their memberships removed.

Why, in a book about parenting, would we talk about adults who leave the Church? Because how we parent, and the way in which our children come to understand the gospel of Jesus Christ, helps to prepare them against the forces that will pull and tug at the very elect. Developing divine-esteem provides a proper foundation leading to greater spiritual maturity. That maturity then enables them to handle the difficult questions that can arise.

There are three general reasons Saints leave the Church. For our purposes, we will only mention the first two and then focus primarily on the third.

1. Unworthiness and Sin

Sin and its attendant guilt can wear like an anvil around a member's neck. "The guilty taketh the truth to be hard, for it cutteth them to the very center" (1 Nephi 16:2). The Holy Ghost will continue to remind someone they have done wrong until they repent or ignore it long enough that their heart grows cold. As a young missionary, I found that investigators who suddenly changed their minds, just before baptism, often had sins they had not yet confessed. Once we helped them complete their repentance, they felt much more comfortable around other members of the Church.

It is easy for us to presume, when someone leaves the Church, that they are leaving because of sin. Regardless of whether that presumption is right or wrong, we place ourselves in the undesirable position of judging those who need our love and support.

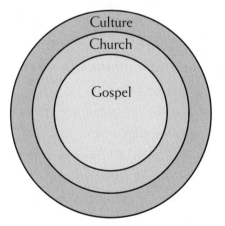

Figure 13

2. Environmental Reasons

As illustrated on the previous page, the gospel of Jesus Christ consists of eternal principles, covenants, and ordinances. Those bedrock verities do not change from "eternity to eternity" (D&C 76:4). The gospel is administered by The Church of Jesus Christ of Latter-day Saints. Certain aspects of the organization or programs of the Church will change to meet the needs of the Saints at any given moment. But the Church is the only organization on the earth today that holds the keys and is authorized to administer the saving ordinances of the gospel.

Surrounding the Church and gospel is our Mormon culture. Nonmembers, gazing in at the Church, view it through the window of the culture that surrounds it. New members, learning about the plan of salvation (the gospel), also learn about the concepts of bishops, stakes, PPIs, and home and visiting teaching. In addition, they are introduced to the pervasive and peculiar (as the world views it) culture that defines us as Latter-day Saints. For example, it is with humor that we speak of Utah as the Jell-O Belt of the United States.

Our Mormon culture is highly correlated, well-established, and family focused. Sometimes, if we are not careful, it can also be unyielding to special needs or circumstances. Some Saints leave the Church, not because of sin, but simply because they are not comfortable within the culture. Unless a ward family goes out of its way to be overly accepting, those who are single, those who struggle with same-sex attraction, or those who are socially awkward, for instance, can have a difficult time feeling part of the larger group.

As we've discussed earlier, young men who do not like Scouting or sports can have problems getting close to their peers in the Young Men program. In some wards, because of established tight-knit friendships and bonds, some newcomers may have difficulty finding a warm reception.

3. Intellectual Reasons—The Difficult Questions

This is the information age. The Internet has put at our fingertips a greater store of knowledge than ever before in the history of the world. In seconds we can navigate between Web sites, exploring the endless data available to us. In addition to the Internet, books, magazines, and media resources continue to expand at a dizzying rate.

As part of this explosion, there is more information available about the Church than ever before. Knowledgeable of this fact, the Church has worked hard to increase its accessibility in the media and on the Internet, using the technology of mass communication to share the gospel with the rest of the world.

At the same time, Lucifer has marshaled his forces in the battle for hearts and minds. Anyone who has simply searched the Web for "Mormon" can attest that the Internet is also the repository of relentless, virulent attacks against Latter-day Saint doctrines, practices, and beliefs. It provides an easy forum for both those who are honestly trying to reach out and "save" LDS people and those more angry and caustic critics of the Church.

Some attempted exposes are clumsy and naïve; while others, though deceptive, appear sophisticated and well-researched. The most persuasive arguments, as always, come from former members who "leave the Church, but cannot leave it alone." They speak with an air of "experience," lending them more seeming credibility.

Favorite topics of this sort include, but are not limited to, discussions on:

- The nature of God
- The nature of salvation

- The origins of the Book of Mormon
- Nonbiblical scriptures
- The authenticity of the Book of Abraham
- The temple endowment and Free Masonry
- Joseph Smith and polygamy
- Blacks and the priesthood
- Quotes by former leaders of the Church

How our youth learn to handle unexpected questions, discerning truth from falsehood, is critical. Spiritual maturity helps them to not be blindsided or caught off guard. However, many adults in the Church sometimes shrink from trying to answer such questions because we do not know what to say or how to respond. They may be mysteries to us as well. When we fail to provide any answer, though, those asking the questions may assume we are "hiding something" or that there is no satisfactory answer.

Let's now look at how we help prepare them to handle both doctrinal and Church history questions.

What Is Our Doctrine?

Not long ago, as I sat at my office, an acquaintance approached me with a question.

"You're a Mormon, right?" he began, looking a little uncertain.

"That's right," I answered.

"Can I ask you a question?"

"Sure."

He hesitated, as if trying to decide how to phrase his question. Finally, he blurted out, "I'm curious why it is that Mormons worship Joseph Smith instead of Jesus Christ?"

With feigned concern, I responded, "Wow, I didn't know we did! I thought we worshiped the Savior!"

"Well, you pray to Joseph Smith!" This he declared as a statement, not as a question, as if it were a well-known fact.

"Why would we do that?" I smiled. "Salvation comes through Jesus Christ, not Joseph Smith. That's why it's called The Church of Jesus Christ, not the church of Joseph Smith."

My friend's confusion then gave us an opportunity to have a good discussion about what the Church *really* believes, as opposed to the falsehoods told to him at his church. From the moment Joseph Smith walked out of the grove in 1820, Lucifer has been trying to "spin" or define, to the world, what our doctrines are.

Doctrines such as that of the "Holy Trinity" or the importance of baptism by immersion generally do not cause most members much consternation when they are confronted with them. We may not know all the immediate answers, but we are not surprised when accused of believing them. The difficulties occur when researching gadflies uncover this quote, or that, supposedly said by an apostle or President of the Church, which shocks or surprises us. These quotes may appear to reveal previously unknown doctrines, not generally known to the membership of the Church.

Robert L. Millet shares the following experience:

> Some time ago a colleague and I were in southern California speaking to a group of about five hundred people, both Latter-day Saints and Protestants. During the question-and-answer phase of the program, someone asked the inevitable: "Are you really Christian? Do you, as many claim, worship a different Jesus?" I explained that we worship the Christ of the New Testament, that we

believe wholeheartedly in His virgin birth, His divine Sonship, His miracles, His transforming teachings, His atoning sacrifice, and His bodily resurrection from the dead. I added that we also believe in the teachings of and about Christ found in the Book of Mormon and modern revelation. After the meeting, a Latter-day Saint woman came up to me and said, "You didn't tell the truth about what we believe!"

Startled, I asked, "What do you mean?"

She responded, "You said we believe in the virgin birth of Christ, and you know very well that we don't believe that."

"Yes, we do," I retorted.

She then said with a great deal of emotion, "I want to believe you, but people have told me for years that we believe that God the Father had sexual relations with Mary and thereby Jesus was conceived."

I looked her in the eyes and said, "I'm aware of that teaching, but that is not the doctrine of the Church; that is not what we teach in the Church today. Have you ever heard the Brethren teach it in conference? Is it in the standard works, the auricular materials, or the handbooks of the Church? Is it a part of an official declaration or proclamation?"

I watched as a five-hundred-pound weight seemed to come off her shoulders, as tears came into her eyes, and she simply said, "Thank you, Brother Millet" (*The Religious Educator*, vol. 4, no. 3, [Provo, Utah: Brigham Young University Press, 2003], 15).

In order to not be caught up in hysteria or this quote or that, our children need to understand that *living prophets are more important to us than dead ones!* We love and honor the men and women who led the Church in the past. Their teachings help guide us in our search for truth. However, since they are no longer with us, we cannot ask Orson Pratt or Wilford Woodruff what they meant. We do not know the context or if their words were transcribed correctly. As such, we draw deeply from the living waters that flow into the Church today.

What we can do is to run any statement past the test Brother Millet has proposed. When we hear a quote from Orson Hyde, or someone who "knew" Joseph Smith, we can ask: Is this something we hear taught in general conference? Is it found in the correlated materials of the Church? Have our current prophet or apostles said something on the same matter, or used that quote in context with their remarks? If so, it is part of our doctrine. If not, then it's not something for us to worry about.

Our youth (and our adults) should not spend one second defending the Church against statements that are not part of our doctrine. One day we will know why they said what they did, but for now, we look to our current leaders for authoritative answers and not to obscure quotes from the *Journal of Discourses*.

Questions about Church History

When the angel Moroni first visited Joseph Smith, the ancient prophet prophesied that Joseph's name "should be had for good and evil among all nations, kindreds, and tongues, or that it should be both good and evil spoken of among all people" (JS–H 1:33). In fact, the Book of Mormon had not yet been printed before spurious articles, maligning Joseph, began to show up in newspapers in Palmyra and elsewhere.

In our discussion about the rebellion in heaven, we recalled that one of Lucifer's favorite stratagems is to falsely accuse any-one who stands in his way. It is no surprise, then, that he continues to attack, slander, and demean the leaders of the Restoration.

Joseph Smith, and those who served with him, restored the gospel against great odds. They were also very human and, at least partially, the products of their times. It is understandably difficult to interpret some of their actions or behaviors when taken outside the context of those times.

That said, in an informational age, we have available at our fingertips every piece of lint and dirt on every prophet possible. President Boyd K. Packer is one who decries the "lint and dirt" approach employed by some historians. Following the release of a book particularly critical of a former President of the Church, President Packer remarked:

> What that historian did with the reputation of the President of the Church was not worth doing. He seemed determined to convince everyone that the *prophet* was a *man*. We knew that already. All of the prophets and all of the Apostles have been men. It would have been much more worthwhile for him to convince us that the *man* was a *prophet*, a fact quite as true as the fact that he was a man (Lucile C. Tate, *Boyd K. Packer: A Watchman on the Tower* [Salt Lake City: Bookcraft, 1995], 245).

Nonetheless, those digging for dirt will discover and publish what they find. And those findings, accurate or not, end up in anti-Mormon literature and Web sites. As a result, youth and new members—as well as more seasoned ones—can end up hearing about spurious behaviors or beliefs that surprise or shake the unprepared.

Getting Answers

In their search for answers, seekers of truth must keep in mind four important truths:

Truth #1: When we are humble, the Holy Ghost can tell us "the truth of all things" (Moroni 10:5).

The answers to difficult questions, like the search for any truth, can be revealed through the whisperings of the Spirit. These answers come to humble seekers of truth.

I was once approached by a friend of mine who was dating an LDS man she was very attracted to. Not a member of the Church, my friend was having a hard time with some of our doctrines. Particularly, the idea of exaltation and "godhood" was a hard concept for her. It went against everything she'd ever been taught. In asking me to explain it, she told me she was open to understanding more.

As we sat and talked, I asked her if she wanted to someday start a family. She did. I asked her what she would wish for her children. She explained that she would want them to grow up well and be happy. I then asked her, "If you truly love their father, would you want your boys to grow up and be like him?" She agreed she would.

I then explained the Latter-day Saint understanding of our Father in Heaven, His love for us, and His plans for our future happiness. The greatest happiness He could wish for any of us, I told her, was that we become just like He is. If we did so, it would be His greatest compliment and our greatest gift.

As we spoke, the Spirit filled the room. She became misty-eyed, thanked me, and left. In those few moments, she had received both an intellectual understanding and a spiritual confirmation of a truth that had been foreign to her just thirty minutes earlier.

The same doctrinal question has been put to me by those who, as it is said, are often in error but never in doubt. They've asked the question not to get an answer but to convince me of my error. These are they who are "ever learning, and never able to come to the knowledge of the truth" (2 Timothy 3:7). The search for truth does not mean merely looking for confirmation of what we want to believe. If we are humble, the Spirit confirms the truthfulness of a doctrine. If the doctrine is not true, we are filled with a cold uneasiness, confirming the information to be a falsehood.

Some Latter-day Saints mistake the uneasiness that comes from deceptive material as a confirmation that the Church isn't true. *They forget that whenever they read falsehood they will feel worse!* The Holy Ghost cannot bear witness to lies. It is similar to asking whether we feel the Spirit more strongly in the temple or in a bar. If we walk into a bar we will feel the Spirit less. When we read anti-Mormon material we feel less peace and comfort.

Truth #2: We must seek out LDS sources for answers.

Second, an honest seeker of truth must turn to the right sources. My wife, Cindy, and I recently spent an evening with a husband and wife who had just joined the Church. They had been radiant at their baptism and were loved into the ward family. A few weeks later, they stopped attending their meetings. A phone call to them revealed they now had serious reservations about the Church. At their invitation, we went to their house to talk about their concerns.

As we talked, this good sister revealed she had been researching the Church on the Internet and had come across some Web sites that "revealed" all of Joseph Smith's true secrets, the ones "Mormon missionaries won't tell you!" She was horrified. After several days of reading, her peace had fled and she felt depressed and down. She feared she'd been duped. Her main confusion, though, was that her new ward family seemed happy and contented and smart enough to know if they were being lied to.

I asked her if she'd spent much time on the Church's Web site. She hadn't. I asked if she was still reading the Book of Mormon. She wasn't. She smiled sheepishly when I explained that it was a little like wanting to learn about the Catholic Church by asking only Baptists. We then took each of her concerns, one by one, and helped her and her husband see the deceptions and misunderstandings in the things she'd been reading. As we continued to talk and bear our testimonies, they both became visibly more happy and at peace once again. The light in her face returned, and they soon came back to church. She acknowledged she'd been looking at all the wrong sources.

The Church has placed a lot of good information at www.lds.org for anyone with gospel questions. Also, there is additional information available at Web sites such as fairlds.org, which, though not run by the Church, is run by BYU professors and others who update the site with the latest research and information on the complex questions members sometimes struggle to answer.

Truth #3: Spiritual maturity helps us deal with ambiguity.

Earlier, we mentioned that some leave the Church because of differences they have with Mormon culture. The reasoning goes something like this: "The Relief Society president was rude; she was called by the bishop; the bishop must not be inspired for calling someone like her; therefore, there is no inspiration; so the Church can't be true."

Learning to separate the unchangeable, eternal principles of the gospel from the imperfect, human aspects of the culture comes with spiritual maturity. This maturity often follows three recognizable stages.

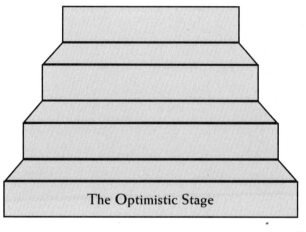

The Optimistic Stage

Figure 14

In the *Optimistic Stage*, or Stage 1 thinking, we view the world idealistically, either good or bad. When we view something as the ideal, we become blind to any fault in it. Incoming freshmen at college or brand-new missionaries often begin at Stage 1 in their spiritual growth. The "letters to the editor" section of BYU's *Daily Universe*, for instance, is filled with Stage 1 students who are "appalled that someone—anyone—would do something that would demean the Lord's University." They expect perfection and have little patience with ambiguity.

At Stage 2, or the *Pessimistic Stage*, we've learned enough to realize that the world isn't perfect and no one has all the answers. Some who pursue a more intellectual path never leave

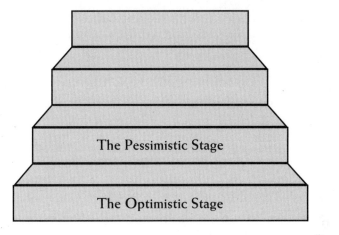

Figure 15

Stage 2 thinking. They remain eternally bound to a cynical view of the world. Everything becomes relative and there are no absolute truths.

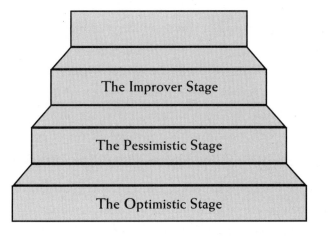

Figure 16

Finally, Stage 3 is the *Improver Stage* (see G. K. Chesterton, *Orthodoxy* [Garden City, N. Y.: Image Books, 1959], 69–71). Speaking of this stage, Elder Bruce Hafen explains:

It seems to me that the most productive response to ambiguity, then, is at level three, where *we not only view things with our eyes wide open but with our hearts wide open as well.* When we do that, there will be many times when we are called upon to take some action when we think we need more evidence before knowing just what to do. Such occasions may range from following the counsel of the Brethren on birth control to accepting a home teaching assignment.

Based on my experience, I believe that it is always better to give the Lord and his Church the benefit of any doubts we may have when some such case seems too close to call. I stress that the willingness to be believing and accepting in these cases is a very different matter from blind obedience. It is, rather, a loving and knowing kind of obedience ("Love Is Not Blind," in *Speeches of the Year, 1979* [Provo: Brigham Young University Press, 1980], 6; emphasis added).

Stage 3 thinking is the level of spiritual maturity that enables us to view early Church leaders not with rose-colored glasses but with loving understanding and gratitude. We can love J. Golden Kimball for his human-ness and sustain him as an inspired Seventy and tireless missionary in the Church. Locally, we can view our bishop, with all his strengths and weaknesses, as deserving of our support in all he asks of us.

In the talk cited above, Elder Hafen goes on to quote G. K. Chesterton, who pointed out:

Some stupid people started the idea that because women obviously back up their own people through everything, therefore women are blind and do not see anything. They can hardly have known any women. The same women who are ready to defend their men through thick and thin . . . are almost morbidly lucid about the thinness of [their] excuses or the thickness of [their] head[s] . . . Love is not blind; that is the last thing that it is. Love is bound; and the more it is bound the less it is blind (ibid., 6).

Truth #4: We must learn to accept that we will not know all things.

Some puzzling questions have no revealed answer. For instance, though I have taught classes on the historical antecedents that helped form the decision making at Mountain Meadows, I readily admit that I have no answers as to *how* the participants justified carrying out that horrible atrocity. Joseph Smith biographer Richard Bushman once responded to a vexing Church history question with, "Right now, I don't see any explanation that will be satisfying to us on the horizon. We're just going to have to swallow it, live with it, digest it and do or die" (www.fairlds.org, "A Joseph Smith Miscellany"). Sometimes that is the only answer.

There is great benefit to our children hearing, from us, after all efforts have been made to find an answer, "You know, I guess this is one we accept on faith." Robert L. Millet has confided:

> I do not hesitate to acknowledge that I have placed many things on a shelf over the past twenty years. A number of those items have come down from the shelf as information and inspiration have brought light and understanding where darkness and uncertainty had been. Some matters will probably stay on the shelf until that glorious millennial day when the God of heaven makes known those things "which have passed, and hidden things which no man knew, things of the earth, by which it was made, and the purpose and the end thereof—things most precious, things that are above, and things that are

beneath, things that are in the earth, and upon the earth, and in heaven." (D&C 101:32–34) (*Steadfast and Immovable: Striving for Spiritual Maturity* [Salt Lake City: Deseret Book Company, 1992], 22).

Ultimately, our job, as parents, is to prepare our youth and students as best we can. We do that by arming them with the correct knowledge about their Heavenly Father, about the reality and effect of the Atonement, and about the efficacy of prayer. We also teach them how to discern truth as well as falsehood. Our goal for them is to be self-sustaining adults, with a firm grasp on the iron rod. We know that mists of darkness will arise, just as Lehi warned us they would. Lehi also informed us that the enticements and arguments coming from the great and spacious building would sound impressive and enlightened. However, he also taught that all their marketing and all their persuasiveness does not change one eternal fact— the fruit of the tree is good, filling those who partake with "exceedingly great joy" (1 Nephi 8:12).

Conversely, "wickedness never was happiness" (Alma 41:10). And the awful truth is, those who get caught up in the dark mists and wander off in forbidden paths place themselves at risk of forfeiting the joy and blessings Heavenly Father intends for them.

As our children spiritually mature, they will recognize that negotiating dark mists and difficult questions are part of our journey through our mortal probation. As we engage in Stage 3 thinking, they will see the joy that comes from keeping both our eyes and our hearts open.

As parents, we must anticipate that difficult questions will arise in those around us and know how we will respond when the time comes.

Fifteen

In Conclusion

The words which I had often heard my father speak concerning eternal life, and the joy of the saints, sunk deep into my heart.—*Enos* 1:3

In the opening pages of the Book of Mormon, Nephi gives us some simple insights into his own conversion. Like his older brothers, Nephi must have faced a culture shock when his father, Lehi, announced they were leaving "the land of [their] inheritance" in search of a promised land (1 Nephi 2:4). Days into the journey, the sand of the desert must have seemed a long way from any promised land. He also watched Laman and Lemuel contending with their father about the hardships of the journey, and specifically about the visions and dreams that led to their hurried exodus.

The question for Nephi appears to have been: Do I agree with my brothers or do I follow my father? Do I obey or do I rebel? His decision to follow would impact countless thousands of his descendants who would bear his name.

How did he decide? In 1 Nephi 2:16 he explains that though he was still "exceedingly young," he was filled with "great desires to know of the mysteries of God." Those righteous desires caused him to "cry unto the Lord" in search of answers. He tells us that in response to his prayers, the Lord "did visit me, and did soften my heart that I did believe all the words which had been spoken by my father."

In a few short words, Nephi provides a blueprint for helping guard against rebellion. The first key is that he was filled with "great desires to know of the mysteries of God." Those desires led him to seek for answers and for God to be able to respond.

Being filled with Nephi-like desires helps to temper the debilitating effect of pride. As we've discussed, children who are filled with pride are at great risk of succumbing to the temptations of pride's author—Satan. In fact, a convincing argument could be made that there is only one sin in all the universe, that of pride.

Nephi's thirst to know invited the softening power of the Lord and helped keep pride's cankering influence from getting root in his soul. All because he had a desire to know.

In this book, we've looked at the ways in which our parenting styles can help us expose children to the Spirit of the Lord and His converting power. Children respond to the Spirit if, as Nephi explains, they have desires to know "the mysteries" of God. *Wonderful*, you might be thinking, *how do I get them excited about God's mysteries when I can't even get them to clean up their room?!* The truth is that children do have mysteries, things they want to know but haven't yet figured out. For instance:

- How do I make friends?
- How do I deal with being different?
- Why do other kids get more toys than me?
- Why can't I just do the things I want to do?
- Why can't I date when I'm twelve?

In other words, kids have a great deal of desire to know *the things that are important to them.* They probably couldn't care less about what direction the Pearly Gate swings, but they do have real concerns that plague them and are important to them. They are *filled* with desires.

Everything we have discussed puts them in a position to get real answers from their Heavenly Father. The problems they have growing up are simply precursors to the larger problems they will have as adults. And, yet, the answers will come from the same place.

If they choose the path of rebellion, if they choose to hold those who love them at a distance, they will find some answers but no lasting peace. Unfortunately, they will not recognize the lack of happiness until after they have become war-scarred as a result of making destructive choices.

The idea of living a surrendered life or being filled with divine-esteem will be less important to a growing child than is solving their everyday problems. Our challenge and opportunity as parents is to teach them the source of the help they need. As they learn to turn to the Lord and trust Him to help them, their hearts will be softened and they will be visited by the God of Heaven. And they will have also avoided the pain rebellious behavior brings.

The "grand key" (to use Joseph Smith's words) of parenting comes in helping children learn to find solutions and intervening only when necessary. It comes in living and demonstrating a surrendered life ourselves. It comes in recognizing our own rebellious behaviors and pleading with heaven for the humility to have them removed. It comes, as one sister put it, "when I come to understand that I don't know what I don't know!"

Parents of extremely rebellious teens will explain that there comes a time when it feels like "resistance is futile"; you've exhausted all of your ideas and are open to any and all input from others who might have a suggestion.

Effective parents maintain a certain element of "futileness." They do the best they can. They recognize they make mistakes and hope to do better next time. But their sense of imperfection, their awareness that "they don't know what they don't know," keeps them open to promptings and whisperings from the Holy Ghost and to inspired suggestions from others.

It is my testimony that imperfect parents, filled with love for their children, will use those promptings to keep trying and keep parenting. The youth of today are strong-willed and divinely appointed by heaven to usher in the Savior's Second Coming. As such, they will be buffeted by Satan's worldly winds and may drift off course, determined to find more "glamorous" ports of call. Others, despite those same parental imperfections, will use their strength to grow to spiritual heights we also cannot possibly imagine.

Our callings, as parents and as youth leaders, is to learn and grow and do the best we can. We do so in partnership with the God of Heaven, our Heavenly Father and their Heavenly Father. His parental skills are perfect in nature; our children were His before they were ours. He will teach us how to teach them, if we'll let Him. He'll also comfort us as often as we need it. And He'll watch over our children when we cannot.

To this end, I pray that you and I will review the points we've discussed and rejoice that we've been called as servants, to labor in our particular vineyard at this point in history with this set of remarkable spirits of God. Rather than feel guilty about things we should or shouldn't have done, we need to accept the Lord's invitation to keep trying to improve as teachers and trainers of youth. He promises that, as we do so, He will "renew [our] strength; [we] shall mount up with wings as eagles; [we] shall run, and not be weary; and . . . shall walk, and not faint" (Isaiah 40:31).

Index